PRESIDENTS
OF THE
UNITED STATES

The classic architecture of The Capitol, Washington, D.C. is clearly depicted in this fine painting *c.* 1835.

PRESIDENTS
OF THE
UNITED STATES

EDWARD GREY

GALLERY BOOKS
An Imprint of W. H. Smith Publishers Inc.
112 Madison Avenue
New York City 10016

First published in 1988 by
The Hamlyn Publishing Group Ltd
Michelin House, 81 Fulham Road, London, SW3 6RB

This edition published in 1988 by Gallery Books
An imprint of W H Smith Publishers Inc.
112 Madison Avenue, New York, New York 10016

© 1988 The Hamlyn Publishing Group Ltd

ISBN 0 8317 7109 7

Printed in Hong Kong

Editor	Isobel Greenham
Art Editor	Pedro Prà Lopez
Production Controller	Audrey Johnston
Picture Research	Angela Grant
Map illustration	Paul Cooper

The Publishers thank the following for providing the photographs in this book:

Associated Press Ltd 127 above & below, 156, 157; BBC Hulton Picture Library 10, 18 below, 91, 97, 99, 105, 109, 121 above & below, 153, (Bettmann Archive) 34, 41 left, 43 right, 59, 76, 102; Black Star/John Olson 135; Bridgeman Art Library (Art Resource/Feder) 17, (Art Resource/White House Collection) 2, 27, 42, (Private Collection) 39; Camera Press Ltd 125, 128, 129, (Bachrach) 124; Culver Pictures Inc 25, 63 & inset, 64, 65; Susan Griggs Agency Ltd (Nick Holland) 6; Robert Harding Picture Library Ltd (Walter Rawling) 45; The Keystone Collection 141, 144, 149 above; The Mansell Collection 49, 61; Mary Evans Picture Library 21, 51 right, 71, 77 below, 81, 88, 107 left; Library of Congress 29; Peter Newark's Western Americana 8, 11, 15, 16, 18 above, 22, 23, 26, 30, 32, 33, 35, 37 left & right, 40, 41 right, 43 left, 44, 46, 53, 56, 66, 69, 73, 75, 77 above, 79, 83, 85, 86, 93, 95 & inset, 101 inset, 103, 107 right, 110, 111, 113 above, 132; Photri 31, 57, 58, 67, 89, 93 inset, 113; Popperfoto 12, 13, 51 left, 101, 114, 115, 117, 119, 122, 131, 138; Rex Features Ltd 137, 143, 145, 149 below, 151, 155; Frank Spooner Pictures 147.

The following pictures are copyrighted by the White House Historical Association:

14, 38, 48, 50, 52, 54, 62, 68, 70, 72, 74, 78, 80, 84, 90, 92, 98, 100, 104, 106, 112, 118, 130, 136, 142, 146, 152.

The following books proved especially useful in the preparation of this volume.

The American Presidents from Washington to Harding, Herbert Agar (Eyre and Spottiswoode, 1933)
Mr President, Maurice Ashley (Jonathan Cape, 1948)
The White House, Kenneth W. Leish (Newsweek, 1972)
The Press and the Presidency, John Tebbel and Sarah Miles Watts (Oxford University Press, 1985)
The Presidents, (Greenwich House, 1984)
The National Experience, various authors (Harcourt Brace Jovanovich, 1981)
The American Nation, John A. Garraty (Harper & Row, 1979)
Longman History of the United States of America, Hugh Brogan, 1985
Washington, the Indispensable Man, James Thomas Flexner (Collins, 1976)
FDR, Ted Morgan (Grafton Books, 1985)
Truman, A Centenary Remembrance, Robert H. Ferrell (Thames and Hudson, 1984)
The Dictionary of Biographical Quotation, Wintle and Kenin (Routledge and Kegan Paul, 1978)
Our Country's Presidents, Frank Freidel (National Geographic Society, 1981)

CONTENTS

INTRODUCTION

From George Washington to Ronald Reagan, the presidents of the United States have been figures involved in a great, continuing experiment. Having liberated themselves from royal tyranny the Founding Fathers did not want to invent a new despotism. Yet they quickly came to believe that an executive was vital to republican government, and the Constitutional Convention created an office of president with formidable authority.

The president was responsible for the "faithful execution of the laws." He had command of the army and navy, was to conduct foreign affairs, and appoint federal judges and other officials. He might veto any law of Congress. Additionally, he was to issue periodic reports on the state of the Union, and recommend "such measures as he shall judge necessary and expedient."

These were extensive powers – yet the office also bristled with institutional safeguards. For example, though the president had control of the armed forces, only Congress had the right to declare war. The presidential veto could be over-ridden by a two-thirds majority of both houses. And the power of impeachment was granted to Congress should any president be deemed guilty of malfeasance in office. In 1868 Andrew Johnson was impeached, and it was the threat of impeachment in 1974 which forced Richard Nixon to resign from the executive office – the only president to do so.

THE EXERCISE OF POWER
Though the system of checks and balances has always tended to impede wild experiment, much about the president's role has depended upon the temperament of the president himself. How much should he interfere with Congress's policy-making prerogatives? At what point does strong leadership challenge the "sacred fire of liberty" on which the Republic was founded?

George Washington and his immediate successors generally exercised restraint as chief executive. But the roughhewn frontiersman, Andrew Jackson, seventh president, created a new and stronger role, stamping the office with elements and his own forceful character. Far more than any predecessors he seized the initiative in policy-making, and he was not afraid to use the presidential veto as a bludgeon to get his way.

Other great energizers – equally controversial in their day – have included Theodore Roosevelt (who called the presidency "Ripping – simply ripping!"), Franklin D. Roosevelt and John F. Kennedy. All considered themselves standard-bearers for cherished principles and were prepared to take risks to see them through. "The important fact," Harry Truman once wrote, "is that the President is the only person in the executive branch who has final authority, and if he does not exercise it we may be in trouble. If he exercises his authority wisely, that is good for the country. If he does not exercise it wisely, that is too bad, but it is better than not exercising it at all."

Examples of weakness are not hard to find in the presidential careers of men like Ulysses S. Grant and the unhappy Warren Harding. But there have been others – men of great ability – who have deliberately kept a lower profile as a matter of political philosophy. Eisenhower, for example, was always one who sought to rule through quiet influence rather than grand gestures. And Calvin Coolidge personified the renunciation of power in office. "Perhaps one of the most important accomplishments of my administration," he once said in a news conference, "has been minding my own business."

PRESIDENTIAL ELECTIONS

As to the means of electing a president, the Constitution established the cumbersome apparatus of the electoral college, by which each state provides electors who in turn vote for candidates. In avoiding the more obvious system of direct vote by the people the Founding Fathers hoped to prevent any mere demagogue from snatching the office of chief executive, or any single interest group from prevailing. The principle of checks and balances operated again, and the system has survived to this day despite criticism of its anomalies. (In 1824, 1876 and 1888 the candidate receiving the largest number of popular votes failed to win a majority of the electoral college and so, therefore, lost the presidency).

How long should a president serve? No constitutional limits were originally placed on the number of four-year terms, but George Washington's well-known tradition of restricting himself to two terms was maintained until the time of Franklin D. Roosevelt.

Controversially, FDR was elected to third and fourth terms. The 22nd constitutional amendment, ratified in 1951, provided that no-one should be elected president more than twice.

THE WHITE HOUSE

Since 1800 the White House – 1600 Pennsylvania Avenue, Washington, D.C. – has been the official home of the president, and successive first families have left their mark on the residence as much as individual executives have stamped the presidency with their character. Thomas Jefferson described the house as "Big enough for two emperors, one Pope and the grand lama." He furnished the building in French style but it was much renovated over the years, especially after the burning of Washington during the War of 1812. Features include the elegant East Room where the seven presidents who died in office laid in state, and the Lincoln Bedroom where Honest Abe signed the Emancipation Proclamation. During World War I, flocks of sheep grazed on the lawn producing wool for charities as President Wilson attempted to release men for the war effort. Under Harry S. Truman in 1952, extensive remodelling was finally completed, and the White House seen today is very much as that renovation left it.

Inevitably, the human details of the First Families' lives have always fascinated the public, whether through the whiff of scandal or the romance of a White House wedding. For the story of the presidency is more than the narrative of a political office; it is the unfolding epic of a nation and the larger-than-life characters who helped to shape its destiny.

GEORGE WASHINGTON

O n April 30, 1789, George Washington, revolutionary general and national hero, was inaugurated first President of the United States. Chosen unanimously by Electoral College vote, the tall Virginian took the oath of office on the balcony of Federal Hall in New York, temporary capital of the infant republic. In his inaugural address, delivered to a joint meeting of the houses of Congress, the great warrior's voice trembled and he shuffled his manuscript from hand to hand. Washington today may seem a remote, ideal figure – protagonist of some eighteenth century costume drama acted out in braided coats and knee breeches – but on that historic day the hero was frankly nervous, aware that he and his country stood on the threshold of a drastic experiment.

The Father of the Republic
Elsewhere, every nation of the known world endured government under the tyranny of kings; Washington was unique among leaders in drawing his power from the people, and as a man of authentic modesty he was awed by the role in which Providence had cast him. Few people could realize, he was to write, "the difficult and delicate part in which a man in my situation has to act . . . I walk on untrodden ground. There is scarcely any part of my conduct which may not hereafter be drawn into precedent."

And it was true – the eyes of the world were on him. Some among his contemporaries expected popular rule to degenerate into chaos and anarchy. Others feared that the

First President 1789-1797

needs of strong government would create a new despotism: might not the President make himself King of America? The idea of an American crown may appear outlandish in retrospect, even faintly ludicrous. Yet it was a real enough prospect in the eighteenth century, and if modern democracy survived and took root on American soil, the fact owes much to the firm and dignified stewardship of one conscientious man who is rightly revered as the Father of the Republic.

His formative years
George Washington was born in a modest house at Bridges Creek near Fredericksburg, in Westmoreland County, Virginia, on February 22, 1732 (under the Julian calendar which still operated in the first half of the eighteenth century his birthday was February 11; the present Gregorian calendar was introduced in 1752 by an act of parliament in Britain, and brought dates forward by 11 days). Everyone today knows the anecdote of his childhood: that being asked how a cherry tree came to be destroyed he replied, "I can't tell a lie, Pa; you know I can't tell a lie. I did cut it with my hatchet." The story first appeared in Mason Locke Weems's *The Life of George Washington* (1800), published directly after the first President's death, and is almost certainly apocryphal. In reality, Washington's father Augustine, a landowner, died when George was 11, and the more dominant influence throughout his childhood may well have been his demanding and possessive mother, Mary Ball Washington.

Washington's schooling was irregular, though he seems to have taught himself a good deal of mathematics, and at 16 he went to live with his older half-brother, Lawrence, at Mount Vernon. In 1748, he went on an expedition to survey the Shenandoah Valley lands of Thomas, Lord Fairfax, who possessed a vast acreage of backwoods territory and who lived at a mansion called Belvoir not far from Mount Vernon. Washington kept a cheerfully ill-spelled diary of this wildernesss trip, recording for example one night in a rude lodging spent naked under "one thread Bear blanket with double its Weight of Vermin such as Lice Fleas &c". The future President was clearly exhilarated and delighted by the whole Shenandoah adventure, and he retained a boyish enthusiasm for the American West and all attempts to open it up.

The young plantation-owner

In the summer of 1752, Washington's half-brother Lawrence succumbed to tuberculosis and George went on to inherit, at the age of 20, the Mount Vernon estate which he expanded through judicious land purchases over many years to come. By his death his holdings amounted to over 100,000 acres, including plantations employing black slave labor. (He viewed the slave system, though, with deepening repugnance as time passed, and was to be alone among the Virginia Founding Fathers in eventually freeing all of his own slaves.)

The young planter's military career started in 1753, when he was sent by Governor Dinwiddie of Virginia to warn the French from encroachments in Ohio country. As a lieutenant colonel charged with constructing Fort Necessity at Great Meadows, Pennsylvania, he clashed the following year with a French and Indian war party. Though acquitting himself bravely, Washington was surrounded at the fort and forced to surrender. In 1755, he accompanied General Edward Braddock on an ill-fated expedition to seize Fort Duquesne; an ambush resulted in defeat, but in fact Washington was to help take that same fort during the Seven Years War (1756-63).

In 1759, Washington married Martha Dandridge Custis, a wealthy widow, and settled down to manage his plantation. When the quarrel with Britain started to brew he was reluctant to press for independence. Nevertheless, the punitive closure of Boston after the famous Tea Party forced him to conclude that opposition to the mother country was the only course; he was chosen as a Virginia delegate to the First and Second Continental Congresses, and as a prominent veteran of the struggles against the French was appointed by Congress on June 15, 1775, to lead the Continental Army.

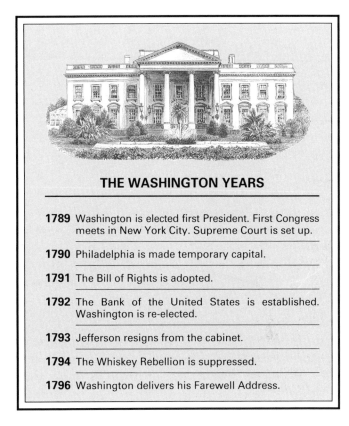

THE WASHINGTON YEARS

1789 Washington is elected first President. First Congress meets in New York City. Supreme Court is set up.

1790 Philadelphia is made temporary capital.

1791 The Bill of Rights is adopted.

1792 The Bank of the United States is established. Washington is re-elected.

1793 Jefferson resigns from the cabinet.

1794 The Whiskey Rebellion is suppressed.

1796 Washington delivers his Farewell Address.

Military achievements

A detailed account of Washington's career as Commander in Chief lies outside the scope of this book. Critics have suggested that he was never, in fact, a great tactician: experienced only in wilderness warfare he knew precious little of how to handle big armies, and tended to listen too attentively to the often squabbling – sometimes intriguing – generals around him. As a result, he often erred on the side of caution and delay instead of acting boldly and decisively. But such critcisms ignore the key facts of his position. Washington had at all cost to keep American public opinion on his side; he could not afford to sustain heavy military or civilian casualties, for any major discouragement might strain loyalties and cause his untrained army to melt away.

In this context, Washington's supreme achievement was to maintain unity, holding the confidence of troops and people and binding all to the national cause throughout the early defeats and frustrations of what was inevitably to be a long war. A strict disciplinarian, he nevertheless earned the warm regard of his men by insisting on better treatment for them from Congress. And toward the end of the war he showed real military flair. The decisive battle was to come in the fall of 1781, when Washington led a combined

Franco-American army against the entrenched position of Lord Cornwallis at Yorktown. Some 8,000 British soldiers were forced to surrender there, and the campaign virtually ended hostilities (although they did not cease formally until April 19, 1783).

The unanimous choice for President

Soon after the war ended Washington resigned his commission and returned to Mount Vernon determined, he wrote to his French ally and friend the Marquis de Lafayette, to be free of the bustle of army and public life. "I am not only retired from all public employments, but am retiring within myself, and shall be able to view the solitary walk and tread the paths of private life with heartfelt satisfaction. Envious of none, I am determined to be pleased with all, and this, my dear friend, being the order of the march, I will move gently down the stream of life until I sleep with my fathers."

It was not to be. Washington's rural tranquilities were interrupted when he was asked to chair the Constitutional Convention of 1787. Reluctantly he agreed, and the soldier's prestige unquestionably gave the public confidence in the new Constitution. Washington also helped to get the Constitution ratified in the state conventions the following year, and though he seems sincerely to have believed that he would afterwards be allowed to return to private life, there was an inexorable logic in what happened next. The Constitution provided for a legislature of two houses and an executive at whose head was to be an elected President.

Everyone knew that Washington must be the first choice for the office, and though he spoke of reluctance – and in no way campaigned for the presidency – he emerged as the inevitable and unanimous choice when the ballots were officially counted in the Senate on April 6, 1789. (John Adams, with 34 electoral votes, won the vice presidency, an office whose chief duty was to preside over the Senate.)

The presidency carried substantial powers. Besides executing laws made in the two houses, the President headed the armed forces, presided over foreign relations and appointed federal judges and other officials. He had the right to veto any law of Congress (unless overridden by a two-thirds majority of both houses) and was expected to deliver periodic reports on the State of the Nation, potentially recommending programs for new legislation.

With such authority vested in the person of one man, the method of election was made deliberately cumbersome. The idea was to prevent any very controversial candidate from slipping into power at the head of a crowded field. Each state appointed a number of "electors" who would vote for two people for President. In the event of the frontrunner failing to secure an overall majority when the electoral vote was counted, the House of Representatives would choose the President from among the five leading candidates. In Washington's case, overwhelming support precluded any need for deliberation by the House – and bloc support in a swiftly emerging two-party system has meant that only two elections have been so fragmented in outcome as to have gone for settlement to the House.

The Boston Tea Party. American patriots resented a Tea Act imposed by Britain and on December 16, 1773 a group dressed as Mohawk Indians boarded ships in Boston harbor, broke open 342 tea chests and dropped them overboard. Washington did not condone the action; but British reprisals made him more militant. In the aftermath he offered to raise 1,000 men at his own expense and march them against Boston's military dictator, Major-General Gage.

Political conflict

After Washington took the oath of office at the Federal Hall, there were hopes that harmony would succeed in political life. The President himself was a strong force for unity, aiming for an even balance in his appointments and firmly believing that as President he should stand aloof from sectional strife. But discord arose immediately between two fundamentally opposed schools of thought personified by two of his ablest ministers: Secretary of State Thomas Jefferson and Treasury Secretary Alexander Hamilton.

Jefferson, a Virginian, throughout his life professed enthusiasm for the common man (for which his model was the white land-owning farmers of the agrarian South); he was suspicious of strong central government, which to him smacked of monarchical tyranny. Alexander Hamilton, in contrast, favored a powerful central government drawing strength from the prosperous commercial classes of the North. The schism between their essentially northern and

The siege of Yorktown in the fall of 1781 marked the climax of Washington's military career. Some 17,000 French and American veterans surrounded a smaller British force under Lord Cornwallis. Two of the enemy's outer defenses were taken at bayonet point, and on October 19, the British capitulated, so virtually ending the war.

southern attitudes was to widen in the following century into the abyss of Civil War. But even in Washington's day the depth of feeling on both sides was manifest.

Hostilities opened over the issue of a proposed Bank of the United States. Hamilton suggested that such an institution be created to serve as "a great engine of state" which would make government loans and service the national debt. The federal government would hold a fifth part of the bank's capital, the rest being in the hands of private businessmen. Opposition arose because of the

George Washington's mansion at Mount Vernon began as a modest 8-roomed dwelling but later expanded. Here Washington often entertained guests, taking tea on the verandah in summer, also enjoying barbecues and clam-bakes. Additionally, Mount Vernon was a base for his favorite pastime of riding to hounds.

influence that these private interests might exert; and also on the constitutional issue of whether the government had the right to incorporate a bank. In the developing debate, Hamilton's group, known as the Federalists, argued that the government had "implied powers" under the Constitution; Jefferson argued for the Constitution's "strict construction" – government must not overstep the limits of its agreed authority. Try as he might to maintain an even balance, Washington had to make choices and effectively came down on Hamilton's side. The Bank was established in 1791.

By no means all measures were so controversial; the Bill of Rights guaranteeing freedom of speech, the press and religion, became part of the Constitution in the same year, and although much discussed never inspired such virulent argument. But a new crisis loomed in 1793, when war broke out between revolutionary France and England. Jefferson and many other Americans had warm feelings toward their fellow republicans in Europe who were, after all, fighting both England and monarchy. But on this issue again, Washington sided with Hamilton, deciding that only the

strictest neutrality would serve American interests. Jefferson now resigned; an opposition to the administration came into being; and suspicions were voiced about Washington himself having monarchical inclinations. The President's hot reply on one stormy occasion is recorded by Jefferson himself. Far from wanting to be king, Washington fumed, "he had rather be on his farm than to be made *emperor of the world*."

A second term

Pushed into standing for a second term of office, Washington was again elected unanimously, but his second four years were marked by much stronger factional attacks.

He supported Hamilton both in suppressing the Whiskey Rebellion (1794) and in concluding a commercial treaty with Britain whose controversial provisions were published in the summer of 1795. Both issues reinforced the increasing perception of Washington as essentially conservative if not openly Federalist in his stance; and his habits of going about in smart black velvet clothing, traveling in a liveried coach and giving formal dinners may well have distanced him somewhat from the common man. Notoriously too, Washington suffered from ill-fitting false teeth, hinged and sprung, which contributed to a slightly alarming facial appearance in the elderly statesman. As Washington approached the end of his second term, potential for his caricature as an old fogy increased.

The Farewell Address

This was the time when he made perhaps his greatest bequest to the nation: a refusal to serve a third term. No one would have greatly complained had Washington served out his days as a national figurehead – indeed there was some pressure on him to do so. But he was firmly opposed to the principle of life presidency, believing that the office should rotate in proper republican manner according to the ballot. His famous *Farewell Address*, written with the help of Alexander Hamilton, stressed the importance of unity as the keystone of American liberty and warned against factional strife. Retiring in March, 1797, to Mount Vernon he was only briefly brought out of retreat the following year when the possibility of a war with France called for him to take up again the post of Commander in Chief. The threat of invasion quickly passed, however, and he returned to his estate.

George Washington died on December 14, 1799, after riding out in snow and succumbing to an acute infection. But he had lived long enough to supervise the planning of a new capital on the Potomac River; the seat of government was moved there in 1800, and it was named in the old hero's honor, Washington, D.C.

Embalmed in legend: this famous picture by nineteenth-century artist Emanuel Leutze evokes the episode when Washington led his men across the ice-choked Delaware River one wild Christmas night, to make a surprise attack on the enemy.

JOHN ADAMS

John Adams

Second President 1797-1801

On the day that John Adams, second President, took the oath of office the tall, dark-suited figure of George Washington was also present in the chamber of the House. All eyes were fixed upon the retiring hero, and many of them were damp with emotion. John Adams – a chubby little man in a pearl-colored suit – could be forgiven for feeling that even in his hour of triumph his thunder was being stolen by the old soldier. And, proud and contentious, the new President did not easily endure slights. "Vanity," he once admitted, "is my cardinal vice and cardinal folly."

A principled laywer

John Adams was born in the small town of Braintree (now Quincy), Massachusetts, on October 30, 1735 (October 19 in the old-style calendar). He trained at the Bar, and it was as a constitutional lawyer that he contributed to the drama of the American Revolution. In 1765, leading the Massachusetts Whigs, he argued before the royal governor against the legitimacy of the Stamp act, on the grounds that there could be no taxation without parliamentary representation. He also published anonymous articles in the *Boston Gazette*, expounding his principles. In 1770, however, Adams defended the British soldiers who fired on civilians during the Boston Massacre, earning the acquittal of the officer and most of his troops. His unpopular stance on this issue showed considerable moral courage – and his success increased his reputation as a lawyer.

Elected to the Massachusetts House of Representatives, Adams was also a prominent delegate at the First and Second Continental Congresses, eloquently urging for a confederation of the colonies and for their separation from Britain. He served on the committee which drafted the Declaration of Independence, and pressed for its adoption in Congress. In 1778, Adams was a commissioner to France; he returned to help frame the Massachusetts constitution; and was again sent over to Europe where he was minister to the Netherlands from 1780-85 and to Britain from 1785-88.

Vice President

John Adams was a candidate in the first presidential election of 1789. Under the prevailing system, members of the Electoral College had two votes for President: if there was a clear majority, the winner took the highest office and the second-placed candidate was made Vice President. Washington, of course, was the unanimous first choice drawing a maximum 69 votes. Adams won the vice presidency, but only on 34 votes; and he began his two-term stint under the tall Virginian nursing some jealousies and suspicions about those who had failed to vote for him.

As Vice President, Adams had little real power, but he made himself useful as a supporter of Treasury Secretary Alexander Hamilton and of the Federalist causes of strong central government and a national bank. Two opposing factions were already emerging in political life, and in the

"We hold these truths to be self-evident..." John Adams stands to the left of the drafting committee as they present their handiwork to Congress in John Trumbull's Declaration of Independence. *With Adams are fellow committee members Roger Sherman, Robert Livingston, Thomas Jefferson and Benjamin Franklin. Though Jefferson was the man chiefly responsible for writing the document it was Adams who led the debate on its adoption, agreed on July 4 1776. (Trumbull, the artist, himself participated in the Revolution in which he served as an aide to General Washington).*

1796 election partisan loyalties came strongly to the fore. On one hand stood Hamilton and the Federalists, certainly conservative but unfairly pilloried as sympathetic to kings and nobility; Hamilton himself was thought so controversial a leader that John Adams was nominated as the Federalist candidate in his place. On the other hand were the Republican-Democrats, championed by Thomas Jefferson and supporting individual rights while caricatured as bloodthirsty radicals.

The Federalist President
In the Electoral College, John Adams won a majority of 71 to 68 over Jefferson, so becoming President. But there was an irony in the vice-presidential placing. The Federalist candidate was Thomas Pinckney, Hamilton's preferred choice for leader because, being weaker than Adams, he might be more easily manipulated from backstage. Hamilton got some Federalist electors to vote solely for Pinckney; Adams's supporters retaliated by dropping Pinckney and the result was that Jefferson became Vice President.

In the event, the unlikely partnership of Adams and Jefferson proved tolerable because both men had great personal respect for one another. And, proud though he was, Adams took his obligations to the national interest seriously. Derided as a "monarchist" and dubbed "His Rotundity," he tried hard to improve worsening relations with the government of revolutionary France. But his mission to that country came to grief in the furor known as the "XYZ Affair," in which three French agents (alluded to as X, Y and Z) were sent by the French foreign ministry demanding a substantial bribe as the price of a deal. Adams's mission refused, and when reports of the event were released in the United States a feeling of injured national honor threatened to turn existing hostilities – attacks by French privateers on American shipping – into a full-blooded war.

Adams resisted the warmongers (in his own party) and in 1800 concluded a Franco-American convention. But to combat alien interference in U.S. affairs he did support the Alien and Sedition Laws (1798) threatening freedom of speech and of the press, and giving the President powers to expel aliens. Public disquiet was used as a weapon by the Republicans in the 1800 elections – in which Adams was narrowly defeated by 65 votes to 73 for the opposition.

John Adams spent the rest of his life in retirement. He was married from 1764 to Abigail Smith (their eldest son John Quincy Adams went on to become sixth President). He died at the age of 90, on the same day as Thomas Jefferson, July 4, 1826 – the 50th anniversary of the Declaration of Independence.

THOMAS JEFFERSON

Th:Jefferson

John F. Kennedy's tribute is well known: in 1962, giving a speech at the White House to honor 49 Nobel prizewinners he said, "I think this is the most extraordinary collection of human talent, of human knowledge, that has ever been gathered at the White House – with the possible exception of when Thomas Jefferson dined alone."

The remark captures the multi-faceted quality of Jefferson's character – the sense that he was many brilliant men bundled up in one. As a champion of democracy, chief author of the Declaration of Independence and a President who virtually doubled the area of the United States, he stands among the very greatest figures in American political history. Yet he was more than a statesman: Thomas Jefferson was an architect, scientist, agriculturist, paleontologist, meteorologist, geographer, archeologist and musician. He reconstructed the first mammoth; built the University of Virginia; invented a revolving chair and was intrigued by such things as the difference between the pronunciation of modern and ancient Greek. So diverse was he in accomplishments and in the range of his ideas that many different traditions lay claim to him, conservative and radical alike. Most American statesmen, wrote Henry Adams, could be portrayed with a few broad brushstrokes, but Jefferson, "only touch by touch with a fine pencil, and the perfection of the likeness depended upon the shifting and uncertain flicker of the semi-transparent shadows."

Third President 1801-1809

The early years

He was born on April 13, 1743 (April 2 under the old-style calender), at Shadwell, in Albermarle County, Virginia. His father was a prominent tobacco planter on whose death the 14-year-old Thomas acquired an estate of 1,900 acres, with slaves. This property he expanded considerably in his early manhood; the apostle of the common man was by no means disadvantaged. Jefferson graduated from William and Mary College in 1762, a freckle-faced youth who at 6ft 2in tall, was a fine horseman and expert violinist. His own nature, he often said, inclined him toward the sciences, but soon after leaving college he entered a law office and after five years was admitted to the Bar. In 1770, he started building Monticello, a fine mansion on wooded heights near Charlottesville, which will forever be associated with his name. To it, in 1772, he brought his attractive bride Martha Wayles Skelton; theirs was a happy union and he never remarried after her early death 10 years later. His daughters – and in due course grandchildren – were to be a lifelong source of comfort and delight to him.

The Declaration of Independence

Jefferson entered public life as an elected member of the Virginia House of Burgesses (1769-75) where he became associated with the anti-British faction. As a delegate to Congress in 1775, he was appointed to the committee which drafted the Declaration of Independence, of which he was

Monticello; Thomas Jefferson served as his own architect in creating his Virginia home, which he conceived "rather elegant, and in the Italian taste." Work began with a single pavilion in 1770 but the mansion was repeatedly expanded and renovated to include a lofty salon, library, two wings, octagonal passages and balustrades. In his last years Jefferson seldom left Monticello, which became a place of pilgrimage for visitors and sightseers from all over the country. Soon after Jefferson's death the house was sold to pay his debts.

the main author. This may seem surprising since two other committee members – Benjamin Franklin and John Adams – were certainly his seniors. Nevertheless, it was felt that Jefferson possessed a "peculiar felicity of expression" well suited to the task. The bold yet eloquent language of the Declaration is essentially his (though his preliminary draft was revised in parts by Congress).

As a member of the Virginia House of Delegates (1776-79) and governor of the state (1779-81) Jefferson was the dynamo driving the so-called "Virginia Reformation" – an immense body of reform legislation which was to include the abolition of land-holding privileges, the abolition of primogeniture and the establishment of religious freedom. He resigned as governor in 1781, amid charges that his resistance to the British was ineffectual. These criticisms were unfair in the main, though it is true that Jefferson had no soldierly pretensions.

An ambiguous record on slavery
In his temporary retirement Jefferson wrote *Notes on the State of Virginia*, a book filled with scholarly information and a wealth of speculation and opinion besides. In Congress (1783-84) he drew up an ordinance for the Northwest Territory which forbade slavery after 1800. Adopted in 1787, the measure set an important precedent for the federal control of slavery and has done something to bolster Jefferson's ambiguous record in this field. Critics have often noted that the great libertarian ran his own

plantations by slavery and in all his lifetime only freed a handful of his own slaves. The truth is that while Jefferson did oppose slavery he felt it to be so ingrained a feature of the American plantation system that the task of emancipation must be left to future generations. His own bankruptcy could hardly serve the cause of liberty and "the public mind would not yet bear the proposition of emancipation."

Minister to France
In 1784, Jefferson went to Paris with Benjamin Franklin and John Adams to negotiate commercial treaties. He was minister to France from 1785-89, thoroughly enjoying the position for its opportunities to explore European arts, sciences and cuisine. Jefferson was less smitten by widespread oppression and corruption and came home with a recharged faith in all things American: "My God!" he wrote, "how little do my countrymen know what precious blessings they are in possession of, and which no other people on earth enjoy. I confess I had no idea of it myself."

JEFFERSONIAN DEMOCRACY

On Jefferson's return in 1789, President Washington asked him to serve as Secretary of State in the new national government. Reluctantly he agreed, and in the period that followed there emerged the great conflict of America's early political life: between Jefferson himself, a Virginian favoring the rights of individuals and states, and Treasury

Left: *Explorers Lewis and Clark on the Columbia River. Sponsored by President Jefferson they set out with a party of 34 soldiers and 10 civilians to explore the Louisiana Purchase (see map on p. 20). The expedition received help from Shoshone Indians in crossing the Continental Divide, and reached the Pacific on November 7, 1805 by way of the Columbia.*

Below: *A procession of chained black slaves passes the Capitol, Washington. The 'peculiar institution' of slavery was already rooted in the South by the 1800s, and Jefferson himself used slaves to work his farms at Monticello. He seems, though, to have been a kindly master: a French visitor noted that "his Negroes are clothed and treated as well as white servants should be."*

Secretary Alexander Hamilton, a New Yorker and champion of strong national government.

Hamilton's financial measures were seen by Jeffersonians as enriching the few at the expense of the many. Moreover he was, Jefferson once said, "not only a monarchist, but for a monarchy bottomed on corruption." Around Jefferson, meanwhile, grew up a body of political attitudes known as "Jeffersonian democracy" which deserve some attention. At the heart of the school of thought was respect for individual rights, the rights both of citizens and states to govern their own affairs without federal interference; the less government the better was the simple rule. Jeffersonian democracy stressed the great liberal freedoms: of speech, of worship, of the press. It elevated the common man above all tyrants and to this extent seemed radical – even insurrectionary – in its day. "A little rebellion now and then is a good thing," Jefferson once wrote in a letter to James Madison.

Jefferson held that a strict construction should be put on the Constitution and that government must not overstep the limits of its agreed authority. But the lasting radicalism of his ideas has to be set against attitudes which tie him more closely to his time and his place. By "common man," for example, Jefferson basically had in mind the educated

white landholder of agrarian America. His position on slavery, as has been seen, was unhappily pragmatic from a twentieth-century standpoint, and he never proposed that the right to vote be granted to every property-less member of a city mob. Indeed, he feared the decadent influence of city life on urban workers and commercial classes alike. His whole system was rooted in agriculture. "The greatest service which can be rendered to any country is to add a useful plant to its culture," he once said, and to Madison in 1787 he confided: "When we get piled upon one another in large cities, as in Europe, we shall become corrupt as in Europe, and go to eating one another as they do there."

Jeffersonian concepts of democracy could be – and in time were – manipulated by Southern plantation owners to justify their own reactionary attitudes. But in his quarrel with the Hamiltonians Jefferson seemed entirely radical, and things came to a head in 1793, when war broke out between Britain and revolutionary France. Hamilton and his so-called Federalist party were pro-British. Jefferson's natural leanings were toward the French republic and he proposed that the government adopt an attitude of sympathetic neutrality to it. Unfortunately, the fiery revolutionism of the French envoy to America, Edmond Genet, alarmed the public and damaged hopes for a balanced approach. Jefferson was forced to repudiate Genet and, wearied by this latest quarrel, he resigned in December, 1793, from Washington's administration.

The Democratic – Republican candidate
Jefferson retired to Monticello to enjoy his farm, his family and his books. But he had become so much a rallying point for opposition to the Federalists that political pressures inevitably forced him back to the front of the stage. Jefferson's friends called themselves Democratic-Republicans and, though not organized like a modern national party, formed an increasingly coherent group from about 1793. In 1796, when George Washington retired from the presidency, Jefferson contested the succession with John Adams, the Federalist candidate. Adams won, but on a divided Federalist vote; and with the support of the Democratic-Republicans solidly behind him Jefferson beat the Federalist running mate to become the Vice President.

Jefferson took no active part in the administration, but urged opposition to the Alien and Sedition Acts (1798) and drafted the Kentucky Resolutions which attacked them as unconstitutional. Adams's administration came to grief on these issues of civil liberty and in the bitterly contested 1800 election the Democratic-Republicans emerged as the narrow victors.

There was confusion in the result, though. Democratic-

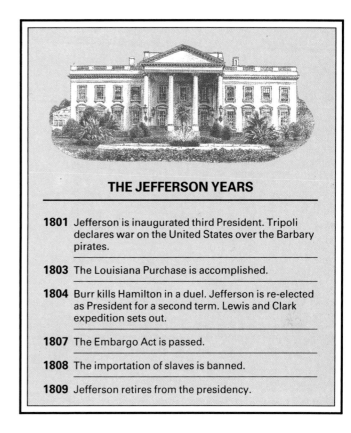

THE JEFFERSON YEARS

1801 Jefferson is inaugurated third President. Tripoli declares war on the United States over the Barbary pirates.

1803 The Louisiana Purchase is accomplished.

1804 Burr kills Hamilton in a duel. Jefferson is re-elected as President for a second term. Lewis and Clark expedition sets out.

1807 The Embargo Act is passed.

1808 The importation of slaves is banned.

1809 Jefferson retires from the presidency.

Republican support was so solid that both of the party's candidates – Jefferson and former Senator Aaron Burr – received precisely equal Electoral College votes for President: 73. It devolved upon the House of Representatives to choose between them and only after further split ballots was the decision made for Jefferson. To avoid a repetition of such annoyances the Twelfth Amendment was drafted (ratified 1804), providing for separate balloting in the Electoral College for President and Vice President.

The new President's reforms
Thomas Jefferson took the presidential oath on March 4, 1801, in the now national capital of Washington, D.C. His now celebrated inaugural address loftily called for a new spirit of harmony and conciliation – "we are all Republicans: we are all Federalists" – but although seeking to unite the country he by no means abandoned his reforming goals. The partisan behavior of Federalist judges under Adams had aroused Republican disquiet and as soon as Congress met, the controversial Judiciary Act of 1801 was repealed. Internal taxation was abolished, too; the Army and Navy were considerably reduced; the theory of state sovereignty was made official doctrine, and within virtually every state

the onslaught on privilege and elitism began.

Jefferson spoke of the "revolution of 1800," but in a sense it was almost more of a reaction – a reaction against the Toryism which had been creeping into American life since the brave days of 1776, when independence was declared. And it was a reaction in style as well as substance. Jefferson repudiated the courtly pomposities which the Federalists had introduced in emulation of English ceremonial. He dressed in plain cloth at the inauguration and afterwards, spurning a coach and six, returned to his lodging house on foot. At the White House, birthday state balls were abolished as were courtly forms of address. No one was His Excellency any more; and when official visitors came to see the President decked out in their gold lace, silk ribbons and dress swords they were surprised to find themselves received by a head of state in a well-worn coat and down-at-heel carpet slippers.

The Louisiana Purchase

The supreme achievement of Jefferson's first administration was the Louisiana Purchase (1803) by which the United States acquired from France nearly one million square miles of territory stretching from the Mississippi to the Rocky Mountains. The price was a modest $15 million, Napoleon needing the money and being unable, in any case, to spare the troops to hold the territory. Ironically, by a strict construction of the Constitution, the federal government had no authority to acquire the new land or make its 50,000 inhabitants citizens. Jefferson, so careful about governmental rights, found himself embarrassed when his

envoys negotiated the purchase on such favorable terms. Eventually he concluded with unaccustomed slyness that "the less we say about the constitutional difficulties the better" and, swallowing his principles, asked the Senate to ratify the treaty.

Lewis and Clark's expedition

In 1804, Jefferson was re-elected President by an overwhelming majority; even John Adams voted for him. Federalism was now in deep decline and received a heavy blow when Alexander Hamilton, its motive force, was killed in a duel with Aaron Burr. Jefferson, meanwhile, augmented his standing by planning the exploration of the vast new territory and its hinterland, sending his private secretary, Meriwether Lewis, with William Clark on their famous expedition (1804-06). The party covered 4,000 miles and returned to great popular acclaim with a vast new body of knowledge about the West, its terrain, flora, fauna and Indian population. Lewis even brought back two grizzly bear cubs which the President kept for a while in a bear pit in the White House lawn.

Problems at sea

Jefferson's second term was not trouble-free, however. It was afflicted in particular by the problems of securing American rights on the high seas. In his first term Jefferson had fought a limited naval war with Barbary pirates who had long been levying tributes on shipping in the Mediterranean. The war was not fully successful, payments still being made as late as 1815, but his policy did display a bold

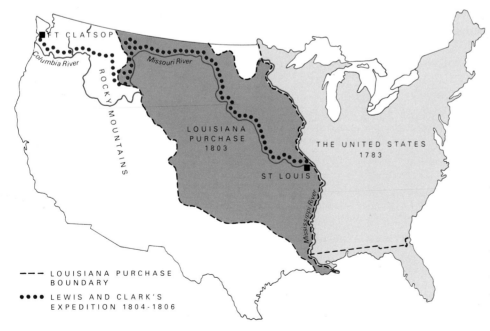

--- LOUISIANA PURCHASE
     BOUNDARY
•••• LEWIS AND CLARK'S
     EXPEDITION 1804-1806

Above right: *The University of Virginia was built to Jefferson's designs within sight of his Monticello home. He supervised every detail of construction from 1819-24; framed its law; became the first rector; and also gathered the faculty of what was in its day the most liberal university in the world.*

Left: *By the Louisiana Purchase of 1803 the United States virtually doubled its area. The region was a magnificent windfall resulting from war in Europe. Jefferson had not planned the acquisition in advance; at his inauguration he told Americans that the nation already possessed all the land that it could need for a thousand generations.*

opposition to blackmail. In his second-term dealing with Napoleonic France and Britain, however, Jefferson had been charged with greater timidity. In 1805, all Europe was drawn into war leaving the United States a lonely bastion of neutralism. American trade was of course very highly valued, but each side insisted on its own commercial terms. Adhering to one system inevitably meant offending against the other, and the peace-loving Jefferson appeared to vacillate as British privateers, especially, plundered American ships, and sometimes even impressed American seamen into their service.

Eventually, as an alternative to joining the war, the Embargo Act (1807) was passed, virtually prohibiting any seaborne trade with foreign nations. It was a daring experiment in peaceful coercion but strongly opposed by northern commercial interests who rendered it almost inoperable through illegal trading and smuggling. Also some critics suggested it was inconsistent with the principles of individual freedom. In the end, shortly before leaving office in 1809, the President was forced to repeal the act, and his double term ended – after the triumphal chords of his earlier years in office – on a minor note.

An active retirement

Jefferson went with no regrets into retirement, eagerly resuming his family life and intellectual pursuits. Until 1815, he was president of the American Philosophical Society, the premier scientific institution of the United States. His great library, which he sold to Congress in 1815, was to form the core of the Library of Congress. He wrote copious letters and completed the work known as the Jefferson Bible, concentrating on the teachings of Jesus.

Above all, in retirement, Jefferson devoted himself to furthering popular education and establishing a university for Virginia, which was chartered in 1819. Architecture was among his keenest interests and the buildings which he designed for the University of Virginia are among the finest products of the American classical revival.

Burdened by financial difficulties in his last years, Jefferson died at Monticello on July 4, 1826, the 50th anniversary of American independence. John Adams, an old political foe who became a personal friend, died on the same day, a few hours later and his last words have often been taken to contain a metaphorical truth: "Thomas Jefferson still survives."

JAMES MADISON

James Madison (signature)

Madison Avenue, New York, heart of America's giant advertising industry, owes its name to a small, careful and thoroughly unshowmanlike statesman who became fourth President of the United States. There was no element of the self-publicist about James Madison; his great contribution to the nation's history was the patient framing of the Constitution, though he is remembered, too, as the unlikely war leader who took the United States into its second armed encounter with Great Britain. The war of 1812 had elements of farce and triumph about it – it was known as "Mr. Madison's war."

Early interest in theology
James Madison was born at Port Conway, in King George County, Virginia, on March 16, 1751 (5 March under the old-style calendar). His father owned sizable estates in Orange County, and in 1769, James entered the College of New Jersey, later to become Princeton University. Graduating

Fourth President 1809-1817

in 1771, he studied theology, perhaps in hope of entering the ministry. He was a member of the Orange County Committee of Public Safety and in 1776, was chosen to sit in the New Virginia Constitutional Convention. Madison was a delegate to the Continental Congress from 1780-83 and when his term ended he went back to Virginia to take up the study of law. There he was elected to the House of Delegates, and was especially prominent in helping to bring about the Annapolis Convention (1786) and its historic sequel, the Philadelphia Convention of the following year.

Drafting the Constitution
The Philadelphia Convention opened on May 25, 1787, with 55 delegates present to "consider the exigencies of the union". There were two notable absentees, John Adams and Thomas Jefferson – who were both on missions abroad – but George Washington was there and presided over what can only be described as an extraordinarily talented group of people who included Madison himself, Benjamin Franklin, Alexander Hamilton, James Wilson, Gouverneur Morris, John Rutledge, Roger Sherman, George Mason and Luther Martin. The average age was low, yet these mainly young and often unruly talents remained fully conscious of their responsibilities. Madison himself expressed a general opinion in declaring at one stage that they were deciding not only on immediate issues but the fate of republican government "for ever."

The aim of the convention was to draft a constitution for the new United States. Most present agreed about the key issue: somehow they must devise a federal system in which sovereignty was divided between the states and the central government. Authority should be drawn from the people, but no section of the population, no matter how large, must be allowed to ride roughshod over the rest. In essence, the task involved many reconciliations of conflicting interests, and no issue proved tougher than the question of who, precisely, should control the national government. The Virginia Plan, drafted by Madison, proposed that representation in the national law-making

body should be apportioned by population; so, the larger states would have more representatives. The New Jersey Plan, in contrast, proposed that each state be given equal representation whatever its size. The compromise reached, after long debate, was that population should determine places in the lower house (the House of Representatives); in the upper house (the Senate) each state would contribute two members regardless of its size.

Many other differences arose, especially in regard to slavery. For example, should a slave be counted as a unit of population? If so it would boost the representation of southern slave-holding states – but also give them an extra burden of federal taxation. The compromise adopted here was the so-called federal ratio, by which each slave was counted as three-fifths of a person for purposes both of representation and taxation.

On abolition of the slave trade a decision was postponed by a clause making it illegal for Congress to ban the traffic before 1808. This was one compromise which Madison disapproved, being a firm opponent of slavery. Nevertheless, the final document was signed by 39 of the 42

"Mr. Madison's War" was a mixed experience for the United States, but there were moments of triumph. Commanding naval operations on Lake Erie Captain Oliver Hazard Perry managed to capture the British fleet in a fierce engagement on September 10, 1813. (About a quarter of Perry's men were black; "skin color", he said, "no more indicated a man's worth than the cut of his coat.")

remaining delegates on September 17 and probably owes more to Madison's thought and provisions than to any other individual contribution. Afterwards, too, Madison did as much as any man to achieve its ratification, collaborating with Alexander Hamilton and John Jay in writing *The Federalist*, a series of papers defending the document. In short, just as George Washington is remembered as the Father of the Republic, so Madison can fairly be described as the Father of the Constitution.

An active Congressman
The Constitution came into effect in 1789. Madison in that year proved a very active member of the House of

Representatives and among other things he proposed the first ten amendments to the Constitution which were the basis of the Bill of Rights. He became, however, increasingly disturbed by Hamilton's financial measures and joined Jefferson's Democratic-Republican opposition. After briefly retiring from public life he attacked the Alien and Sedition Acts, drafting the Virginia Resolution (1798) supporting the states' rights against the high-handed abuse of federal powers.

Madison was married from 1794 to Dorothea (Dolly) Payne Todd, a widow of considerable charm whose buxom figure was often compared with the slight frame of her 5ft 6in husband. ("Jemmy Madison," wrote Washington Irving, "Oh poor Jemmy, he is but a withered little applejohn.") And as one of Jefferson's closest friends and supporters Madison was appointed Secretary of State when Jefferson won the 1800 presidential election.

Secretary of State for Jefferson

The two men worked very closely together, their character traits neatly complementing one another: Thomas Jefferson, the visionary, needed the calm, practical intelligence of his aide. Madison assisted in the Louisiana Purchase, for example, and was kept especially busy in trying to protect American neutrality on the high seas against the blockades and violations of Britain and Napoleonic France. Their Embargo policy was unsuccessful, and it is a tribute to the immense popularity of the retiring President that when Jefferson stood down, Madison – his chosen successor – won the 1808 presidential elections with a handsome 122 of the 173 electoral votes.

The build up to war

Dutiful and intelligent as he was, President Madison inherited continuing difficulties in foreign policy. In place of the blanket Embargo on maritime trade he introduced a Non Intercourse Act prohibiting trade only with Britain and France. But it proved hard to enforce, and Napoleon eventually succeeded in tricking Madison into applying a boycott to Britain alone. American ports were closed to His Majesty's ships, and pressure for war against Britain built up within the United States.

Warlike feelings were especially strong in the West, where the Indians were beginning to resist white settlement stirred up (it was believed) by the scheming British in Canada. At the Battle of Tippecanoe in November, 1811, General William Henry Harrison dispersed a potentially very dangerous confederation of tribes rallied by the Shawnee chief Tecumseh. Skirmishes, however, continued and anxieties remained. Eventually, on June 1, 1812,

Madison succumbed to the mood of belligerence and advised Congress to declare war against Britain. Approval was duly given – but only on very close votes in the Senate and the House.

THE WAR OF 1812

"Mr. Madison is wholly unfit for the storms of War," Henry Clay was to write. "Nature has cast him in too benevolent a mold. Admirably adapted to the tranquil scenes of peace – blending all the mild amiable virtues, he is not fit for the rough and rude blasts which the conflicts of nations generate." But if the President was unfit, so too was the nation as a whole. No preparation had been made for the War of 1812 and from the outset its conduct was mismanaged. Detroit and several other Northwest forts fell in the first summer, while American offensives failed miserably. By the end of the year His Majesty's navy was sealing a blockade of American ports. Madison was re-elected in 1812, but with continuing disasters the Federalists in New England started calling for his resignation, even raising the prospect of secession.

The ultimate humiliation occurred in 1814 when, supported by a fleet, a force of 4,000 British troops marched on Washington, D.C., seized the national capital and burned public buildings. Before putting the White House itself to the torch, a British admiral stole one of the President's hats as a souvenir, also taking a cushion from Dolly Madison's chair. The officer subsequently drank a mocking toast to the absent "Jemmy" adding what an onlooker described as "pleasantries too vulgar for me to repeat."

An honorable peace with Britain

A stalemate ensued, however, and by the Treaty of Ghent signed on Christmas Eve, 1814, relations between Britain and the United States reverted to their prewar condition, no territory being won or lost by either side. Fifteen days later – oblivious of the peace treaty – Andrew Jackson led the Americans to a famous victory over a larger British army at the Battle of New Orleans.

The honorable peace and the late flourish of a military triumph for the United States helped to restore Madison's standing. It also finished off the Federalists (who had been predicting calamitous defeat). Just about everyone in American politics professed democratic beliefs, and "Mr. Madison's War" also showed the governments of Europe that the U.S. republic was here to stay. Ironically these very facts helped Madison to adopt measures which were traditionally associated with the Federalists. In 1816, a second Bank of the United States was established, and in the same year Madison signed a protectionist tariff act. Last but not least, Britain and the United States grew closer together now that all prospect of returning to colonial rule became virtually unimaginable.

Madison retired in 1817 to his estate at Montpelier. In 1826, he succeeded Thomas Jefferson as rector of the University of Virginia, and his later years were also distinguished through his editing of his papers on the Federal Convention of 1787. He died at Montpelier, aged 85, on June 28, 1836.

The burning of Washington, August 1814. President Madison had gone to Bladensburg 7 miles away and his wife Dolly fled the executive mansion taking with her a large portrait of George Washington for safe keeping. Not long afterward British troops set the capital alight. The President's House was left a burned-out shell and would have been totally destroyed but for a lucky rainstorm which doused the flames.

JAMES MONROE

James Monroe (signature)

Fifth President 1817-1825

Good fortune smiled on James Monroe's administration. The United States was both peaceful and prosperous during his two terms, its growing population spreading westward into newly acquired lands which offered seemingly limitless opportunities. The time has been dubbed the "Era of Good Feelings" and Monroe himself was well suited to the role of supervising the young republic's growth. Neither a brilliant orator nor an especially skilled politician he nonetheless possessed qualities of sincerity and sound judgment which matched the needs of the nation. He was the Union's great consolidator, "entitled to say," wrote John Quincy Adams, "like Augustus Caesar of his imperial city, that he had found her built of brick and left her constructed of marble." Moreover, in the Monroe Doctrine he gave his name to a principle which was to serve future Presidents as a keystone of U.S. foreign policy.

The valiant soldier

James Monroe was born at Monroe's Creek, in Westmoreland County, Virginia, on April 28, 1758, to a father of Scottish and a mother of Welsh descent. He was educated at the College of William and Mary and fought in the 3rd Virginia Regiment during the revolutionary war. Monroe saw action at Harlem Heights, White Plains, Trenton, Brandywine, Germantown and Monmouth. From 1780, he studied law under another prominent Virginian, Thomas Jefferson, for whom he developed a lifelong respect and friendship; Jefferson in turn admired Monroe as "a man whose soul might be turned wrong side outwards without discovering a blemish to the world."

Formative political years

Monroe was elected to the Virginia House of Delegates in 1782 and served in Congress from 1783-86. As a U.S. Senator from 1790-94 he opposed Federalist plans for a national bank and was generally critical of Washington's administration. He was minister to France from 1794-96 and after serving as Governor of Virginia from 1799-1802 returned to France in 1803 to help in the negotiations which achieved the Louisiana Purchase. After further missions to Spain in 1804 and Britain from 1805-06 Monroe sailed home to the United States. He served Virginia again in the House of Delegates and as governor, resigning to be Madison's Secretary of State (1811-17). After Washington, D.C., was burned by the British he briefly combined his duties with those of Secretary of War.

During these formative years in public life Monroe achieved only a mediocre reputation; when it was announced in 1816 that he was to stand as a presidential candidate the colorful, combative Aaron Burr referred to him in a letter as "one of the most improper and incompetent that could be selected. Naturally dull and stupid; extremely illiterate; indecisive to a degree that would be incredible to one who did not know him . . ." Such charges are certainly exaggerated: it is true that Monroe

lacked a forceful manner and dazzling intellect, but his more patient virtues were acknowledged in a tribute by John C. Calhoun who declared, "I have known many much more rapid in reaching a conclusion, but few with a certainty so unerring."

Number 1600 Pennsylvania Avenue – better known as the White House. President Monroe moved into the rebuilt mansion in the fall of 1817. Gleaming white paint covered marks of the earlier fire; hence the term White House, in general use from Monroe's era (but not officially adopted until 1901).

The "Era of Good Feelings"

In the presidential election, Monroe received 183 electoral votes to the meager 34 of his Federalist opponent, Rufus King. The disparity reflects the near total collapse of organized opposition to the Democratic-Republicans more than the qualities of the incoming President. But Monroe's eight years were genuinely distinguished by a new spirit of national unity which was noted from the very outset. Typically, Monroe opened his presidency not with any rush to present state papers but with a goodwill tour of New England, once the hostile heartland of Federalism. Everywhere he was warmly greeted and it was in Boston that a journalist on the *Columbia Centinel* first spoke of a new "Era of Good Feelings." The mood of reconciliation was also personified by the rekindled friendship of two old political opponents – the former Presidents, Thomas Jefferson and John Adams – who after a decade of cold animosity began a warm and voluminous correspondence.

Monroe himself reached the presidency at the age of 61, and had something of the air of an eighteenth-century throwback about him, the powdered hair and cocked hat reinforcing the formal manners learned during long years in the diplomatic service. He entered a White House rebuilt since the disastrous burning of Washington, and he and his wife Elizabeth, to whom he was married from 1786, refurnished the mansion in the most elegant French style with Aubusson rugs, candelabra, porcelain and items of bronze-doré. After the simplicities of Jefferson and the spontaneities of buxom Dolly Madison, the Monroes restored a hint of pomp to the office of President, their dinner parties suffering somewhat from rigid solemnities. "Not a whisper broke upon the ear to interrupt the silence of the place," complained a congressman, "and everyone looked as if the next moment would be his last."

It was all faintly nostalgic and reassuring, though, and seems not to have greatly troubled anyone. Indeed, such was the absence of ill will that in 1820, Monroe was re-elected by every vote except one – only the New Hampshire elector cast a vote against him, and that on the grounds that nobody should share with George Washington the honor of a unanimous vote.

The acquisition of Florida

Monroe's foreign policy was marked by several important achievements which include the acquisition of the Floridas. In the course of the first Seminole War (1816-18) a small army under General Andrew Jackson moved into the Spanish colony in pursuit of the fleeing enemy. Spain now recognized her inability to defend and govern the area and ceded it to the United States under the Transcontinental Treaty of 1821.

Also of major consequence was the Rush-Bagott Agreement (1817) by which Britain and the United States peacefully demilitarized by Great Lakes, limiting armaments to 100-ton vessels: one each on Lakes Champlain and Ontario and two on the upper lakes. Ratified by the Senate in 1818, the agreement is regarded as a model of effective disarmament. Stage by stage the entire U.S./Canadian border was later demilitarized, while offshore fishery disputes were also settled in a spirit of friendship.

The Missouri Compromise

Not so lasting in effect was the Missouri Compromise which only temporarily defused the explosive political issue of slavery. Missouri was a new state formed from the Louisiana Purchase, and before its admission in 1820, the slave and free states of the Union were evenly matched at 11 states each. Clearly the new state was liable to tilt the balance, and since many of its settlers were slave-owners it seemed that Missouri must give a majority to the slave states in the Senate. Deadlock was reached over its application for statehood until a compromise was devised, by which Missouri did enter the Union as a slave state but Maine, having been separated from Massachusetts, was also admitted as a counterbalancing free state to maintain equilibrium in the Senate. To provide against further strife, Congress also adopted a proposal banning slavery forever from any other part of the Louisiana Purchase north of 36°30′ north latitude.

A depth of passionate feeling was buried to achieve the Compromise and the dispute did not bode well for the future. The controversy, said Thomas Jefferson, "like a fire bell in the night, awakened and filled me with terror." Nevertheless, agreement had been reached and tempers cooled for the time being.

THE MONROE DOCTRINE

Though personally opposed to slavery, President Monroe had himself abstained from intervening in the Compromise debates. But his name is intimately connected with a famous message to Congress, delivered on December 2, 1823, embodying what is known today as the "Monroe Doctrine." Its text proclaimed that the American continents, "by the free and independent condition which they have assumed and maintain, are henceforth not to be considered as subjects for future colonization by any European powers." The United States would not interfere with any existing European colonies in the Western Hemisphere, but if European powers tried to extend their control to countries there independent, it would be considered an act of unfriendliness toward the United States itself.

The message was issued in direct response to two particular issues. The Russians had lain claim to fishing rights off the northwest coast of North America; and there was some general concern at a possible European attempt at reconquest of former Spanish colonies in Latin America. Drafted by Secretary of State John Quincy Adams, the statement had Monroe's full endorsement and basically stated that Americans wanted to work out their own destiny without interference. In fact, it attracted little attention at the time, either at home or abroad.

But the significance of the Doctrine deepened as the decades passed and the United States grew in power. It was revived, for example, by President Polk to repudiate European intrigues over the annexation of Texas, and to

Florida Indians dressed in deer skins stalk their prey in this early print. Florida had a mixed population, numbers of local Seminole Indians being swollen by fugitive Negroes who had fled the United States to seek sanctuary. Before Spain ceded the territory there was considerable toing and froing across the border wtih Georgia. In the first of the so-called Seminole Wars (1816-18) U.S. troops made punitive raids; marauding blacks and Indians struck back.

counter proposals by de Lesseps for a French-built Panama Canal. President Theodore Roosevelt carried its implications beyond a simple warning to Europe to keep its hands off Latin America; by the "Roosevelt Corollary" (1904) he justified direct U.S. intervention in the affairs of Latin American countries on the grounds that the nation could under certain circumstances act as the Western Hemisphere's "international police power." Indeed, the Cuban crisis of the 1960s and Nicaraguan events of the 1980s can be interpreted as progeny of the Monroe Doctrine.

Such developments lay far beyond the horizon of James Monroe and his contemporaries. Besides lending his name to the famous principle of foreign relations, the President himself initiated few policies, preferring to steer a steady course in the name of national unity rather than crusade for any doctrine. In fact, like his fellow Virginian republicans Jefferson and Madison, he proved more flexible in office than his states' rights pedigree might have suggested. In particular, Monroe could see the need for federal aid to improve communications in the ever expanding republic, and though it went against his traditions he authorized substantial expenditure on transportation projects.

In 1825, at the end of his second term, James Monroe retired to his home at Oak Hill, Virginia. Four years later he served on the Virginia convention called to amend the state constitution. Toward the end of his life he was plagued by financial difficulties and forced to ask Congress to repay him for expenses incurred in office. He died, aged 73, in New York City on July 4, 1831.

JOHN QUINCY ADAMS

John Quincy Adams.

"I am a man of reserved, cold, austere, and forbidding manners: my political adversaries say, a gloomy misanthropist, and my personal enemies an unsocial savage," John Quincy Adams once wrote in his diary. History shows him to have been honest and able, with great vision of America as a continental nation. Yet the forbidding quality which America's sixth President diagnosed in himself proved a serious political liability. He was seen as a vinegary Old Puritan; he possessed a talent for making enemies, without the warmth to command loyalty from his friends. And although he was unquestionably a great statesman, he was neither great – nor even competent – as a President of the United States.

Son of the second President
John Quincy Adams was born on July 11, 1767, at Braintree (Quincy), Massachusetts, the son of Abigail and John Adams – America's second President. In 1778, when his father sailed for France to serve in the American commission, John Quincy accompanied him and so gained his education in Europe. There, too, he started to keep a diary which still survives as an important documentary record of his time. The young Adams subsequently returned to Massachusetts, graduated from Harvard in 1787, and went on to study law. From 1794, he was American minister successively in the Netherlands and in Prussia. In 1801, he came back to New England and from 1803-08 he represented Massachusetts as a Senator.

Sixth President 1825-1829

Adams at this time was a Federalist, but he always pursued an independent line in the Senate: approving the Louisiana Purchase, for example, and generally supporting Republican foreign policy. His stance created hostility within his own party and he resigned his seat in 1808. In the same year Adams attended the Republican caucus which nominated Madison for the presidency, so becoming a Republican. From 1809-17, under Madison, he was American minister to Russia and Britain; and from 1817-25 he was Monroe's Secretary of State.

Secretary of State
This was his time of greatness: as Secretary of State Adams played a key role in the shaping of modern America. In 1818, he negotiated the boundary with Canada along the 49th parallel, with a ten-year joint occupation with Britain of the Oregon Country. In the following year, by mercilessly hard bargaining, he negotiated the acquisition of Florida from Spain, and a boundary to the Louisiana Territory which included a vast area extending beyond the Rockies to the Pacific. By this "Transcontinental Treaty" (1819) Adams had opened a mighty corridor to the western seaboard and he regarded the achievement with justifiable satisfaction. "The acquisition of a definite line of boundary to the (Pacific)," he wrote in his diary, "forms a great epoch in our history."

It was Adams too who, as Secretary of State, was chiefly responsible for formulating the Monroe Doctrine (1823) repudiating any future colonization of the Americas by

The Smithsonian Institution, Washington D.C. was founded by a bequest of Englishman James Smithson to create an establishment for the "increase and diffusion of knowledge among men." Strong opposition came from people who denied Congress's constitutional right to accept the endowment. As ex-president, however, John Quincy Adams proved a valiant champion of the institution which was established in 1846. (In this picture the modern Museum of History and Technology dominates the foreground.)

European powers. And with such a formidable set of achievements under his belt, his presidency was to be all the more disappointing.

An unhappy presidency

The presidential election of 1824 was contested in the Electoral College by Andrew Jackson (99 votes), Adams himself (84 votes), William Crawford (41 votes) and Henry Clay (37 votes). Jackson had notched up the highest tally but since there was no clear majority the decision was put to the House of Representatives which, under the Constitution, had to choose from among the three front-runners. Clay, the losing candidate, gave his support to Adams who then won on the first ballot. Jackson felt cheated, and his supporters became virulent in their hostility to the incoming President. When Clay was made Secretary of State their rancor increased; charges of corrupt bargaining were laid against Adams who then had to endure the additional aggravation of congressional investigation into his appointments.

Ironically, as a President, Adams showed a distinct and disastrous reluctance to find jobs for his partisans, or to remove opponents from office. It was an issue of principle – he did not believe in parties or sections. But his refusal to build up support contrasted with the grandeur of his conception of the President's role. Adams proposed to use the federal authority to initiate a host of useful projects ranging from roadbuilding to the founding of a national university. These were interpreted with some suspicion by the many Americans who feared strong national government. His father had often been accused of conservative – even monarchical – tendencies and the same worries were now being voiced about him.

Hounded by vengeful Jacksonians, lacking a strong party faction and without any wide popular support, John Quincy Adams found himself thwarted at every turn and endured so unhappy a presidency that, it is recorded, he came to doubt the existence of God and the purposefulness of life. The one significant event of his administration was the passage of a bill raising tariffs, the so-called "Tariff of Abominations," introducing high duties on raw wool, flax, hemp and several other commodities to protect the factional interests of American producers who were based chiefly in the north and west of the country.

The 1828 election was a shameful affair, fought between Adams and Jackson with lies and personal smears spread by both sides. Jackson won (178 to 183); and it is a measure of the bitterness aroused that Adams refused to attend the inauguration ceremony.

A bequest for the Smithsonian Institution

Nevertheless, Adams did not abandon politics; on the contrary, in 1831, he entered Congress where he served with great distinction for 17 years, an outspoken opponent of extending slavery and of the "gag rules" by which pro-slavery members tried to stop abolitionist petitions from being alluded to in Congress. In a different sphere the ex-President was also the man chiefly responsible for ensuring that the Smithsonian Institution was established, from a bequest to the nation.

John Quincy Adams was married from 1797 to Louisa Catherine Johnson. In February, 1848, at the age of 80, he suffered a stroke in the House; he died two days later in the Speaker's Room.

ANDREW JACKSON

Andrew Jackson

As the hero of New Orleans and the first President to come truly from the common people, Andrew Jackson – "Old Hickory" – was swept into office on a tide of popular enthusiasm the like of which had not been seen before. A boisterous mob descended on Washington, D.C., for the inauguration on March 4, 1829, folk sleeping where they could for a chance to watch the frontiersman take the oath. Daniel Webster observed, "I have never seen such a crowd before. Persons have come 500 miles to see General Jackson, and they really seem to think that the country has been rescued from some dreadful danger."

After the inaugural ceremony people rushed to the White House reception where something close to a riot broke out: liquor was spilled in the crush; dishes were shattered; fights erupted and women fainted. In all the eagerness to catch a glimpse of the President, mud-stained boots trampled on damask satin covered chairs and with the physical safety of the 61-year-old incumbent in jeopardy, aides formed a human chain to keep the mob back. Andrew Jackson, who had earlier been smuggled into the Capitol via the basement, now made his escape from the White House by a back door to spend his first night as President in Gadsby's Hotel.

A popular choice
A rugged individualist, brusque, forceful – even uncouth – Jackson continues to exert his fascination to this day. He

Seventh President 1829-1837

unquestionably strengthened the role of President and it was under his auspices that a vigorous new national party system took shape, appealing to an ever-larger electorate because property requirements for voters were being eliminated in many states. When Jackson was elected for his first term, 56 percent of adult white males voted – more than twice the percentage four years earlier. His victory was celebrated as a triumph of the new democracy, and "Let the people rule!" was his slogan.

Yet Jackson was no modern incarnation of egalitarian feeling. By the time he contested the presidency he was a major slaveholder; and a tough master, too – he had once advertised for a runaway offering the captor a double reward if he would administer 100 lashes to the fugitive. In his dealings with American Indians, moreover, Jackson was entirely callous, forcing mass removals while speaking of his "red children." Suspicious by temperament he shunned many a man of talent, preferring to rely on a "kitchen cabinet" of loyal subordinates. And in rewarding his supporters with government posts he legitimized the office-grabbing practices of the spoils system.

The young frontiersman
Andrew Jackson was born at the Waxhaw settlement in Lancaster County, South Carolina, on March 15, 1757, to lowly Irish immigrant parents. He grew into a quick-tempered youth who eagerly answered the call to arms

against the Redcoats, taking part in the Battle of Hanging Rock when only 13. An episode from the following year deeply imprinted his character: captured by the British, Jackson was ordered to black the boots of an officer and when he refused received a blow across the face with the flat of a saber. Jackson bore the scar to his dying day, and retained an enduring dislike of the British.

The young frontiersman read law in Salisbury, North Carolina, opened a practice in 1787, and the following year moved to Nashville as the prosecuting attorney of what was to become Tennessee. In 1791, he married Rachel Robards, a woman who had been victim of an earlier, unhappy marriage and who had been led to believe that her first husband had obtained a divorce. In fact, the divorce was not finalized until two years later so that Jackson and Rachel had to go through a second marriage ceremony, albeit quietly, in 1793. Cruel charges of adultery were later raised to damage Jackson's political prospects, and he fought a number of duels to defend his wife's honor against slights, real or imagined.

"Old Hickory"

In 1796, Jackson helped draft the Tennessee constitution and for a year he held the state's single seat in Congress. He was a judge of the Tennessee supreme court from 1798-1804, and championed Aaron Burr in the famous trial of 1807: Burr had been involved in a conspiracy to create an independent nation in the West, was indicted for treason but acquitted. Jackson's own hot-blooded and quarrelsome nature led him into an assortment of duels and private disputes in the years which followed, but in 1813-14 he won a reputation for toughness and military prowess in leading the campaign against the Creek Indians whom he defeated at Horseshoe Bend, Alabama. It was then that the popular nickname "Old Hickory" was first applied, and later that year he was appointed a major general to fight against the British in the War of 1812.

THE BATTLE OF NEW ORLEANS

Jackson shot to national prominence as the hero of the Battle of New Orleans, an engagement fought two weeks *after* peace was negotiated at the Treaty of Ghent (December 24, 1814). But neither Jackson nor his opponent knew of the ceasefire. The Westerner's task was to defend the Gulf Coast against an anticipated attack, and when the Redcoats arrived under Packenham, Jackson directed his force of some 4,500 backwoods fighters against superior British numbers. Convinced that the undisciplined Americans would flee before a show of strength, Packenham led his men against the patriots' position in a fixed-bayonets frontal attack at dawn. Stiffened by Jackson, however, the

The inauguration riot, March 4, 1829. Although only the "officially and socially eligible" had been invited to the White House reception there was no way of preventing crowds of boisterous admirers from gaining access to the executive mansion and running amuck.

A bitter defeat

Jackson again became a Tennessee Senator from 1823-25 and in 1824 was a presidential candidate. Such was his prestige that in a four-cornered fight he won the highest number of votes in the Electoral College. However, he lacked an overall majority, which meant that the decision must be put to the House of Representatives where he was defeated by John Quincy Adams. There was bitterness in the Jackson camp afterwards; their man seemed to have been cheated and throughout the presidency of John Quincy Adams the Jacksonians kept up a fierce and obstructive opposition. Jackson himself, temperamentally suspicious to the verge of paranoia, believed that there had been a plot against him, and that Henry Clay had used his influence in the House to swing support behind Adams on promise of receiving the office of Secretary of State.

Everything conspired to make the election of 1828 the most acrimonious yet seen. Questions of policy were not much discussed; the contest was fought on personalities with Adams pilloried as an aristocrat and squanderer, and Jackson as a barbarian demagogue – and adulterer. This last was a deeply wounding charge. Jackson won the election but Rachel died three months before the inauguration, her death hastened (Jackson believed) by the smears spread in the campaign. On the day of his riotous inauguration, Jackson was dressed in mourning black and still grieving for his beloved wife.

The self-made man

It seemed to some fastidious observers that the rule of "King Mob" had arrived on that tumultuous day. But though Jackson was an authentic son of the frontier, ill-educated and with many a roughhewn Western mannerism – such as tobacco-chewing – he was by no means a fiery revolutionary. On the contrary: through speculation in western lands he had become the rich proprietor of a great Tennessee plantation called The Hermitage, and he was the master of many slaves. Jackson was the very archetype of an American self-made man; and as observers were to learn increasingly in the nineteenth century, a self-made man of the lowliest origins might turn out as reliable a conservative as any privileged aristocrat.

At the White House Jackson entertained lavishly, but he

Americans did not turn tail. Instead, they held their positions and delivered such a withering hail of fire that the Redcoats sustained over 2,000 casualties to only a dozen suffered by Jackson's men.

It was a stirring victory, and in 1818 Jackson made himself conspicuous again through invading the Spanish colony of Florida in pursuit of fleeing Indians, outlaws and slaves during the Seminole War. The action provoked controversy, not least because two British subjects were hanged as spies during the operation. However, the result was that Spain acknowledged her inability to administer the colony. Negotiations for its purchase were opened; Florida was won for the Union; and in 1821, Jackson was made military governor of the territory.

did so without stiff ceremonial, preferring a more comfortable environment. One visitor has described a typical evening there, with a fire blazing in the grate, women sewing and children playing about regardless of affairs of state. "At the farther end of the room sat the President in his armchair, wearing a long loose coat and smoking a reed pipe, with a bowl of red clay; combining the dignity of the patriarch, monarch and Indian chief. Just behind was Edward Livingston, the Secretary of State, reading him a dispatch from the French Minister for Foreign Affairs. The ladies glance admiringly now and then at the President, who listens, waving his pipe toward the children when they become too boisterous."

A new generation of Americans loved this combination of the heroic with the homespun. Jackson had a true mass appeal: although he drew his support especially from the farming south and west any average citizen could identify with the easy style, and Jackson was fully conscious of his image. Sometimes, it seems, he even feigned his uncouth fits of temper simply to get his way.

Andrew Jackson rallies his men at the Battle of New Orleans, January 8, 1815. The British battalions advanced packed four ranks deep into a murderous fire. "They couldn't stand it," wrote an American regular. "In five minutes the whole front of their formation was shaken as if by an earthquake . . . No such execution by small arms was ever done before."

The "kitchen cabinet"

His "spoils system" owed much to his temperament: a forceful individualist he placed a high store on personal loyalty, putting it above status or ability. In assuming office he candidly intended to punish those who had attacked him during the campaign and to fill offices with his own partisans. Jackson did not truly invent the system; others had operated it before. But what he did was to elevate it almost to a high principle of statecraft. He believed that by a regular house-cleaning the corrupt and inept would be eliminated; that by rotating office more people would participate in government. The danger, of course, was that efficient public servants would be dismissed with the dross and that their experience would be lost to the nation. Mere spoilsmen certainly prospered – in the spring of 1829, a host of Jacksonian supporters descended on the Capitol, "lank, lean, famished," in the words of a disdainful Henry Clay, and shouting, "Give us bread! Give us treasury pap! Give us our reward!" It has to be said that in choosing heads of departments Jackson appointed many such loyal, lackluster party men and that in his informal council, known as the "kitchen cabinet," only Martin Van Buren had real ability.

Personal factors hugely influenced appointments, especially during the Eaton Affair. Jackson's friend, John Henry Eaton, Secretary of War, had married a brunette named Peggy O'Neale whose first husband, it was said, killed himself because of their illicit liaison. The wives of Vice President John C. Calhoun and other Cabinet members publicly shunned Mrs. Eaton in Washington. But remembering how his own marriage had been blighted by rumors of adultery, Jackson was staunch in the lady's defense. In 1831, he entirely disbanded his first Cabinet to purge the gossiping offenders. Calhoun, in particular, became a sworn enemy while Van Buren (a widower with no snooty wife for embarrassment) supported Mrs. Eaton and became the grateful President's heir apparent.

The modern concept of national parties owes much to Jackson. It was under his administration that the Jeffersonian Democratic-Republican party divided into the pro-Jackson Democrats and so-called National Republicans lead by Henry Clay. Moreover, from 1832, presidential candidates were no longer nominated by congressional caucuses but by national conventions.

A financial crisis

In 1832, Jackson won re-election, defeating Henry Clay by a large majority: the great issue of the contest, and of his second term, was the Bank of the United States. Basically Jackson had a frontiersman's mistrust of paper money and

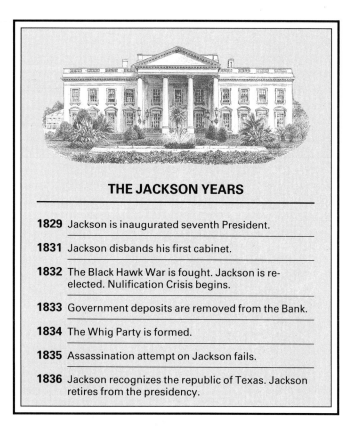

THE JACKSON YEARS

1829 Jackson is inaugurated seventh President.

1831 Jackson disbands his first cabinet.

1832 The Black Hawk War is fought. Jackson is re-elected. Nulification Crisis begins.

1833 Government deposits are removed from the Bank.

1834 The Whig Party is formed.

1835 Assassination attempt on Jackson fails.

1836 Jackson recognizes the republic of Texas. Jackson retires from the presidency.

all commercial banking, and suspecting that the privileged institution of the great Bank was working against him he vetoed its re-charter. In 1833, Jackson ordered its government deposits to be transferred to selected state banks, and as funds were withdrawn the Bank fought back, pressing the state banks to convert their own notes and checks into specie, gold or silver. A crisis ensued, petitions being presented to Congress and opposition mounting especially in the Senate. But Jackson dug in his heels. "I am fixed in my course as firm as the Rocky Mountains," he told Van Buren. And after a long struggle the Bank was destroyed.

Strong leadership

Another great trial of strength was the Nullification Crisis which began in 1832, when South Carolina tried to nullify the tariff laws and refused to collect imports. Jackson recognized a serious threat to the Union and showed no hesitation in wielding the full might of the federal authority. He threatened military action; he threatened to hang Calhoun (who had reluctantly condoned the southerners). In the end, South Carolina's jittery radicals took refuge in a face-saving compromise.

In 1836, Jackson recognized the Republic of Texas which

had declared itself independent after the siege of the Alamo. The adventure seemed somehow in keeping with the Jacksonian frontier spirit of bold enterprise and personal initiative. But in offering his own, unique brand of strong leadership Jackson had made enemies aplenty. In 1835, he narrowly escaped an assassination attempt. His political opponents, meanwhile, took to speaking of him as "King Andrew" and, likening themselves to the British party which had opposed monarchical tyranny in the eighteenth century, they styled themselves the Whigs. Theirs was an ineffectual coalition while the hero still presided at the White House. But when Jackson stepped down after his second term their prospects began to look brighter. Van Buren, "Old Hickory"'s hand-picked successor, won the

1836 election with the well-organized Democratic machine behind him. But he lacked Jackson's mass appeal and in 1840, the Whig party was to win the presidency for its own candidate by using precisely the style and methods which the Jacksonians had initiated.

All this was for the future. Jackson left office more popular than ever but retired in ailing health and mourning his niece Emily Donelson, who had served as his official hostess after Rachel's death, and who succumbed to tuberculosis late in 1836. Nevertheless, Jackson lived on in retirement to the age of 78, an ever idolized, ever idiosyncratic national figure whose approval was still sought by aspiring politicians. He died at The Hermitage on June 8, 1845.

Above: *Black Hawk, chief of the Sauk and Fox, led an Indian rising in 1832. Defeated, he was taken to President Jackson in Washington. His spirit remained unbowed: "I am a man and you are another," he told Jackson with dignity.*

Left: *The Battle of Bad Axe (1832) ended the Black Hawk War with ruthless slaughter. The campaign had begun when Chief Black Hawk rallied tribes to try and win back Indian lands from settlers on the east bank of the Mississippi. After some initial success in raids the rising was decisively suppressed by the militia.*

MARTIN VAN BUREN

Eighth President 1837-1841

Nicknamed the "Little Magician," Martin Van Buren was known to his contemporaries as a skillful manipulator of political machinery – a sly puller of party wires. And though these charges may mask the statesmanlike resolve which he undoubtedly showed as President, an almost engaging quality of craftiness still lingers about his political memory. "He rowed to his object with muffled oars," was the memorable comment of John Randolph of Roanoke.

The machine politician

Martin Van Buren was born on December 5, 1782, at Kinderhook, New York, to a farming family of Dutch descent. Having trained for the law he was admitted to the Bar and served as surrogate of Columbia County, N.Y., from 1808-13. In 1812, he entered the state senate, and was U.S. Senator in 1821, and re-elected in 1827. He was briefly Governor of New York in 1829, but in March of that year he resigned the governorship to become President Jackson's Secretary of State.

Throughout the 1820s, Van Buren exhibited both the personal charm and political foxiness which were to be his hallmarks. It is hard to discover his attitudes to the issues of the day precisely because he took trouble to avoid taking up a position; if a fence was in the offing Van Buren could be relied on to sit upon it. But what he lacked in policies he made up for in friends; Van Buren was a key member of the Albany Regency, a powerful grouping of New York politi-

cians who, as much as anyone, were responsible for establishing the "spoils system" in U.S. political life. He became the archetype of a machine politician, promising office as reward for support.

As Secretary of State, Van Buren made himself the most valued member of Jackson's so-called "kitchen cabinet" of close friends and advisers. He supported Jackson's opposition to the Bank of the United States, and in 1832 was elected Vice President, easily outsmarting Calhoun in the struggle to become heir apparent. Jackson himself was determined to make Van Buren his successor, and in 1835 the Democratic convention was unanimous in nominating him for President.

Jackson's protégé becomes President

Andrew Jackson's prestige and support also secured victory for Van Buren in the presidential election of 1836, when he received 170 electoral votes against the 73 cast for General William H. Harrison, his leading Whig opponent. But the margin of victory in the popular vote was narrow, and Van Buren took office at a difficult time, with the Panic of 1837 seizing the nation. The crisis had begun in 1836 under Jackson, when land speculators who had earlier been buying public land with paper money were required to pay in specie: gold or silver. Prices plummeted and the land boom ended as hordes of bank depositors tried to withdraw their gold or silver. In the panicky spring of 1837, every bank in the country was forced to suspend specie payments.

Advice on the Prairie *by William Ranney (1813-1857), an artist well known for genre paintings of the West. Pioneer families with their wagons pressed westward in great numbers during the early decades of the nineteenth century. The homesteaders bought virgin land from the government, then mortgaged the land to borrow cash from local banks. With this paper money they could then buy more land from the government – and so the spiral of purchases continued, until Jackson's government got jittery and insisted on payment for public land in gold or silver. Land prices immediately plummeted, creating the panic which rocked Van Buren's administration.*

The crisis initiated a nationwide depression. Banks and business became bankrupt, thousands of speculators lost money on land and the country as a whole suffered the worst depression in its history so far. Van Buren firmly refused to acknowledge responsibility for the country's general economic condition; his policy was to let the panic sort itself out without interference by federal government. In fact, by 1838, a revival was underway and the banks were again making specie payments. But the following year a sharp drop in the price of cotton triggered a further general price decline and the depression continued.

Van Buren cannot be held responsible for either financial crisis (nor for the growing tensions between the Northern and Southern wings of the Democratic Party over the contentious issue of slavery). Indeed, the firmness of his resolve on financial matters was admirable, and for four years he struggled to secure the passage of his Independent Treasury Bill, finally succeeding in 1840. The new law severed all connection between banks and the federal government. In future, all payments to the government were to be made in hard cash, revenues being stored in specially constructed government vaults situated in different parts of the nation.

The first modern presidential campaign

But the president's firmness did not make him popular. On the contrary, he was widely perceived as indifferent to the people's fate – a perception which his Whig opponents were quick to exploit. They nominated General William H. Harrison in 1840, cynically billing him as a homespun log cabin frontiersman for contrast with the remote, luxuriating Van Buren. "Van, Van, Van is a used up man," was their chant. In vain did the President try to speak of the issues; in the first modern presidential campaign with mass rallies, parades and sloganeering he was soundly beaten, receiving only 60 electoral votes to the 234 secured by his opponent.

Van Buren was a victim of his own electoral approach in which policies counted for nothing beside the imperative of the political machine. After the election he retired to Kinderhook hoping to be nominated in 1844. However, he failed to win the required two-thirds majority in the Democratic convention, chiefly through opposing the annexation of Texas. In 1848, he was nominated by the Free Soil faction, but ran without success. At the outbreak of the Civil War he lent support to President Lincoln.

Van Buren was married in 1807 to Hannah Hoes; he died at Kinderhook on July 24, 1862.

WILLIAM H. HARRISON

W H Harrison

A President for only one month, William Henry Harrison scarcely had time to make his governmental mark. Inaugurated on March 4, 1841, he passed away on April 4, so achieving melancholy distinction both as the first President to die in office, and as holder of the shortest presidency. Pneumonia was the immediate cause of his demise, but it is fair to speculate that in reality "Old Tip," as he was known, succumbed in part to the heavy burden of office.

Son of Benjamin Harrison

He was born at Berkeley, in Charles City County, Virginia, on February 9, 1773, son of prominent politician Benjamin Harrison who had signed the Declaration of Independence. William Henry began his military career at 18 as ensign in the 1st regiment at Fort Washington in Cincinnati. Having seen service and risen to the rank of captain he left the army in 1798 to become secretary to the Northwest territory, and territorial delegate to Congress in 1799.

The Battle of Tippecanoe

It was as first governor of the newly created Indiana territory (1800-12) that he made his reputation. White settlers had long been teeming into the fertile region of the Ohio Valley and by force, bribery and deceit wresting land from the Indian inhabitants. Through a series of mercilessly negotiated treaties Harrison kept up the pressure, opening vast areas to white settlement in the name of "civilization."

Ninth President 1841

Resistance sooner or later was inevitable, and the Indians found a leader of genius in the Shawnee chief Tecumseh, who through brilliant oratory sought to bind all of the peoples east of the Mississippi in one grand tribal confederation to drive the whites from their lands. In this he was assisted by his brother, a crusading medicine man known as The Prophet, and by 1811 many thousands of Indians were flocking to their cause.

Harrison responded by advancing with a party of troops and militia to the Tippecanoe river where the brothers had their camp. Tecumseh himself was away rallying support, and the Prophet led a rash attack on the white men's position. Harrison replied by destroying the Indian camp, although he suffered a heavy loss of men, but though the episode was not entirely decisive it did break the Indians' confidence. The Battle of Tippecanoe was a great triumph for Harrison, the future cornerstone of his political career.

In the War of 1812, Harrison was made a major general and given command of all troops in the Northwest. He routed the British at the Battle of the Thames (1813) and went on to become a Congressman from 1816-19 and Senator from 1825-28 for Ohio. In the presidential elections of 1836 he emerged, somewhat surprisingly, as the frontrunner among the Whig candiates opposing Van Buren. His appeal lay in his very lack of such annoyances as policies; like a lesser version of his fellow westerner Andrew Jackson, Harrison was seen as a plain, honest

The Battle of Tippecanoe made Harrison's name. Tecumseh, his Shawnee opponent, here wears British tunic and medal (British intrigue was blamed for Indian unrest).

and down-to-earth military man with no doctrinaire commitments attached to him.

The creation of "Old Tip"

Harrison lost in 1836, but his "old soldier" appeal was shrewdly manipulated by the Whigs in the election of 1840. A fully-fledged two-party system now operated nationwide, with political machines working on both sides. The Democrats had succeeded under Jackson and his protégé Van Buren by largely ignoring issues and getting a bandwagon rolling. The Whigs in 1840 simply copied their tactics. The suave, subtle President Van Buren had presided over a country gripped by economic depression. The Whigs offered no true antidote but a figurehead whom the disgruntled electorate could applaud – General Harrison, all-conquering Hero of Tippecanoe, the trusty frontiersman, "Old Tip."

Some conscious image-building was required to turn Harrison into a horny-handed son of toil for contrast with the remote and effete New York aristocrat which Van Buren was made out to be. After all, as son of a very eminent Virginian, Harrison was by no means lowly born. So when the Democrats derided the Whig candidate as a "log cabin and hard cider" contender Harrison's supporters gleefully accepted the tag, parading miniature log cabins in their processions and serving hard cider at their rallies. Mass meetings were key features of the campaign, while songs,

chants and slogans drowned all attempt at serious discussion. For a balanced ticket, the Whigs ran former Democrat John Tyler of Virginia as vice-presidential candidate, and the cry of "Tippecanoe and Tyler Too!" was incessantly heard.

The ballyhoo greatly increased public interest in presidential elections, the huge turnout amounting to four-fifths of all eligible voters. "Old Tip" won by a popular margin of 150,000, and the electoral vote was a resounding 234 to 60.

The shortest presidency

"General Harrison was sung into the presidency," wrote a contemporary. But the sequel was anticlimactic. Many a political debt had been incurred in the course of the campaign, and the 68-year-old general was besieged by office-seekers greedy for the spoils of success. Harrison did not conceive himself as a commanding executive figure, and a bitter power struggle was fought out for real leadership by the charismatic Kentuckian, Henry Clay, and Daniel Webster, another prominent Whig, who was made Secretary of State. "Old Tip" himself had been exhausted by his many "stump" speeches in the campaign and he had no reserves of energy to fight illness when it struck. He died precisely 31 days after inauguration.

William Henry Harrison was married from 1795 to Anna Symes; their grandson Benjamin Harrison became the 23rd President.

JOHN TYLER

John Tyler

W hen President William H. Harrison, "Old Tip," succumbed to pneumonia only a month after his inauguration the spotlight turned suddenly on his Vice President, John Tyler, the first man to claim the presidency by right of succession. A former Democrat, he had been chosen by the Whigs only to create a balanced ticket for Harrison and he had no party machine fully behind him. Repudiated by the Democrats he also fell foul of the Whigs, whose real leader in Congress was Henry Clay. Laboring under these disadvantages, John Tyler proved a worthy if unspectacular President, and was memorable chiefly as the man who signed the resolution annexing Texas.

Stubborn and independent

He was born at Greenway, in Charles City County, Virginia, to a father who was governor of that state. Having trained in law, John Tyler began political life as a member of the Virginia House of

Tenth President 1841-1845

Delegates from 1811-16. He served in Congress from 1816-21, in the Virginia legislature from 1823-25 and was Governor of Virginia from 1825-26.

As a U.S. Senator from 1827-36, John Tyler exhibited both doctrinaire consistency and a stubborn independence of mind. He was, for example, a typical states' rights southerner and always opposed to high tariff. Though a Democrat in origin he was hostile to Jackson because of the way in which the President used the veto and the spoils system and so joined the emerging Whig party in the mid

1830s. These credentials made him an asset to the Whigs in the famous election of 1840 when he was chosen to be Harrison's running mate as a man of principle – who could carry the South for them. The campaign, with its mass rallies and sloganeering was a triumphant success. But no one anticipated Harrison's sudden demise, and serious difficulties arose when in April, 1841, Tyler was elevated to the office of the presidency.

President by right of succession

Did he even have the right to call himself President? John Quincy Adams thought not: Tyler, he complained, "styles himself President of the United States, and not Vice President *acting as* President, which would be the correct style." But this was mere quibbling beside the jealousies which his promotion inspired within the Whig party. Tyler kept the Cabinet which Harrison had appointed but was soon clashing with the flamboyant Henry Clay and other Whig leaders. Clay in particular proved a thorn in his flesh, announcing in Congress his own wide-ranging nationalist program which included a plan to set up a new Bank of the United States.

Van Buren's Independent Treasury Act was repealed without much controversy, but Tyler twice vetoed Whig attempts to push through a new Bank bill. In reply, the entire Cabinet, with the exception of Secretary of State Daniel Webster, resigned. This was in September, 1841; for the rest of his presidency Tyler was party-less and forced to garner support where he could.

His record, though, is one of steady achievement. In 1842, Tyler ended the second Seminole War which had cost the United States some 1,500 soldiers and some $40 million. In the same year the Webster-Ashburton treaty with the British settled a longstanding boundary dispute between Maine and New Brunswick. Tyler also reformed the Navy and refused to operate the spoils system, keeping many able ministers abroad at their posts instead of touting their jobs among his partisans.

The annexation of Texas

His supreme achievement, though, was to open negotiations for the annexation of Texas. Americans had been settling the area from the 1820s, and two attempts had already been made to buy it from Mexico. The Mexicans would not sell and the Texans eventually rebelled. Despite the celebrated loss of the Alamo they went on to win victory in 1836, when Texas became an independent republic under the governorship of Sam Houston.

A plebiscite immediately demonstrated that most Texans favored annexation by the United States, but fearing war with Mexico both Jackson and Van Buren were reluctant to respond. There was another obstacle, too: Texas was essentially pro-slavery and its annexation might cause sectional strife. Nevertheless, Tyler as a southerner was keen both for annexation and the prestige it would bring

his administration. "If the annexation of Texas shall crown off my public life," he said, "I shall neither retire ignominiously nor be soon forgotten."

Negotiations for annexation began in the spring of 1843 and were completed in 1845 by the controversial figure of John C. Calhoun, a doughty spokesman for the South and for slavery. His association with the move caused disquiet. The Whig and Democrat heavyweights Clay and Van Buren came out against annexation and with a forthcoming national election, northern and western Senators prevented the treaty's ratification.

Texas now became a key issue in the election. Tyler, who lacked a party, was persuaded to withdraw as a candidate and James K. Polk – a Democrat strongly favoring annexation – won the presidency in a closely fought contest. Tyler took this as a vindication of his policy, and before he left office persuaded Congress to accept Texas by joint resolution.

So Texas was won for the Union. Tyler played no great part in political life afterward, until 1861 when he chaired a Washington conference called to avert the Civil War. When it failed he joined the secessionists and was a member of the provisional Confederate Congress. Tyler was twice married: to Letitia Christian from 1813, and to Julia Gardiner from 1844. He died on January 18, 1862, in Richmond, Virginia.

JAMES K. POLK

The first "dark horse" among presidential candidates, slightly built and mediocre in intelligence, Tennessee's James Polk proved to be one of the White House's surprise successes. Dogged determination and a willingness to work hard were his great qualities, along with a stubborn belief in the United States's "Manifest Destiny" to spread across the North American continent. The phrase was coined by pressman John O'Sullivan, but Polk is the figure forever associated with it. Under his administration more than a million square miles were added to the United States; he has been called "The Continentalist."

A Tennessee lawyer

James Knox Polk was born in Mecklenburg County, North Carolina, on November 2, 1795, to farming parents of Scottish-Irish descent. In 1818, he graduated from the University of North Carolina and he afterwards moved to Nashville, Tennessee, to study law. Polk was a member of the Tennessee state legislature from 1823-25; he was a Congressman from 1825-39 and was then Speaker from 1835-39, retiring to become the Governor of Tennessee.

Polk was an able enough governor but, as a Jacksonian Democrat (dubbed "Young Hickory" because of Jackson's support), he was disadvantaged by the tide of opinion flowing for the Whigs, and was defeated in 1841. When he lost a further bid for re-election in 1843 it seemed almost that his political career was over. Polk's vault to the

Eleventh President 1845-1849

forefront of national politics owes everything to a single issue – the issue of territorial expansion.

The Texas question was at the heart of the matter. In 1844, the state was still pressing for annexation, a goal for which the outgoing president, John Tyler, was striving. But the Whig leader Henry Clay and the Democrat Martin Van Buren found the issue an embarrassment. Annexation opened the possibility of a war with Mexico, and of upsetting the balance of slave and nonslave states in the Union. Both men issued statements opposing annexation, and though Clay was duly nominated presidential candidate by the Whigs, the expansionist lobby was so strong among the Democrats that Van Buren was denied the nomination. The Democratic party convention was deadlocked, and it was in this context that the "dark horse" James Polk emerged to win the nomination. Polk was unequivocably committed to expansion in general – and in particular to the immediate annexation of Texas. He, therefore, swept the convention floor.

Polk was not everyone's idea of an ideal contender. "A more ridiculous, contemptible and forlorn candidate was never put forth by any party," someone wrote in the *New York Herald*. "Mr Polk is a sort of fourth or rather fortieth rate lawyer and small politician in Tennessee, who by accident was once Speaker of the House... He was rejected even by his own State as Governor – and now he comes forward as candidate of the great democracy." But

public feeling was turning strongly in favor of expansion and in the closely fought presidential election of 1844, the failed governor Polk went on to beat the heavyweight Clay by a narrow margin: 38,000 out of 2.7 million votes in the country (170 to 105 votes in the Electoral College).

The capture of Mexico City, 1847, by U.S. troops under General Winfield Scott. It was President Polk who led the United States into the Mexican War – a conflict quickly won against a weak enemy, which brought vast territorial gains.

Texas and Oregon

President Polk was 49 when he assumed office and he devoted the next four years of his life entirely to the presidency. It has been said that he only left his desk at the White House for a total of six weeks through his entire term. His wife Sarah, whom he had married in 1824, doubled as his private secretary and theirs proved a very sober First Family. Sarah banned cards, dancing and wine from the White House; the couple had no children to bring laughter to its corridors, and the Polks are memorable chiefly among White House historians for introducing piped gas to the mansion.

Politics was everything to Polk, and Texas was the first issue on his agenda, though in reality the question was virtually settled before his inauguration. Polk's victory was taken as a verdict in favor of annexation and the outgoing president John Tyler asked Congress to take Texas by joint

resolution: by December, 1845, it had achieved statehood.

Oregon was the next priority. The northwestern wilderness had for decades been jointly occupied by the British and Americans with no line of division agreed. American expansionists believed that the United States should control the whole area, and the claim to it was part of the Democratic party platform in 1844. Indeed, in his inaugural address the President referred to the United States's "clear and unquestionable" title to the territory. However, stubborn as he was, Polk was keen to avert war with England and proposed the compromise of continuing the line of the 49th parallel to the ocean. Richard Pakenham, British minister in Washington, rejected the proposal, insisting on a more southerly division at the Columbia River. Polk then withdrew his offer and in a famous phrase concluded that "the only way to treat John Bull was to look him straight in the eye." He recommended to Congress that the British be

Miners in the Sierras during the California Gold Rush which began in 1849. Hordes of prospectors swarmed to the gold fields equipped with pickaxes, shovels and pans. The local Spanish-American population was swamped by the newcomers, and some ethnic strife accompanied the legendary gambling, robbery and hard-drinking mayhem of the gold rush days.

given a year's notice to end the joint occupation.

Happily, the British retreated from a showdown and returned to the offer of a compromise. Polk also withdrew his most belligerent stance and the long boundary dispute ended with a treaty ratified in June, 1846. The border was to follow the 49th parallel but dip at Puget Sound to leave Vancouver Island to the British. A few fervent expansionists condemned Polk for betraying the claim to all of Oregon, but in general the treaty was welcomed. After all, there was little in the wastes of northern Oregon to warrant armed conflict with Britain; and besides, the United States was already at war with Mexico and much more was at stake in this encounter.

THE MEXICAN WAR

Historians disagree about the fundamental cause of the war with Mexico. For some it lies in the Mexicans' foolish pride in repudiating the Texas annexation. Others trace the cause to Polk and a cynical readiness to take up arms against a weak enemy (the young Congressman Abraham Lincoln was among those who considered the war to be immoral). Clearly, with goodwill on both sides, fighting might have been avoided. A spirit of adventurism, however, triumphed over the will to peace – giant slices of land were the prizes of victory.

The trouble began as soon as Congress voted for the annexation of Texas. The Mexican response was to break off diplomatic relations with the United States. Texas itself was meanwhile ambitiously claiming the Rio Grande as its southwestern boundary (instead of the Nueces River as under Spanish rule), and in bold support of the Texans' claim Polk sent General Zachary Taylor with some 1,500 men into the vast disputed area between the two rivers. When a secret mission aiming at a negotiated settlement failed – and a belligerent new government in Mexico laid claim to the whole of Texas – Polk decided on war.

With a force now swollen to 4,000 men, General Taylor massed his troops on the north bank of the Rio Grande. Hostilities opened when Mexican troops crossed over to attack a U.S. patrol. "War exists," Polk told Congress, "and notwithstanding all our efforts to avoid it, exists by the act of Mexico herself." On May 13, Congress formally declared war, authorizing recruitment of 50,000 soldiers and the raising of $10 million for military purposes.

In the campaigns which followed the American armies easily defeated the Mexican forces, the United States's superior equipment, resources and generalship all playing parts in the victory. Polk himself ably assisted in the planning of military operations, hoping for speedy results which would force the Mexicans into territorial concessions. Senator Thomas Hart Benton, in fact, specifically recorded that the President wanted "a small war, just large enough to require a treaty of peace, and not large enough to make military reputations dangerous for the presidency." A party point: America's two leading generals, Zachary Taylor and Winfield Scott, were both Whigs. Polk, a Democrat, did not want to see either of them sweep into office on the wings of illustrious victories as Generals Jackson and Harrison had.

The war ended with a masterly campaign led by Scott against Mexico City. In March, 1847, he landed his army near Vera Cruz and forced that city's surrender with minimal loss of men. Advancing slowly on the Mexican capital through hostile terrain, he won a decisive victory at Cerro Gordo and, reinforced by new arrivals in August, fought his way into Mexico City on September 14. Mexico surrendered not long afterwards, and by the treaty of Guadalupe Hidalgo (February, 1848) the United States made vast gains. Not only was the Rio Grande boundary secured, but California and New Mexico were won, too. It was a triumph of Manifest Destiny – or land-grabbing depending on your perspective – and gave the United states a wholly new Pacific profile.

Retirement
Polk's eventful administration accomplished more than territorial gains. The independent treasury system was finally established, for example, and the tariff was reduced – both targets which Polk had set himself in his first annual message. But geographical expansion was the overwhelming achievement, and a Midas touch was added as pure bonus with the gold strike in California in 1848. Prospectors were already hurrying to the new territory in December of that year when Polk referred to the discovery in his annual message. Presidential confirmation of the strike greatly boosted the gold rush, and in 1849, some 70,000 Americans invaded California, scouring the streams and canyons in the western slopes of the Sierras for the Mother Lode's glittering harvest.

No great luster surrounds Polk's memory, though. Considering his achievements he remains a curiously unfeted figure who inspired little affection in his own day, and less attention from posterity than other more charismatic White House occupants. Yet his industry was tremendous: Polk worked himself virtually to death in the presidential office and refused nomination to a second term. In March, 1849, he retired to his home in Nashville, and he died there of heart failure only three months later, on June 15, 1849. He was 53 years old at his death.

ZACHARY TAYLOR

A successful general and honest man, Zachary Taylor was propelled by shrewd Whig politicians to the presidency despite his own complete lack of experience in public affairs. "Old Rough and Ready," as his troops called him, had spent his entire career in the regular Army and as President won some attention by letting his campaign horse graze on the White House lawn. Nobody doubted Taylor's warm heart or integrity, but he did not possess the subtlety to cope with the deepening crisis over slavery. Commenting on the President's lack of sophistication, Horace Mann, the great educationalist, wrote that Taylor "talks as artlessly as a child about affairs of state, and does not seem to pretend to a knowledge of anything of which he is ignorant. He is a remarkable man in some respects; and it is remarkable that such a man should be President of the United States."

Twelfth President 1849-1850

disputed Texas border of the Rio Grande. An attack on one of his mounted patrols sparked open hostilities and despite the difficulty of protecting his supply line Taylor won striking victories in May, 1846, at Palo Alto and Resaca de la Palma. News of these triumphs spread nationwide and already a number of Whigs began to see in the military hero a potential candidate for the presidency. Taylor's reputation only increased when he took Monterey later that year and won a decisive battle against Santa Anna at Buena Vista (February, 1847) despite heavy odds of three to one against him.

Taylor was not brilliantly skilled as a military strategist; his nickname of "Old Rough and Ready" testifies to a lack of science, and he certainly made mistakes – at Monterey, for example, where his lack of experience with artillery caused him to rely on a bayonet assault with unnecessary loss of life. But he was unquestionably popular with his men, commanding both affection and respect, and at Buena Vista his inspiring presence probably tipped the balance for victory. In fact, such was his reputation after that particular battle that President Polk, partly fearing that the Whig soldier's popularity might threaten the Democratic succession, gave control of the final campaign against Mexico City to General Winfield Scott.

The stratagem made no difference. In the elections of 1848, the Whigs did run Zachary Taylor as their presidential candidate, and a split in the Democratic party helped the

The military hero

Zachary Taylor was born in Orange County, Virginia, on November 24, 1784, and was brought up in Louisville, Kentucky, where his father became collector of the port. Taylor had only a rudimentary schooling and joined the Army in 1808. He served in Indian campaigns and was appointed a major in the War of 1812, but all through his long military career he made no great impression until the Mexican War of 1846-48 – at which time he was well into his sixties.

When the conflict arose, Taylor was sent to protect the

old soldier to win the presidency by 1.36 million votes to the 1.22 million polled by Lewis Cass for the Democrats (163 to 127 votes in the Electoral College).

During the campaign, Zachary Taylor had professed himself a Whig but "not an ultra Whig." He had never even bothered to cast a vote in an election, and he consciously strove for a nonpartisan presidential role, pledging himself in his inaugural address of March 5, 1849, to "the welfare of the whole country, and not to the support of any particular section or merely local interest." Unhappily, the country itself was far from whole, and uniting the nation required more deftness of thinking than the President's military mind could offer.

California and New Mexico
The great issues of Taylor's presidency were the newly acquired areas of California and New Mexico. Making them territories would mean reopening the slavery debate, for Congress would have to decide whether they should or should not operate the slave system. Taylor's solution had a soldierly simplicity to it: admit California – and in due course New Mexico – directly as states and allow the inhabitants to decide for themselves on the issue.

Southern slave holders were appalled by the plan for as

Zachary Taylor spurs his men to victory at the Battle of Buena Vista (1847), fought near Saltillo during the Mexican War. Success gave the United States control of northern Mexico.

Taylor himself knew well enough, the proposed new states had no slave plantations and would ban slavery – so destroying the balance of slave and free states in the Senate. The scheme was received by them with particular bitterness because Taylor himself was a Southerner and a slave-holder. Alternative proposals were advanced in a long and stirring Senate debate of 1850, and it became clear that most members favored some kind of a compromise. Yet, with the unity of the nation in jeopardy, Taylor stubbornly adhered to his own plan, and the deadlock was broken only by a sudden, unexpected event.

On a scorching 4th of July, having unwisely consumed raw fruits and cold liquids while suffering from a bout of typhus fever, President Taylor took sick. He died five days later, on July 9, 1850, having served only 16 months of his term, and it was left to his successor, Vice President Millard Fillmore, to look for conciliation.

Zachary Taylor was married from 1810 to Margaret Smith and had six children, three of whom outlived him.

MILLARD FILLMORE

Millard Fillmore (signature)

The 13th president of the United States, Millard Fillmore was unlucky in inheriting a crisis far beyond his powers to resolve. The issue of slavery in the 1850s was beginning to tear the nation apart, and Fillmore's attempts at conciliation only alienated both sides. "At a time when we needed a strong man," Harry S. Truman was to say, "what we got was a man that swayed with the slightest breeze. About all he ever accomplished as President, was to send Commodore Perry to open up Japan to the West, but that didn't help much as far as preventing the Civil War was concerned."

A New York apprentice

Millard Fillmore was born in Cayuga County, New York, on January 7, 1800, to parents of English descent. At age 15 he was apprenticed to a clothier with tasks which included carding and dyeing wool. Before his term was complete, however, Fillmore bought himself out of the apprenticeship and turned to the study of law, supporting himself partly by teaching school in Buffalo. Admitted to the Bar in 1823, he became a member of the state assembly from 1829-32, and served in Congress from 1833-35 and 1837-43.

Fillmore was a Whig who opposed the admission of Texas as a slave territory and took an anti-slavery stance on a succession of other key issues. His approach, though, was more moderate than that of many New York anti-slavery men. He also favored a protective tariff and in 1843, as chairman of the House Committee on Ways and Means,

Thirteenth President 1850-1853

championed an appropriation of $30,000 petitioned by inventor Samuel Morse to defray the expense of his new telegraph. Despite opposition, the appropriation was passed and the first, historic line from Baltimore to Washington was opened the following year.

In 1844, Fillmore was defeated as Whig candidate for the governorship of New York, but he was chosen as running mate for General Zachary Taylor in the presidential election of 1848. When the old soldier entered the White House, Fillmore as his Vice President, presided in the Senate over the great debates of 1850 on the Compromise. The controversy centered on the extension of slavery to the lands won from Mexico in the War of 1848, including California. President Taylor, whose own plans conflicted with those of the majority on Capitol Hill, died suddenly with the issue unresolved, and it was left to Millard Fillmore to break the deadlock.

The Compromiser

On July 10, 1850, on the day after Zachary Taylor's death, Millard Fillmore took the oath of office. Unlike his predecessor he was pliable to Congress and smoothed the path for the Compromise measures, all of which he had passed and signed by September 1850. California was admitted as a free state; the emptier territories of New Mexico and Utah were created with no restrictions on slavery; the Texas boundary was settled; the slave trade was abolished in the District of Columbia; and a much stricter

Above; *Harriet Beecher Stowe, whose* Uncle Tom's Cabin *was published under the presidency of Millard Fillmore, and did much to expose the sufferings of Negroes in the South.* **Right;** *The illustration shows the slave girl, 'Topsy'.*

fugitive slave law was passed.

The package won a lot of support from moderate opinion at first and the Compromise was celebrated in mass meetings around the country. But it was not long before trouble started to brew again, and President Fillmore's reputation was an early victim. Southern "fire-eaters" condemned the measures and Fillmore lost standing among Northern anti-slavers, especially through signing the rigorous new Fugitive Slave Act. Citizens could now, for example, be compelled by threats of fine or jail to assist in the capture of fugitives; runaways could be sent back South without jury trial or the right to testify on their own behalf. Feelings were inflamed: Harriet Beecher Stowe dashed out her *Uncle Tom's Cabin* in direct response to what she called the "nightmare abomination" of the Act and, published in 1852, her blockbuster caused a furor.

As Harry S. Truman said, Fillmore's only true achievement was to send Commodore Perry on his historic mission to Japan, where he opened ports to U.S. trade. Perry arrived in Edo Bay in July, 1853, carrying with him letters from President Fillmore to the Emperor. But in reality, American whaling and manufacturing interests lay behind the mission's initiation: it was no brainchild of Fillmore, whose career was already on the downturn as Perry steamed with his warships into the bay. In 1852, Fillmore had failed to secure the Whig nomination for the presidency and by March, 1853, he was out of office.

His public life was not entirely over, however. In 1856, Fillmore was nominated for President by the American "Know Nothing" party, a coalition which owed its name to the members' practice of claiming to know nothing when asked about the party. In the election of that year, Fillmore came a poor third.

Millard Fillmore was twice married: to Abigail Powers and to Caroline Carmichael McIntosh. He had two children and died of a stroke in Buffalo in March 8, 1874.

FRANKLIN PIERCE

Franklin Pierce

A handsome, soft-spoken man fond of good company and eager to please, Franklin Pierce came from obscurity to win the presidency; and to obscurity he returned after serving his single term. The main achievement of his administration was the Gadsden Purchase by which some 45,000 square miles of territory in the southwest was bought by the United States from Mexico. Otherwise, Pierce has been consigned by history to the succession of ineffectual Presidents powerless to stem the tide flowing toward Civil War. He is memorable almost for being so forgettable. "Pierce was either the worst, or he was the weakest, of all our Presidents," said his contemporary, Ralph Waldo Emerson.

A New Hampshire Democrat

Franklin Pierce was born at Hillsboro, New Hampshire, on November 23, 1804, to a father who became Democratic Governor of the state. Entering Bowdoin in 1820, he made friends with the young Nathaniel Hawthorne (who was to become his biographer), and on graduating four years later Pierce turned to the study of law. He was admitted to the Bar in 1827, and was in the state legislature from 1829-32. As a Congressman from 1833-37 he supported President Andrew Jackson, and he went on to enter the Senate as its youngest member, serving from 1837-42.

In 1846, Pierce enlisted for the Mexican War, and he took part in the eventual advance on Mexico City. During the campaign, however, there occurred an event which

Fourteenth President 1853-1857

Pierce's enemies were to turn against him – he fainted on the field of battle. When his presidential nomination was announced, the Boston *Evening Journal* was to charge him with cowardice; Pierce hotly replied that he had been thrown from his horse the previous day and had fought on in pain, against the advice of his superior, so accounting for the "fainting spell." Whatever the truth, the episode placed a note of ambiguity against his otherwise commendable military record.

After the war, Pierce led Democratic support in New Hampshire for the 1850 Compromise and, with the candidacies of the party's heavyweights – Lewis Cass, James Buchanan and Stephen A. Douglas – blocked by factional rivalries, Pierce came through as a "dark horse" to take the nomination. "We Polked you in 1844 and we shall Pierce you in 1852" was the Democratic party campaign slogan, referring to the earlier dark horse victor. And indeed, fragmentation of the Whig party allowed Franklin Pierce to win the presidential election by a handsome 254 electoral votes to 42 (with a margin of more than 200,000 in the popular vote) against his Whig rival General Winfield Scott.

The young President

Aged 48 at his inauguration in March, 1853, Franklin Pierce was the youngest man yet to have entered the White House, and his engaging manner endeared him at first to many. But smiling agreeableness began to look increasingly like

weakness as the months passed; and it became known that Pierce's "conviviality" stemmed in part from too great a fondness for the bottle.

He began his term aggressively in foreign policy, with proposals for territorial expansion. The main aim was to acquire Cuba from Spain, but his intention of taking the island by force if necessary – embodied in the so-called Ostend Manifesto (October 1854) – came to nothing when the project was leaked prematurely. The President was forced to disown it.

In 1853, Pierce more successfully accomplished the Gadsden Purchase at a cost of $10 million. But any reputation he might have earned from the acquisition was overshadowed the next year when he signed the controversial Kansas-Nebraska Act. This measure opened the two new territories for settlement, with the issue of slavery to be decided by the local inhabitants. Sponsored by Stephen A. Douglas, it stirred passionate animosity because it repealed part of the carefully achieved Missouri Compromise (1820) passed during Monroe's Presidency, which prohibited slavery in the territories north of latitude 36°30'. Under the new act, Kansas would get a pro-slavery government despite lying above the 36°30' line which was supposed to keep it slave-free. An undeclared war between partisans of the two sides broke out within "Bleeding Kansas," and the nation lurched ominously to the threshold of the Civil War.

In the turmoil, the anti-slavery Whigs formed the new Republican Party, Franklin Pierce, whose stance favored the slave-holders, lost both support among Northern Democrats and all credibility as a candidate for a second term. Caricatured as a drunk helpless at the helm of state, he did not seek renomination but left office ignominiously in 1857. During the Civil War he resurfaced momentarily as a savage critic of President Lincoln, but otherwise Pierce sank to a remarkable depth of political obscurity in retirement at Concord, New Hampshire.

Franklin Pierce was married to Jane Means Appleton and had two children. He died at age 64, on October 8, 1869, of natural causes.

JAMES BUCHANAN

James Buchanan

Much was expected of James Buchanan. The United States's only bachelor President came to the White House at a time when the Union was in danger, and slavery for the first time the major issue of a presidential campaign. Buchanan was conscientious and patriotic, with a great breadth of political experience. Yet, in the end, he lacked the strength of character to meet the crisis, submitting increasingly to a cabinet dominated by Southerners who ultimately abandoned him anyway. Republican opponents contemptuously derided him as "Doughface" for his vacillations and it is true that while condemning secession he took no measures to stop it: in the last months of his term the Confederacy was born.

Congressman and diplomat

James Buchanan was born in Franklin County, Pennsylvania, on April 23, 1791, to parents of Scottish-Irish descent. Graduating from Dickinson College, he went on to study law and was admitted to the Bar in 1812. Buchanan was in the state legislature from 1814-16 and in Congress from 1820-31. Andrew Jackson appointed him minister to Russia 1831-33 and he returned to serve as a U.S. Senator from 1834-45. Buchanan became prominent as Secretary of State in the administration of Polk from 1845-49, supporting the Tennessee President's vigorous program of expansion, and as minister to Britain in 1854, he helped to draw up the Ostend Manifesto which favored the acquisition of Cuba by force if necessary.

Fifteenth President 1857-1861

On his return to the United States, Buchanan won the Democratic nomination for President, helped by the fact that he had been abroad during the heated debates on the Kansas-Nebraska bill and so avoided much of the controversy. The election of 1856 turned into a three-cornered fight, with Buchanan facing Republican candidate John C. Frémont and ex-President Fillmore for the so-called "Know-Nothing" party, an oddball alliance of anti-immigrants, former Whigs and voters simply fearing disunion. The essential struggle, though, was between the Republicans, strong in the North, and the Democrats dominating the South. The Democrats' strategy was to present themselves as the party of national unity, claiming: if Frémont won, the South would secede. The Democrats were better organized, too, and they carried the day, with Buchanan receiving 174 electoral votes to Frémont's 114 (and Fillmore's paltry 8). The incumbent lacked an overall majority of the popular vote, and in many states the margin of victory was extremely narrow.

The bachelor President

Aged 65 at his inauguration, Buchanan was a heavily built man, and always charming and courteous. He in no way shunned women's company nor did he lack female admirers but, by some chance, never married and so earned the unique distinction of occupying the presidential office as a bachelor. His niece, Harriet Lane, acted as First Lady, and

won a reputation as a hostess despite the troubled times.

Not even Washington's fashionable society, though, could ignore the storm clouds gathering over the Union. Buchanan came to office with violence flaring in the "Bleeding Kansas" controversy and before he could address that issue, the Dred Scott case exploded. On March 6, 1857, only two days after the inauguration, the Supreme court ruled that the slave Dred Scott could not sue in a federal court for his freedom, on the grounds that Negroes were not citizens within the meaning of the Constitution. Northern feeling was outraged when the President supported the ruling, and further alienated when he used his influence to get Kansas brought into the Union under a pro-slavery constitution – against the wishes of most settlers. This measure put Buchanan up against fellow Democrat Stephen A. Douglas, champion of popular sovereignty, and in their clash the Democratic party was ruined as a national machine.

In October, 1859, John Brown's celebrated raid at Harper's Ferry began the countdown to open hostilities. In the elections of the following year the divided Democrats were beaten by Abraham Lincoln for the Republicans. The

Old Kentucky Home Life, 1859, a scene from the South on the eve of Civil War, depicted by painter J. Eastman Johnson.

last, fateful events of Buchanan's term occurred with Lincoln already waiting in the wings, for "Honest Abe's" victory prompted South Carolina to secede from the Union, and the other states of the lower South swiftly followed. Buchanan, still officially holding power in the winter of 1860-61, denied the states' right to secede, but he also denied that as President he had any authority to act against them. The Southern members of his own cabinet – who had pressed their own advantages in the name of the Union – now resigned to join the secessionists and it was a distraught and dithering Buchanan who finally left office on March 4, 1861, telling Lincoln, "If you are as happy, my dear sir, on entering this house as I am in leaving it and returning home you are the happiest man in the country."

Afterwards, James Buchanan retired to his home at Wheatland, Pennsylvania, where he offered such support as he could to the Union. He died there on June 1, 1868.

ABRAHAM LINCOLN

Abraham Lincoln

Studying likenesses of the later Lincoln – the famous photographs by Mathew Brady, for example – it is easy to believe that even without the 16th President's innumerable biographies his portraits alone would mark him out as someone special among occupants of the White House. The eyes and gaunt cheekbones combine with the beard to stamp his face with Old Testament gravity. Yet there is worldly humor in the set of the mouth and in the quizzical arching of an eyebrow. A strange figure, really: leaner, somehow, than any politican ought to be, and with hints of the prophet – or hobo – about him.

Lincoln was, in fact, a blend of contradictory traits. Physically he was tough: a 6 foot 3 inch Illinois log-chopper fond of good company and bawdy talk. Yet he was also a very private man, secretive even, and prone to paralyzing spells of black depression. Then there was his attitude to religion: a vein of authentic spirituality permeated his character but, in an age of hellfire revivalism, he maintained a stance of gentle skepticism, never uniting himself to any church.

Lincoln, the great Emancipator, has been idolized for his integrity as a statesman. Yet he was also a politician's politician, knowing instinctively how to tailor a speech for his audience; rarely going further along any road than they were prepared to follow. Coarse, compassionate, simple and shrewd he remains the most enigmatic of the White House occupants. He was also, in many people's judgment, the

Sixteenth President 1861-1865

greatest of all the Presidents – a towering figure on the stage of world history.

A frontier childhood

Abraham Lincoln was born in a farmhouse log cabin in what is now Larue County, Kentucky, on February 12, 1809. His father, Thomas, was something of a wastrel who tried his hand at farming and carpentering around Kentucky before settling at Pigeon Creek in southern Indiana when Abraham was 7 years old. The future President's mother, Nancy Hanks, came from a humble Virginia family and was illegitimate (her natural father being, by romantic tradition, an aristocrat). Nancy died two years after the move to the forest wilds of Indiana and the young Abraham received very little formal schooling. He did, however, become expert with an ax, for clearing timber was his main task from the moment of arrival at Pigeon Creek.

Not long after Nancy's death, Thomas Lincoln remarried taking as his new bride a widow, Mrs. Sarah Bush Johnston, a warm-hearted and practical person who had a favorable influence on Abraham. He grew to be a lanky, easy-going youth with a reputation for storytelling and mimicry. At 19, cutting loose from the family, he went on a trip to New Orleans, but two years later he pushed westward with the rest of the Lincolns to Illinois, where he put his axman's expertise to use on a contract to split 3,000 fence rails; hence his future tag of "The Railsplitter" in political life.

After a second trip to New Orleans, Abraham Lincoln

The emancipation of slaves, proclaimed in 1863, was Lincoln's supreme achievement; this print shows scenes before and after. (The proclamation did not apply to all states, however; full abolition came only with the 13th Amendment of 1865.)

made his home at the frontier settlement of New Salem, Illinois, where he earned his living as manager of a general store, was a postmaster and a surveyor. He also ran into a group of local young toughs known as the Clary Grove Boys and, having defeated their best man in a wrestling match, won both their friendship and their support as he embarked on a career in smalltown politics.

"Honest Abe"

In 1832, Lincoln enlisted as a volunteer in the Black Hawk War and the Clary Grove Boys, joining too, elected him captain of their company. During that year he also stood, unsuccessfully, for the state legislature but in 1834, he stood again and won a seat as a Whig. Barely 25 and impoverished, he studied law at home to further his career, and gaining admittance to the Bar in 1837 he took up a partnership in a law office at Springfield, Illinois.

It was at Springfield that Lincoln became engaged to Mary Todd, a lively young woman of good family ("One 'd' is good enough for God," Lincoln joked, "but not for the Todds"). In due course she would become his wife, but before their marriage there occurred a disturbing event: in 1841, Lincoln suffered something like a nervous breakdown which plunged him into a depression so deep that he could speak of himself as "the most miserable man living." The engagement was temporarily broken off. And though the black spell passed and the reconciled couple were married in November, 1842, Lincoln never lost the fear of his own melancholy streak. His "cat fits" of depression and indecision were to recur.

Lincoln was in Congress from 1847-49 where he served without particular distinction as an orthodox party wheel who took the conventional Whig line on most issues. Afterwards he returned to Springfield and devoted himself

A Federal camp on the Pamunkey River, Cumberland Landing, Virginia, photographed in May 1862. Superiority in numbers and materials were major factors in the North's eventual victory.

to an increasingly prosperous legal career. "Honest Abe" won a reputation both for his integrity and for lucid powers of argument which made him a formidable jury lawyer. Lincoln was never florid: he cut straight through the legal niceties and this simple, penetrating style was to serve him in good stead on his re-entry to the political arena.

The slavery debates

The issue which brought Lincoln back to politics was the slavery controversy, revived by the Kansas-Nebraska bill of 1854. Lincoln's attitude to the problem had never been extreme. He was not an abolitionist, for example, nor did he champion full social or political equality for Negroes. Iconoclasts have delighted in exposing traces of conventional nineteenth century white supremacism in his attitudes; he had even represented slave-holders reclaiming runaways in court cases. And certainly, in his own day there were plenty more radical campaigners whose views on race accord better with those of the twentieth century.

Nevertheless, Lincoln did see the institution of slavery as morally wrong, and he believed that opening Kansas and Nebraska to it would be quite unjustified. When Stephen A. Douglas promoted the controversial bill, Lincoln replied to him in a now celebrated speech at Peoria in October, 1854, which entirely revitalized his political career. Though failing in a bid for the Senate in 1855, he joined the new

Republican party the following year and was considered as a possible candidate for the vice presidency. In 1858, Lincoln stood again for the Senate, in opposition to Stephen A. Douglas, and he opened his campaign with another historic speech. "A house divided against itself cannot stand," it began. "I believe this Government cannot endure permanently half slave and half free."

There followed a series of seven public debates with Douglas which are today regarded as classics. Lincoln condemned slavery's inhumanity: "If slavery is not wrong, nothing is wrong," he once said. But his position with regard to Southern whites was understanding rather than priggish or vindictive, and he fully acknowledged the difficulties of attempting a sudden dismantling of the slave system. Emancipation, he believed, would come in God's good time; Lincoln's purpose was to oppose slavery's extension. The institution was wrong and "one of the methods of treating a wrong is to make provision that it shall grow no larger."

As it happened, the more cynically pragmatic Douglas won his re-election to the Senate, but Lincoln had more than held his own in the debates and become a national figure. His eloquence and moderation recommended him to Republican politicians and in the convention of 1860, he was given the presidential nomination.

In the campaign of that year the Democratic party was split between its Northern and Southern wings, and with a fourth Constitutional Union candidate also contesting the presidency it was unlikely that any one would win a popular majority. But Lincoln, standing on a clean-cut platform

Federal soldiers destroy the railroad tracks at Atlanta during Sherman's notorious march to the sea. His punitive measures hastened the war's end – but left the South embittered.

opposing slavery in the territories, won a majority in the Electoral College with 180 votes to the 72 polled by his nearest rival, Southern Democrat John C. Breckinridge.

For the South the result was alarming: an anti-slaver would occupy the White House. Almost immediately, South Carolina seceded from the Union and by February the rest of the lower South had followed.

The coming of war
Lincoln took up the reins of government on March 4, 1861, but in the months between his November victory and his inauguration the seceding South had already inaugurated its own president, Jefferson Davis. Lincoln's behavior during the eventful interim period inspired no confidence.

THE WAR LEADER

Gentle and humane by nature, Lincoln made an improbable commander-in-chief and yet, in the titanic conflict which followed he showed an increasingly masterful firmness. As Congress was in recess until July, 1861, he was forced to act on – and exceed – executive authority, summoning the militia, proclaiming a blockade and suspending *habeas corpus*. Then, after some temporary loss of confidence due in part to congressional interference, Lincoln assumed supreme control of the war effort. He learned to follow his own judgment and, considering himself military executive of a democracy in jeopardy, took on near dictatorial powers.

Through Lincoln's initiative a potentially disastrous war with England was avoided. In November, 1861, a Northern warship stopped a British vessel on the high seas and arrested two Confederate envoys; it was Lincoln who ordered their release – so defusing the situation.

It was Lincoln too who championed the controversial Ulysses S. Grant as a soldier who, whatever his drinking habits or unkempt appearance, could win battles. When someone complained of his fondness for whiskey, the President said that if he knew Grant's favorite brand he would send a barrel of it to others among his generals.

Above all, Lincoln will be remembered for his Emancipation Proclamation of January 1, 1863. This was by no means a brainchild of the President: slaves were being proclaimed free by some Union generals as soon as they captured enemy territory and, in fact, Lincoln tried to check these random emancipations. Despite pressure from abolitionists he delayed the key measure until he judged the time ripe to take action from a position of strength. Victory at Antietam gave him the pretext, but even then he emancipated slaves only in Southern areas still in rebellion against the Union; the act did not apply in the border states (which he was anxious not to alienate); and the phrasing of the document stresses more than once the act's purpose as a "necessary war measure," as if shy of its humanitarianism.

Nonetheless it was an historic document, and Lincoln paused before signing it. "I have been shaking hands since nine o'clock this morning and my right arm is almost paralyzed," he explained. "If my name ever goes down in history it will be for this act and my whole soul is in it. If my hand trembles when I sign this Proclamation, all who examine the document hereafter will say, 'he hesitated'."

In the event, Lincoln's hand was steady.

The bitter end

Behind the masterful public figure was a tender family man who experienced private tragedy in the White House when

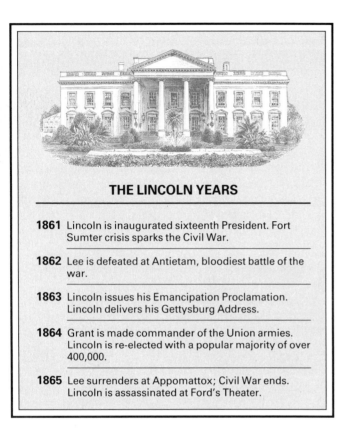

THE LINCOLN YEARS

1861 Lincoln is inaugurated sixteenth President. Fort Sumter crisis sparks the Civil War.

1862 Lee is defeated at Antietam, bloodiest battle of the war.

1863 Lincoln issues his Emancipation Proclamation. Lincoln delivers his Gettysburg Address.

1864 Grant is made commander of the Union armies. Lincoln is re-elected with a popular majority of over 400,000.

1865 Lee surrenders at Appomattox; Civil War ends. Lincoln is assassinated at Ford's Theater.

He made only a few vacuous speeches on his way to Washington, otherwise giving an impression of total ineffectuality. His inaugural address, however, made an impression. Though conciliatory in tone it contained notes of steely resolve: denying that he intended to interfere in any way with Southern institutions, he nonetheless declared the secession illegal – its very concept the "essence of anarchy" – and he pledged himself to maintaining the possessions of the federal government.

Events at Fort Sumter in Charleston harbor triggered the cataclysm. When Lincoln sent food supplies to the beleaguered federal garrison there, the Confederates took the reprovisioning to be an act of war and opened fire. Lincoln replied by calling for troops, and he went on to fight the Civil War, not (as naive versions sometimes suggest) in order to end slavery, but to save the Union and the democratic authority vested in its government. This, to Lincoln, was the all-important point. "The central issue pervading this struggle," he wrote, "is the necessity of proving that popular government is not an absurdity. We must settle this question now, whether, in a free government, the minority have the right to break up the government whenever they choose."

one of his two beloved sons, Willie, died of typhoid. Afterwards, Mary Lincoln's grief made her temperamentally unstable. Yet Lincoln kept to his rigorous routine, rising early and putting in an hour's desk work before breakfast; then receiving calls; lunching frugally; signing commissions; dealing with correspondence; writing speeches and – at night – crossing the White House lawn to the War Department where he worked often to the early hours of morning. Besieged by office seekers and supplicants for promotion, he never lost his sense of humor. In 1863, having succumbed to a mild attack of smallpox, Lincoln quipped that at last he had something to give everybody.

In November of that year Lincoln delivered the brief, immortal Gettysburg Address, one of the world's great statements of democratic faith. Re-elected in 1864 with a popular majority of over 400,000, Lincoln entered his second term committed to reconstruction and conciliation toward the South, promising "malice toward none" in his second inaugural. On April 9, 1865, a month after that address, General Lee surrendered at Appomattox Court

The assassination at Ford's Theater, April 14, 1865. Lincoln had come to watch Our American Cousin, *a comedy so entertaining that the bodyguard left the door of the box to watch – giving the assassin John Wilkes Booth his chance.*

House. The devastating four-year war which had cost 600,000 American lives was over.

Five days later, while Lincoln was watching a play at Ford's Theater in Washington, the crazed actor and secessionist John Wilkes Booth stole into the President's box and shot him in the back of the head. Lincoln died early the next morning, on April 15, 1865, without regaining consciousness. He was the first presidential victim of assassination and mourners came in their thousands to view the body which lay in state on a black-draped catafalque in the White House. Afterwards, Lincoln's body was returned to Illinois for burial, and with it were interred the best hopes for forgiveness in the aftermath of war. The peace, all now knew, would not be easy.

ANDREW JOHNSON

Andrew Johnson (signature)

A stubborn, self-taught loner, Andrew Johnson rose to the White House from a background of illiterate poverty and always saw himself as champion of the poor white class from which he came. Lincoln's assassination gave him the presidency and his short term proved eventful: the 13th Amendment abolishing slavery was ratified, for example, and the Alaska Purchase was achieved. But personality flaws marred Johnson's career: insecure about his origins he tended almost neurotically to excoriate "stuck-up aristocrats;" he was willful, tactless and inflexible. In the end Andrew Johnson is remembered not for achievement but for his failed policy of reconstruction – and also as the only President before Richard Nixon to face impeachment.

"These traitorous aristocrats"

Andrew Johnson was born at Raleigh, North Carolina, on December 29, 1808. The son of an inn porter he was apprenticed at age 10 to a tailor and had no formal schooling, learning instead to read and write in what little spare time he enjoyed. As a teenager, Johnson ran away, settling eventually at Greeneville, Tennessee. But he continued for many years to support himself by his trade, and in his later political speeches often fondly recalled how the coats which he made as a tailor were always good fits.

Elected mayor of Greeneville in 1830, Johnson became active in local and state politics, serving in the House of Representatives from 1843-53; as Governor of Tennessee

Seventeenth President 1865-1869

1853-57 and as a U.S. Senator from 1857-62. A Jacksonian Democrat, he supported John C. Breckinridge against Lincoln in the presidential election of 1860. However, Johnson did not believe that Lincoln's victory justified secession. He became conspicuous as the only Southern Senator to stand by the Union during the Civil War, and as a courageous military governor of Tennessee from 1862-64 proved a real asset to Lincoln's government.

In 1864, Johnson was chosen as Lincoln's vice-presidential running mate. The idea was in part to create a balanced "Union" ticket, Johnson being a lifelong Democrat who might attract votes other than Republican. He was certainly no radical as far as the great issue of race was concerned: working to further the interests of the small farmer he opposed slavery only as an institution which entrenched the privileges of the detested Southern planter class. "Damn the Negroes," he once exclaimed during the War, "I am fighting these traitorous aristocrats, their masters."

Impeachment

Johnson was inaugurated in April, 1865, with the nation mourning Lincoln's assassination. Reconstruction, inevitably, was the priority and Johnson's statements seemed to promise a very hard line against the South. Johnson came to office, in the words of one *Harper's Weekly* journalist, metaphorically "foaming at the mouth" against those traitorous aristocrats; and Northern radicals rejoiced.

The senate chamber during the historic impeachment trial of President Andrew Johnson in 1868. Also shown is a ticket of admission to the proceedings.

Yet the early rhetoric came to nothing. Johnson in reality adhered to Lincoln's policy of moderation, clinging to it with such intransigence that as events changed he was seen to be maintaining a stance clearly favoring the Southern whites at the expense of the freed black populations. In May, 1865, Johnson issued a general amnesty to all Confederates except certain leaders if they would ratify the new 13th Amendment abolishing slavery. In response, the new Southern governments accepted abolition – but they also enacted codes curtailing freed Negroes' liberties. The South, it seemed, was planning to perpetuate slavery in disguised form: Northerners were outraged. And Johnson, who refused to change his stance, came into headlong conflict with the majority of Republicans in Congress.

Congress's strategy was to pass a series of measures restoring military control and protecting the black populations in the South. Johnson vetoed them, including the important Civil Rights Act giving Negroes citizenship, which became the 14th Amendment. Taking a step without precedent for a major piece of legislation, a two thirds majority in Congress overruled the presidential veto – and the Act became law in defiance of the White House.

The struggle climaxed when Johnson dismissed Edwin Stanton, Secretary of War, who had radical sympathies. Congress took the sacking as a pretext for impeachment proceedings under the Tenure of Office Act (forced through to protect cabinet officers from dismissal without senatorial approval). The impeachment was a drastic and obviously partisan measure and it failed – but only by a single vote. Johnson completed his term much embittered, and with no real hope of nomination for a second term. The importance of his one glittering achievement – Alaska's purchase from Russia for $7.2 million – was not appreciated at the time; Secretary of State William Seward arranged the acquisition in 1867, and the new, frozen hunk of America was derided as "Mr Seward's Icebox."

Andrew Johnson was married from 1826 to Eliza McCardle and had five children. He was elected a Senator a few months before his death on July 31, 1875, of a stroke.

ULYSSES S. GRANT

One of the world's greatest generals and one of the United States's worst Presidents, Ulysses S. Grant has always made an awkward American hero. A stubby little man with a scruffy beard, rumpled suit and inordinate fondness for the bottle, he scarcely looked the part of military commander. Yet commander he was: possessing strategic insight; capable of handling large armies; flexible when necessary; relentless in pursuit of his objective. The Union's victory in the Civil War owed much to Grant's steely determination, and his Confederate foe, General Robert E. Lee, was to pay him this tribute: "I have carefully searched the military records of both ancient and modern history, and never found Grant's superior as a general."

The formidable war record, though, only sharpens the disappointments of Grant's eight years in presidential office. In the White House he proved weak, naive – and disastrous in his choice of advisers.

Eighteenth President 1869-1877

A succession of scandals shook the nation during his two terms, although Grant's integrity was never doubted his poor judgment was evident to all. The lion of war was a lamb-like Chief Executive, and he retired from office with relief: "I never wanted to get out of a place as much as I did to get out of the Presidency," he said.

The call to arms

Ulysses Simpson Grant was born at Point Pleasant, Ohio, on April 27, 1822, to a family of Scottish descent. His father,

Jesse Root Grant, was the local tanner. His name at birth was Hiram Ulysses Grant, but he was known in boyhood as simple Ulysses and acquired the new middle name of Simpson (from his mother's family) when he was entered for West Point in 1839.

At the military academy Grant showed no particular promise: though a good horseman he ranked overall 21st in a class of 39. Nevertheless, he served gallantly under Generals Taylor and Scott during the Mexican War, attaining the rank of captain. And when the fighting was over he married Julia Boggs Dent who was to bear him four children.

It was in the tedium of a lonely post in Oregon that Grant gained a reputation for drinking: in 1854, allegations about his intemperance forced him to resign his commission. In the years which followed he failed at a series of occupations: farming; real estate; clerical work. In frustration he moved eventually to Galena, Illinois, where his father and brothers ran a leather store. In 1860 Grant took up employment as a clerk and seemed at that time destined for mediocrity.

The Civil War changed his fortunes. Grant answered the call to arms promptly in 1861, and was appointed colonel of the 21st Illinois Volunteers; then made a brigadier-general. In the western theater he won victories at Fort Henry and at Fort Donelson which he took with 15,000 Confederate prisoners, earning himself the name of "Unconditional Surrender Grant."

Grant in Civil War days: he stands (in the hat, at center) among members of his staff at Cold Harbor, north of Richmond, where a costly battle was fought in June 1864.

The commander in chief

At Shiloh (April, 1862) Grant was taken initially by surprise, slogging through to eventual victory despite heavy losses. The number of casualties did nothing for his reputation, but the fact that he was capable of winning – whatever the cost – had brought him to the attention of President Lincoln who was then in dire need of battlefield successes. In July, 1863, moreover, Grant captured the strategic Confederate stronghold of Vicksburg by an audacious encircling maneuver which gave the Union control of the Mississippi. It was a turning point of the Civil War, and after further success at Chattanooga in November, Lincoln placed Grant in command of all the Union armies.

Early in May, 1864, Grant began the final, remorseless drive to Richmond, the Southern capital, with General Sherman pushing simultaneously on Atlanta. It was a campaign of sustained aggression in which Grant deployed his superior forces with ruthless determination. When critics complained of the terrible casualties he remained undaunted. "I propose to fight it out on this line, if it takes all summer," he reported back to Washington after one sequence of costly engagements. And in the end, "Butcher" Grant's ugly, unyielding war of attrition succeeded. Richmond fell on April 3, 1865; six days later, Robert E. Lee surrendered at Appomattox. In victory, Grant was magnanimous: reminiscing with Lee about service in Mexico he required only that Confederate soldiers lay down their arms and go home; they were allowed to keep their horses.

"LET US HAVE PEACE"

In the aftermath of war and the Lincoln assassination, Grant became embroiled in President Johnson's savage wrangle with Congress. Johnson dismissed Secretary of War, Edwin Stanton, without notifying the Senate, and appointed Grant as his successor. But Grant accepted only under protest, and willingly gave the appointment back to Stanton when Congress took up arms on the dismissed minister's behalf. So, Grant earned the truculent President's bitter enmity.

As a war hero, all knew, Grant would make an attractive presidential candidate. Had it not been for the rift with Johnson he might well have run for the Democrats, but now the Republicans gathered him to their bosom and he was nominated unanimously at their convention in May, 1868.

Grant's victory over the Democratic candidate, Horatio Seymour, seemed almost inevitable. Presenting himself as a be printed? Or should "sound" currency be restored?

Grant offered no coherent program. Lacking political experience and any personal enthusiasm for politicking, he left such problems largely for Congress to decide. Nor did he surround himself with skilled advisers. His cabinet appointments were frankly baffling to observers for their mediocrity (*"Who in the world is Borie?"*, the New York *Herald* queried, alluding to the rich, obscure Philadelphia merchant Adolph E. Borie with whom Grant played cards and who was appointed Secretary for the Navy). A host of appointments also went to kinfolk of Grant and his wife, and though such nepotism was not unknown in Washington it was particularly disquieting because of the absence of any compensating talents around the White House.

Corruption in the Gilded Age

With no one standing firm at the helm of state, corruption ran riot. Materialism anyway was flourishing in the aftermath of a war which had cheapened life and overstretched the values of honor and self-sacrifice. This was the so-called Gilded Age, when fortunes were made suddenly and enjoyed ostentatiously. Grant himself acquired a taste for luxury and though not personally implicated in the scandals around him never found it easy to resist gifts from favor-seekers, whether of fine cigars, or racehorses, or entire houses. The White House itself was elaborately refurbished in the gilt-and-chandelier "steamboat palace" style, and very lavish entertaining was done there.

And the reek of scandal was everywhere. Grant's sister, Jennie, was married to Wall Street speculator Abel Rathbone Corbin, an associate of notorious stockmarket swindlers Jay Gould and James Fisk. The three sharks, often seen in the President's company, cornered the New York gold supply and sent its price sky-high, causing a national panic, before the Treasury took action. The notorious Credit Mobilier scandal of 1872 tainted Congress more than the Executive; but searching questions were asked when Grant's private secretary, Orville E. Babcock, was implicated in the Whiskey Ring Affair, a distillery conspiracy which cost the government millions in revenue. Then Secretary of War, William W. Belknap, was found to have accepted bribes while managing Indian affairs; in 1875 he resigned to avoid impeachment.

The white South fights back

The worst scandals broke during Grant's second term; he was re-elected by increased majorities in 1872. But in the last years they detonated amid such press fury that attention was diverted from events in the South.

In March, 1870, the historic 15th Amendment had been

Klansmen depicted in 1868. Under Grant, Congress passed two Ku Klux Klan acts (1870 and 1871) to try and protect Negro voting rights from Klansmen's interference.

nonpolitical, nonpartisan candidate and campaigning under the slogan "Let us have peace," Grant did indeed win: by 214 electoral votes to 80. But the margin of victory in the popular vote was much narrower: only 52.7 percent of ballots cast. The public was nervous of Republican radicalism and, in fact, without the support of new black votes in the South, Grant would have lacked a majority.

As President, moreover, Grant inherited a plethora of difficulties. Violence was rife in the white South where domination by Northern "carpetbaggers" was resented and the freed Negro population was feared. The Ku Klux Klan arose in this context, its phantasmagorically-clad night-riders beating, mutilating and murdering victims on a terrifying scale. There were economic problems, too. Western farmers, for example, were suffering from a long decline in commodity prices; the high tariff was hotly debated; and there was controversy, too, over the handling of wartime "greenback" paper money. Should more dollars ratified to protect black (male) voting rights. But though Grant acquiesced in the Republican Congress's radical reconstruction program, he gradually lost enthusiasm for sending federal troops to support flimsy carpetbag regimes. So, in truth, did the Northern public. The white south recovered its confidence, and hooded Klansmen working by night gave way to open parades of white racists who publicly intimidated Negro voters to the point where they simply stayed home at elections.

Grant's unhappy presidency came to an end in 1877, amid talk of seething corruption, and with a financial panic (1873) having inaugurated an economic depression. In his last message to Congress, the President admitted that "mistakes have been made as all can see" but laid the blame on his assistants. Out of office, heaving a metaphorical sigh of relief, he embarked on a world tour. His personal popularity had never entirely waned and in 1880

serious moves were made by Republican "Stalwarts" to nominate him for a third term. They failed, however, and to supplement a dwindling income Grant put all his property into the banking house of Grant and Ward. In 1884, the bank collapsed and the former President was left penniless, suffering from a cancer of the throat which was to prove fatal eventually. Nonetheless, he managed despite the pain to write his two-volume *Personal Memoirs*, admired among military biographies for their modesty and simplicity of style. Grant finished the work only four days before his death at Mt. McGregor, New York, on July 23, 1885.

Vicksburg, 1863: the Union victory here was one of Grant's supreme triumphs as a military commander; he showed no such flair in the years of presidential office where, someone complained, he had "not an idea above a horse or a cigar."

RUTHERFORD B. HAYES

R B Hayes (signature)

Nineteenth President 1877-1881

Campaigning for President in the hundredth year of the Republic, Rutherford Hayes is chiefly remembered as the victor of a deadlocked contest: the hotly disputed election of 1876. The former Governor of Ohio was afterward pilloried in the opposition press as "The Fraudulent President," "His Fraudulency" and "Rutherfraud." As judgments on his character the charges were unfair: Hayes was honest, able and serious-minded in his approach to politics. In office he ended the era of Reconstruction and he reformed the civil service to the annoyance of office seekers. Yet the disputed election remains controversial to this day, most modern analysts agreeing that his opponent *was* defrauded of the presidency. Historian Hugh Brogan has gone so far as to call the result the most outrageous piece of election-rigging in American history – "which is saying something."

The disputed election

Rutherford Birchard Hayes was born in Delaware, Ohio, on October 4, 1822, graduated from Kenyon College in 1842 and from Harvard Law School three years later. He was city solicitor of Cincinnati at the outbreak of the Civil War and proceeded to serve with the 23rd Ohio Volunteers. Hayes was several times wounded and rose to the rank of major general before the war was over. Entering politics as a moderate Republican, he served in the House of Representatives from 1864-67 and was three times elected Governor of Ohio in 1867, 1869 and 1875. His campaign in

the state for "sound money" gave him a national reputation, and in 1876 he won his party's nomination for the presidency over the more colorful James G. Blaine who had been tainted by association with a railroad securities swindle. Both parties opted that year for unblemished candidates, the Democrats nominating the reforming governor Samuel J. Tilden of New York who had broken up the Tammany Hall "Tweed Ring" in his city. The public had a craving for clean candidates, shell-shocked as it was by recent revelations of corruption in the Grant era.

The campaign, though, was bitterly fought, the Democrats sensing the possibility of victory in a presidential election for the first time in two decades. And as the returns came in it did indeed look as if their man had won; so much so that on election night Hayes and his supporters went to bed convinced of their defeat, and newspapers announced a triumph for Tilden.

Tilden had in fact won a 51 percent majority of the popular votes, and with 184 electoral votes he was only one short of the 185 needed for victory. Hayes, in contrast, was conceded only 165 electoral votes. He would need every one of the remaining 20 contested votes if he was to steal victory.

However, all of the contested votes lay in states under Republican government: South Carolina, Louisiana, Florida and Oregon. And with their hands on the election machinery, Republican managers cynically invalidated Democratic ballots wholesale on grounds of fraud and intimidation

against black voters in the three Southern states. Republican electors cast the votes for Hayes; outraged Democratic electors cast them for Tilden; and with inauguration day fast approaching a special electoral commission was set up by Congress to decide the disputed cases. Evidence of chicanery was revealed on both sides; pressure on the commission was intense; and in the end, by a vote of 8 to 7, all of the contested returns were awarded to Hayes.

The Compromise of 1877

Congress was in uproar and there was talk of filibustering to paralyze the government of the country. But in the end the Democrats settled for expediency in the Compromise of 1877, by which they would accept Hayes as President if he would promise to withdraw federal troops from the Southern states and allow them to manage their own affairs. The compromise was agreed after long-drawn-out negotiations, and on March 2, 1877, Hayes was formally declared elected – only two days before he took office.

As President Hayes honored his promises to the Demo-

Women members of the temperance movement, in action at an ale and whiskey store in the 1870s. Crusaders had support in the White House where the Hayes banned all wines and spirits.

crats. The last carpetbagger governments vanished from the old Confederate capitals and tensions between the white North and the South eased considerably. Conciliation, however, was achieved at the expense of the former slaves, now abandoned by the North and relegated increasingly to inferior status. In other respects Hayes proved a capable, conservative President who reformed the civil service and supported "sound money," resuming monetary specie payments. He also restored some homely sobriety to the White House. The new First Family lived simply and Hayes's wife Lucy was nicknamed "Lemonade Lucy" for a rule banning alcohol from the mansion. The couple had eight children.

Refusing to stand for a second term, Rutherford B. Hayes retired to his home at Fremont, Ohio, where he died on January 17, 1893.

JAMES A. GARFIELD

James A. Garfield.

"**M**y God! What is there in this place that a man should ever want to get into it?" fumed President Garfield not long after entering the White House – and so adding himself to the growing company of men who found the office a near-intolerable ordeal. Pressure from office-seekers was the cause of his outburst: Garfield came to power in the Gilded Age when spoilsmanship was at its most blatant and issues of policy were deemed virtually negligible in the scrambling for political favor. As President, Garfield is in fact memorable only as a martyr to the system of patronage: shot while entering a railroad station by a crazed office-seeker, he died after serving less than five months of his term.

The Ohio canal boy
Born in the frontier town of Orange, in Cuyahoga County, Ohio, on November 19, 1831, James Abram Garfield grew to personify the log-cabin-to-White-House le-

Twentieth President 1881

gend. He came from a poor farming background and endured years of childhood hardship, his father dying when Garfield was only 2 years old. His schooling was only rudimentary and at 16, the future President left home to tramp the countryside seeking what work he could find. For some time before sickness drove him home Garfield worked as a canal bargeman. Later he struggled to get himself educated and eventually managed to work his way through Williams College, from which he graduated at age 25.

Garfield was a member of the Disciples of Christ and

developed powers of oratory as a lay preacher. Pursuing a career in teaching he also entered politics as a Republican with strong feelings against the slave system. A big, broad-shouldered man, compelling through his eloquence, Garfield entered the Ohio senate in 1859, and spoke firmly against secession. Offering his services to the Union at the outbreak of the Civil War he became a colonel in the 42nd Ohio Volunteers. Garfield served at Shiloh, Rosecrans and Chickemauga, rising to the rank of major general.

In 1863, Garfield resigned his commission to take a seat in the House of Representatives. He proved a skilled parliamentarian, becoming leader of the Republicans in the lower house. Garfield was accused of corruption during the Credit Mobilier scandal of 1874, but defended himself successfully and held onto his seat: the sum he allegedly gained was a mere $329 – paltry by the corrupt standards of the day.

Garfield was a member of the electoral commission which decided the disputed presidential election of 1876, and was finally elected to the Senate in 1880. At the Republican convention of that year the party was divided into two factions. The so-called "Stalwarts," led by New York spoils baron Senator Roscoe Conkling, proposed to run General Grant for a third term (against the unwritten code, observed since Washington's time, prohibiting three tenures of office). The "Half-Breeds," equally committed to spoils but rather more discreet, favored James G. Blaine of Maine. Treasury Secretary John Sher-

man hoped to win as a compromise candidate, but when it became clear that none of the three could get a majority the Blaine-Sherman forces united under the slogan "Anything to beat Grant!" and rallied behind the experienced Garfield. He was nominated on the 36th ballot and in the election defeated the Democrats' General Winfield Scott Hancock by an electoral vote of 214 to 155 (with a wafer-thin margin of only 7,000 votes in the popular ballot).

Assassination

Competition for the spoils of office marred Garfield's presidency from the outset. To appease the Stalwarts, Grant's supporter Chester A. Arthur had been nominated for the vice-presidency. But the arch-spoilsman Conkling was enraged when Garfield gave the key post of Collector of the Port of New York to a Half-Breed who was Conkling's leading opponent in that state. Garfield also took a stand by pressing for investigation of a post office scandal. In short, Stalwart hostility to the new President was intense by the time the fateful 2nd of July, 1881 came around.

On that day, as Garfield arrived at Washington railroad station en route to watch exercises at Williamstown,

Assassination: President Garfield is shot by the crazed Charles J. Guiteau in Washington only months after his inauguration.

Massachusetts, the President was shot in the back by a disgruntled office-seeker named Charles J. Guiteau. The assassin, clearly unbalanced, had earlier been pestering officials in Washington in hopes of an appointment – and had been turned down. He professed himself a Stalwart but there was no evidence of a conspiracy.

Unlike Abraham Lincoln, the earlier presidential victim of assassination, Garfield did not die immediately but endured many weeks of pain and discomfort. Infection set in and reports on the President's condition were relayed to the public in such a ceaseless stream that the stricken Garfield observed, "I should think the people would be tired of having me dished up to them in this way." In September, to escape the hot summer in Washington, the patient was moved to a New Jersey cottage where, it was hoped, the ocean air would revive him. It failed.

James A. Garfield was married from 1858 to Lucretia Rudolph. He died on September 19, 1881.

CHESTER A. ARTHUR

[signature: Chester A. Arthur]

Twenty-first President 1881-1885

Few Presidents have been greeted on attaining office with more suspicion than Chester Alan Arthur. Emerging from the murky playground of New York State politics he had held the vice presidency for purely factional reasons and reached the White House only because his predecessor, President Garfield, was assassinated. Arthur's polished manners, plump cheeks and luxuriant side-whiskers did nothing to allay people's concern: as a friend and lieutenant of New York's czar of patronage, Roscoe Conkling, he seemed the very archetype of the spoils politician, and the *Tribune*, in the summer of 1881, pictured him standing under a sign which read, "political dickering and other dirty work done here."

Yet in office Arthur became a different man. While continuing to live an elegant life he behaved with dignity and courtesy; worked conscientiously; administered efficiently; and (by a startling irony) is remembered above all as the man who rescued the civil service from the worst abuses of the spoils system. He might almost be said to have reversed Lord Acton's famous maxim that "power tends to corrupt;" in Arthur's case, power uncorrupted.

The spoilsman
Born at Fairfield, Vermont, on October 5, 1830, Chester Alan Arthur was of Irish-American parentage and graduated from Union College in 1848. He studied law in New York, was admitted to the Bar in 1854, and won a name for himself in the "Lemmon slave case" by which it was decided that slaves passing through New York were to be considered free. In 1855, winning another decision, he obtained a ruling that Negroes were to be treated the same as whites on New York City streetcars.

During the Civil War Arthur rose to the post of Quartermaster General of New York. He was already acquainted with Roscoe Conkling and in the words of Herbert Agar, "quickly learned more than is good for a man to know about New York State politics." Arthur, it should be said, was never personally financially dishonest. But he was well aware of the multitudinous ways that public money moved into private hands, and seems to have relished the maneuvering and wire-pulling of party politics. In 1871, President Grant served him the most appetizing dish on the office-seeker's menu, appointing him Collector of the Port of New York. The custom house had long been notorious as a center for the distribution of jobs to the party faithful, and Arthur made no move to clear it up.

President Hayes, attempting to reform the civil service, forced Arthur's resignation as Collector in 1879, and the spoilsman afterwards worked with other Republican "Stalwarts" to bring back the more amenable General Grant as a presidential contender. When Garfield won the Republican nomination in 1880, Arthur was given second place on the ticket to conciliate the defeated Stalwarts – and so it was that he stood waiting in the wings as Garfield's presidential tragedy was acted out.

The reformer

When "Chet" Arthur took up the reins of office the public watched his moves with apprehension – and with fascination, too. His plans for the White House involved total redecoration: 24 wagonloads of old furniture and clothing were removed and auctioned off to make way for opulent new furnishings. Stylish entertaining returned to the mansion: Arthur's wife Ellen, who had borne him three children, had died in 1880, but his sister served as an accomplished hostess. A French chef was brought in to preside in the White House kitchen – and Conkling's steward was filched to govern the household.

But Conkling himself was not invited in to preside in the same way over patronage. Arthur used his own judgment, surprising many people by his restraint in distributing offices and by the number of Garfield's appointees whom he retained. More, he astounded critics by telling Congress of his belief that appointments "should be based upon a certain fitness." In 1883, he firmly supported the Pendleton Act classifying about 10 percent of government jobs as

Brooklyn Bridge, the steel and cable suspension bridge spanning the East River was opened by Arthur in 1883 and considered an engineering miracle. American cities were taking modern shape: the first metalframe skyscraper was built in Chicago in 1885.

appropriate for competitive examinations and setting up a civil service commission to supervise them.

Arthur did more besides, urging tariff reform, for example; pressing for prosecutions in the "Star Routes" postal fraud; calling for the construction of a modern Navy. But though his name was put forward for renomination in 1884, any hopes of a second term had been dashed by his desertion from the Stalwarts. The spoilsmen had turned against him; and Arthur was soundly beaten at the Republican convention by the magnetic James G. Blaine.

Chester A. Arthur nonetheless left the White House a more respected figure than he had entered it. His health was failing, however, and he died on November 18, 1886.

GROVER CLEVELAND

Grover Cleveland [signature]

A mold-breaker in many senses, Grover Cleveland entered the White House as the first Democrat to be elected in 28 years. He was also the first – and to date the only – President to serve two nonconsecutive terms (so counting both as 22nd and 24th President). Above all, though, Cleveland was distinguished in his own day by his honesty. A short, heavy-set figure weighing over 240 pounds and with determination set firm in his moustachioed face, he had a look of tough self-sufficiency which caused H. L. Mencken to write in 1933 that "his whole carcass seemed to be made of iron. There was no give in him, no bounce, no softness. He sailed through American history like a steel ship loaded with monoliths of granite."

Cleveland was a conservative. He was no great orator; added no new territories to the Union; pushed through no earth-shattering legislation. And yet in the Gilded Age of spoilsmanship and suave chicanery he rendered invaluable service to the country simply by reaching the White House and presiding there without finagling. The Statue of Liberty was dedicated under Cleveland's first administration, and on a human scale the President too was a symbolic figure – a stolid little monument to integrity.

Twenty-second President 1885-1889
Twenty-fourth President 1893-1897

A Buffalo clerk

Grover Cleveland was born in Caldwell, Essex County, New Jersey, on March 18, 1837, the son of a Presbyterian minister. (He was, in fact, christened Stephen Grover Cleveland, but dropped his first name on entering public life.) From 1855, he worked as a clerk in a Buffalo law office and was himself admitted to the Bar in the same city some four years later.

Cleveland took no active part in the Civil War but stayed at home to support his mother. He was made district attorney of Erie County in 1863 and elected sheriff in 1871 despite the fact that he stood as a Democrat in a nominally Republican county. Already his obvious integrity was proving capable of winning votes and compensating for a certain dourness and lack of social grace. Buffalo at this time was a rowdy waterfront community laboring under corrupt Republican city government, and in 1881 a group of civic reformers chose Cleveland as their candidate for mayor. Again, despite his Democratic platform, he won – and as mayor quickly gained a name as a businesslike reformer of independent spirit. His success resulted in his election the next year to the governorship of New York. Cleveland's refusal to play the party games of patronage and spoils brought him into open conflict with Tammany Hall, but civil service reformers united behind the governor; businessmen found his conservatism very much to their liking; and a public longing for clean politics turned to him with great enthusiasm. In 1884, Cleveland received the Democratic nomination for President, and he went into the election with real prospects of success.

A mudslinging campaign

The Republicans had been damaged by the defection of a large group of anti-corruption activists known as the Mugwumps, who campaigned in the election for the Democrats. The two parties, then, were very evenly matched, but since neither Cleveland nor his Republican opponent James G. Blaine had any major policy innovations to offer the contest degenerated into a mudslinging fight that was dirty even by the standards of the day.

Blaine, though a brilliant and charismatic leader of his party, was tainted by charges of corruption in a scandal revolving around the granting of congressional favors. Cleveland, of course, was above suspicion as far as his personal finances were concerned. But he was no prig: he played poker, smoked cigars – and his rotund figure

European immigrants arrived in human flood in the late nineteenth century, including many Greeks, Italians, Hungarians and Slavs from peasant eastern and southern Europe. A literacy test for the newcomers was debated by Congress in 1896 and 1897, but the bill limiting entry was vetoed by President Cleveland.

betrayed the prodigious quantities of beer and sausage which he routinely consumed. These were forgivable, even likeable, traits. But he had committed one real indiscretion in fathering a child years beforehand by a widow named Maria Crofts Halpin.

The Buffalo *Evening Telegraph* broke the story during the campaign, in a piece headed "A Terrible Tale: A Dark

Chapter in a Public Man's History." And the Republicans pounced gleefully on this scandalous revelation.

Faced with a tirade of abusive slogans from the Republican opposition Cleveland acted with complete openness and honesty. He admitted that he had known the widow and, though the child's paternity was by no means certain, it transpired that he had made full provision for the child's welfare. "Tell the truth," was Cleveland's simple advice to his supporters on the issue, and his candor may have earned him as many friends as detractors. Ultimately, though, Cleveland was probably elected because a Republican parson, speaking in the critically important state of New York, referred to the Democrats as the party of "Rum, Romanism and Rebellion," so alienating the city's many Roman Catholics. The result was very close, Cleveland winning by fewer than 25,000 popular votes (219 to 182 votes in the Electoral College).

A White House wedding

Grover Cleveland at his inauguration was 48 years old and still a bachelor. True to his mold-breaking form, however, he delighted the society columnists by becoming the first and only President to get married in the White House. The date was July 2, 1886 and his bride was the lovely young Frances Folsom, who was the daughter of his former law partner. She became a much admired First Lady and was to bear five children.

Otherwise, Cleveland's first term passed without great drama. The President worked hard for reform in the civil service, extending the system of competitive examinations begun under his predecessor, President Arthur. He also examined pension bills with unusual diligence, vetoing a host of awards granted as favors to the undeserving; and in general confirmed his existing reputation as an honest and industrious public servant. In February, 1887, he signed the Interstate Commerce Act, giving the federal government powers to regulate the anarchic railroad industry.

Cleveland was renominated by the Democratic convention in 1888, but lost the election of that year to Republican Benjamin Harrison on the tariff issue. (Acknowledging that that the tariff was bringing in an unnecessarily large surplus revenue Cleveland had proposed moderate reductions; publication of the so-called "Murchison letter" from the British minister, however, gave the impression that the president was lowering the tariff only to serve English interests.) The Clevelands duly vacated the White House, but in leaving Frances Cleveland told a steward to take good care of the furniture and ornaments, "for we are coming back just four years from today." Those words proved prophetic. In 1892, after one administration under

the weak and colorless Harrison, Grover Cleveland was returned to the White House with 277 electoral votes to the Republican's 145 (and a popular margin of over 360,000).

Gold bugs and silver Democrats

Cleveland's second term opened with the country on the edge of a financial panic which was to cause the failure of over 15,000 businesses. A conservative in money matters, Cleveland blamed the inflationary Silver Purchase Act of 1890, by which the government bought double quantities of silver bullion every month and coined it into silver dollars. Cleveland himself, believed in a single gold standard, and secured the act's repeal in 1893. But his policy only

A cartoon of 1886 congratulates Grover Cleveland on his unique White House wedding to pretty, 21-year-old Frances Folsom. The ceremony was held in the Blue Room, amid garlands of roses and pansies.

THE GREATEST CURIOSITY OF THE NINETEENTH CENTURY.

An anti-Democrat cartoon of 1894 complains that Cleveland has failed to look after business interests.

easily won over his audience; the silverite platform was adopted; and Bryan was nominated for the presidency. In response the most ardent gold bugs left the party and, calling themselves the National Democrats, ran their own candidate in the coming election.

Cleveland, confessing himself dazed by the whole situation, was swept aside by the tide of passion. Before his term ended, however, he had won some popularity by intervening in a long-standing boundary dispute between Venezuela and British Guyana. Invoking the Monroe Doctrine, the President sent some very haughty notes to England which pleased jingoists in the public. Nevertheless, the bulk of his own party had disagreed with him on his commitment to lower the tariff as well as on the silver issue, and he left office a solitary figure, on March 4, 1897.

In retirement, Grover Cleveland lived at Princeton, New Jersey, an unusually respected elder statesman who contributed articles to the press, was much consulted on public affairs, and was in great demand as a speaker. He died on June 24, 1908, at the age of 71.

resulted in a drain on the Treasury's gold reserve – and also a dramatic rift in his own party.

The so-called silver Democrats, strong in the farming South and West pressed for silver coinage. The "gold bugs," representing Eastern business, supported Cleveland. In 1894, against a background of severe depression, with rural discontent and labor unrest, an army of unemployed demonstrators marched on Washington to be dispersed by club-wielding police. In the same year Cleveland ordered federal troops to Chicago to break the Pullman strike. Increasingly, the President appeared callous rather than courageous and the silver Democrats gained strength in the party at the expense of "His Obstinacy."

At the 1896 Democratic convention, the messianic young orator William Jennings Bryan spoke to deafening applause in the silverite cause, warning: "You shall not press down upon the brow of labor this crown of thorns. You shall not crucify mankind upon a cross of gold!" The youthful zealot

The unemployed march on Washington, 1894, was broken up amid scenes of violence.

BENJAMIN HARRISON

Bnj Harrison

Twenty-third President 1889-1893

Having served a single term sandwiched between the two administrations of Grover Cleveland, Benjamin Harrison always was a forgettable President. At 5 feet 6 inches he was physically inconspicuous and his cold, reserved temperament did nothing to compensate. Harrison was an "iceberg" – he "sweated iced water" – according to contemporaries. No one doubted his intelligence, and he came to office untainted by any hint of scandal. But his presidential reticence only served the interests of congressional wheelers and dealers. The pension list hugely expanded under Harrison's administration; spoilsmen got back into business; and the President's attempts at civil service reform were so ineffectual that the youthful and energetic Theodore Roosevelt, serving on the Civil Service Commission, was moved to speak of the Chief Executive as a "cold-blooded, narrow-minded, prejudiced, obstinate, timid old psalm-singing Indianapolis politician."

Posterity is not quite so harsh in its judgment, but Harrison still ranks down among the average-to-poor Presidents. Some good things and some bad things were accomplished under his administration: Harrison had precious little to do with any of them.

Ancestral echoes

Benjamin Harrison was born at North Bend near Cincinnati, Ohio, on August 20, 1833. He was the grandson of General William Henry Harrison, the 9th American President; and great-grandson of the Benjamin Harrison who signed the Declaration of Independence. Such pedigree inclined future opponents to take him for a man of privilege, but in reality the family fortunes had declined somewhat over the decades. The young Benjamin was brought up on a farm and taught at the local log schoolhouse; he became a keen reader, though, and with help from a tutor entered Miami University, Ohio. Graduating in 1852, he studied law, was admitted to the Bar in 1853, and went on to practice in Indianapolis.

Harrison was an ardent anti-slaver and in the second year of the Civil War was commissioned as a second lieutenant. He had risen to the rank of brigadier-general by its end, having campaigned in Kentucky and Tennessee, and marched with Sherman on Atlanta. Returning afterwards to law practice, he failed in 1876 as Republican candidate for the governorship of Indiana, but entered the U.S. Senate in 1881 and served there for six years, chairing the committee on territories. In other respects, he attracted little notice: he supported civil service reform; opposed Cleveland's pension vetoes; and in 1887 he failed in seeking re-election.

At this stage it might have seemed that Harrison's political career had petered out. He had little more to offer his party than a good war record and a name in Washington untarnished by charges of corruption. These, however, were luminous qualities to Republican bosses at the time. The ancestral name of Harrison still possessed a certain reso-

The Oklahoma Land Rush of April 22, 1889 was among the most dramatic events of Benjamin Harrison's presidency. On that day some 2 million acres of Oklahoma land were opened to settlers, and all had been claimed within a matter of hours by so-called "boomers." However, the event marked the high point of the western land boom. Worsening climate and a loss of business confidence were to initiate a deep agricultural depression creating bitter discontent among western farmers.

nance; and what was more the general came from Ohio, always a key state in elections (it furnished every successful Republican presidential candidate between Lincoln and Roosevelt). In short, when the Republicans convened at Chicago in 1888, the defeated Senator Harrison was given the presidential nomination.

The Billion Dollar Congress

The election of that year was a low, lackluster affair fought on the issue of tariff which President Cleveland wanted to reduce and which the Republicans, financed by big business interests, wanted to keep high. The results were close and corruption was rampant. Harrison won basically by swinging industrial states in the Northeast, albeit on narrow margins, to end up with a good-looking 233 electoral votes to Cleveland's 168. The defeated President, however, had a popular majority of 100,000.

Congress under Harrison passed some notable legislation. The Sherman Antitrust Act outlawed industrial monopolies; the Silver Purchase Act authorized the government to coin increased quantities of silver in an attempt to help poor farmers. To please the manufacturers, the McKinley Act racked the tariff up to an all-time high; and to please

Union veterans a new Pension Act increased expenditure from an annual $98 million to $157 million. In all, the House for the first time in peace spent $1 billion in a single session, earning itself the name of the "Billion Dollar Congress" – and wiping out a large treasury surplus.

Harrison, though, was not much involved in these affairs; complaining, on the contrary, of his own lack of privacy at the White House he proposed substantial alterations to the mansion. These were refused by the freehanded Congress, though the First Family was given electric lighting. (It worried the Harrisons, who were said to leave the lights on all night for fear of shocks when switching them off.)

The President's wife Carrie, whom he had married in 1853, died in the last year of his term, and though nominated for re-election in 1892 he was defeated by Grover Cleveland. Harrison returned to his law practice but won some some attention again in Paris, 1899, when he represented Venezuela in a boundary dispute with Britain. Afterwards, he returned to Indianapolis.

Benjamin Harrison had remarried in 1896, taking as his bride Mrs. Mary Scott Lord Dimmock, the niece of his first wife. He had three children in all and died at Indianapolis on March 13, 1901.

WILLIAM McKINLEY

William M. McKinley [signature]

As President from 1897-1901, William McKinley took America into the twentieth century. And he presided over another great transition too: under his administration the United States became for the first time a world power. His years in office saw the country go to war with Spain, annex Hawaii, and acquire Puerto Rico, Guam and the Philippines. Triumphantly re-elected, McKinley was assassinated in his second term by a young anarchist, and with such dramatic events crowding his tenure in the White House he might be pictured a bold, provocative figure.

Not so: the 25th President was in himself a mild and cautious man, even castigated by critics for spinelessness. Pressure from a jingoistic press and public pushed him into the Spanish-American War of 1898, and he was personally reluctant to seize lands afterward. In human terms he possessed a kindliness that was wholly admirable: faced with all the burdens of

Twenty-fifth President 1897-1901

a wartime Chief Executive he still found time to care for his frail, epileptic wife, Ida. But he was no visionary. America was forcing its way to the table of great nations; McKinley resembled an old-fashioned usher who was being overtaken by his own hurrying customer.

The McKinley Tariff
William McKinley was born in Niles, Trumbull County, Ohio, on January 29, 1843, to parents of Scottish-Irish descent. His father was an ironmaker who took the family, in 1852,

to Poland, Mahoning County, where William received his schooling. He went on to Allegheny College, Meadville, Pennsylvania, but was forced to leave through ill health. Nonetheless he was sufficiently recovered within a year to enlist to fight in the Civil War, and he served with distinction in the 23rd Ohio regiment under Rutherford B. Hayes, 19th president. By the end of the war, McKinley had risen to the rank of major.

Afterward McKinley pursued the vocation taken up by so many of his presidential predecessors: he studied law. Graduating from Albany Law School in New York, he went on to open a practice in Canton, Ohio, in 1867. That same year he married the delicate society beauty, Ida Saxton. The couple had two daughters, but both little girls died in earliest childhood, and the grieving Ida so deteriorated in mental and physical health that she was left a confirmed invalid, medically depressive and given to epileptic seizures. McKinley remained devoted to her. When he was Governor of Ohio he would break off every day at three o'clock to wave a handkerchief from his office window to Ida at their home nearby. Ida herself had an obsessive need to be with her husband and at receptions – even in the White House – insisted on acting as hostess. Official functions were often awkwardly interrupted as the President, ever alert for signs of a coming seizure, would suddenly place a napkin over her convulsed face and lead her from the room.

McKinley entered politics in Canton as a Republican and

Leon Czolgosz shoots President McKinley at the Pan-American Exposition in Buffalo, New York, on September 6, 1901. One of the two bullets fired entered the abdomen, and despite expectations that the President would recover he collapsed and died eight days later. McKinley had gone to the exposition to deliver an address on the subject of the tariff. Czolgosz was an extreme anarchist, believing in the assassination of rulers on the grounds that all forms of government are oppressive. Anarchist assassins took the lives of many different leaders around the turn of the century, including President Carnot of France, the Empress Elizabeth of Austria and King Humbert I of Italy.

went on to serve in the House of Representatives from 1877-83 and from 1885-91. An ardent protectionist, he became particularly prominent as chairman of the Ways and Means Committee and in that capacity he sponsored the McKinley Tariff of 1890, which raised duties so high that they became, in many cases, prohibitive, causing revenues to fall. The Tariff's unpopularity was a major cause of Republican failures in the congressional elections of that year, and McKinley was himself among the victims, being defeated for re-election.

Nevertheless, as Governor of Ohio from 1892-96, he consolidated his reputation for industry and intelligence,

also coming into close contact with Marcus A. Hanna, an Ohio businessman with ambitions as a political "king-maker." With strong backing from Hanna, McKinley allowed his name to be put before the Republican convention of 1896 as presidential candidate; and with strong backing from Hanna, too, he secured victory on the first ballot.

A front-porch campaigner
The 1896 election aroused furious passions and, for the first time in decades, some serious debate on an issue of public concern. The country was in the grip of an economic slump and the Democratic party had been torn down the middle

on the question of how best to cope with it. Smalltown rural Democrats favored the inflationary solution of coining more silver; businessmen insisted on a strict gold standard. The young silverite orator William Jennings Bryan won the Democratic nomination but caused a mass defection of Democratic "gold bugs," and with such a fragmented opposition the path should have been clear for Republican success.

However, victory was by no means assured. Bryan ran a barnstorming campaign, delivering as many as 30 impassioned speeches a day to mass audiences around the country. The popular response was impressive, threatening to make nonsense of old political voting patterns, and creating some fear of a social revolution.

McKinley countered in very different style. Unable to vie with Bryan for oratory he ran a "front-porch" campaign instead, speaking to delegates on the lawn before his own modest frame house with a calculated air of informality. Funded by Hanna and other conservative businessmen, the Republicans meanwhile pumped out a mass of propaganda conjuring nightmares of Bryanite "anarchism." The campaign succeeded. McKinley won with a plurality of 609,687 and 271 electoral votes to 176. However much Bryan may have stirred hearts, he had failed to sway heads in the industrial Northeast; significantly, he had also failed to win over three key Midwestern farming states – Iowa, Minnesota and North Dakota. The dream of an agrarian presidency was over; the businessmen stayed in business.

AN AGE OF EMPIRES

Soon after his inauguration, McKinley called a special session of Congress: to protect American industry and farming, they passed the new Dingley Tariff (1897) which raised duties on imports to a new high. Later, in 1900, the Gold Standard Act firmly established gold as the backing for U.S. currency. The economy meanwhile picked up, and the issues which had so dominated the election now slipped from the forefront of national consciousness to make way for imperial themes.

The late nineteenth century was an age of empires. The great powers of Europe had long been scrambling for territories in Africa and Asia, and there was a widespread feeling that young America was missing out on the spoils. Foreign footholds could serve strategic as well as commercial purposes, and Cuba had for decades been a focus of attention, lying as it did so close to the beckoning finger of Florida. The island's Spanish administration was decaying: from 1894, the Cubans had been in revolt and reports of Spanish atrocities filled the pages of the press. Newspapers

clamored for something to be done to aid the rebels, while McKinley made every effort to avoid intervention. His stance earned him the contempt of the young Theodore Roosevelt, who was to say that McKinley had "about as much backbone as a chocolate éclair." And the President had other critics too; in his own administration, in Congress, and above all in various newspapers owned by millionaire William Randolph Hearst.

McKinley finally succumbed to the warmongers when the U.S. battleship *Maine* was sunk by a mysterious explosion in Havana harbor. After much inner debate, he sent a message recommending intervention to Congress; in response the two Houses recognized Cuban independence, and authorized the use of force to expel the Spanish.

The Spanish-American War cost the United States 5,000 lives, mostly through typhoid, malaria and yellow fever, but it generated its own heroic lore, too, through the exploits of the volunteer unit known as the Rough Riders with Theodore Roosevelt as second-in-command. And it ended in American victory: by the peace terms agreed in Paris in December, 1898, Spain ceded Puerto Rico, Guam and the Philippines to the United States. Spain also gave up sovereignty of Cuba, which was freed – under U.S. jurisdiction. During the course of the war, the Hawaiian Islands, long under American influence, were also annexed, so that at the threshold of the twentieth century, the United States was a major international power, its flag flying over bases in the Caribbean, the Pacific and Far East.

"I went down on my knees"
Not everyone applauded these gains. Anti-imperialists regarded them as immoral and unconstitutional, the seizure of the Philippines provoking particular criticism. The archipelago lay at such distance from the United States that its future statehood was inconceivable: the sizable ethnic population would then be vassals, wholly against the spirit of American democracy. McKinley, by his own account, agonized for many nights over the fitness of the decision. "I am not ashamed to tell you," he said, "that I went down on my knees and prayed to Almighty God for light and guidance more than one night."

In the end, however, he decided that taking the Philippines was the United States's moral obligation. To give them back to Spain would not help the inhabitants; nor were the people ready to govern themselves. As an unblushing White-Man's-Burdenite, McKinley concluded that the United States's duty was to "educate the Filipinos, and uplift them and civilize them and Christianize them." So he instructed his commissioners in Paris to take the archipelago, paying Spain $20 million for it in conciliation.

The USS Maine *is blown up in Havana harbor, Cuba, February 15, 1898. McKinley ordered the battleship to the harbor in order to protect American citizens after rioting had broken out. The ship's sinking was a prime cause of the Spanish-American War – 260 officers and enlisted men perished in the explosion. The exact cause of the calamity has never been discovered but the Spanish government was held guilty by a belligerent press, and* "Remember the Maine" *was an often repeated slogan.*

The result was that Filipino nationalists revolted, waging a three-year guerilla war which took 70,000 American troops to contain.

McKinley was now committed to expansion nonetheless. Negotiations began in 1900 for the construction of an isthmian canal, and the President backed a new "Open Door" policy to China, which sought equal commercial opportunities with other great powers in that country. In 1900, U.S. troops participated in the allied march on Peking during the Boxer Rebellion.

In the presidential elections of the same year, Bryan, standing again for the Democrats, tried to turn anti-imperialist sentiment to his party's advantage – but failed. Despite the Philippines issue, McKinley was re-elected by increased majorities, and he continued to pursue expansionist policies by backing the Platt Amendment which amended the Cuban constitution to give the United States rights of intervention. He had become a hugely popular President, and on September 6, 1901, a big reception was held for him at the Pan-American Exposition in Buffalo, New York, The crowds were as warm as ever. However, taking advantage of loose security, a young anarchist named Leon Czolgosz was able to fire two shots at close range at the President. "I didn't believe one man should have so much service and another man should have none," the assassin was to explain.

After early hopes of a recovery, McKinley collapsed and died on September 14, just eight days later, with the tragic Ida at his bedside. He was the last Civil War veteran to serve in the White House – and the third president to be assassinated in less than 40 years.

THEODORE ROOSEVELT

Theodore Roosevelt.

Twenty-sixth President 1901-1909

Age 42 at his inauguration, Theodore Roosevelt was by far the youngest man ever to become U.S. President, and he brought an energy to the White House which came from more than youth alone. "Teddy" Roosevelt was one of life's enthusiasts, a rambunctious individualist and a man of action in the boy's storybook mold. As a Badlands cattle rancher, he captured rustlers at gunpoint; as a Rough Rider in the Spanish-American War he personally led the charge up Kettle Hill in San Juan. In the White House, Theodore Roosevelt wholly revitalized the role of Chief Executive, restoring to it much of the prestige lost to Congress through earlier decades of presidential mediocrity. In retirement he went on big game safari in Africa; and not long before his death at 60, when stout and rheumatic, the larger-than-life ex-President could still set out on a hunting trip to Arizona with his sons to find himself, in his own words, "curled up in a blanket on the ground, and eating the flesh of a cougar because there is nothing else available."

Critics in his own day denounced him as rash and aggressive, caricaturing him as a megalomaniac dude cowboy. Yet the charm of the eternal adolescent was evident too, even to such opponents as Woodrow Wilson who conceded, "Yes, he is a great big boy ... I can easily understand why his followers are so fond of him." Because some of "T. R."'s macho posturings appear offensive by late twentieth century standards, they also detract unfairly from his record. Roosevelt, the slaughterer of lions and rhinoceroses, was also a pioneer conservationist to whom America owes many of her finest national parks and nature reserves. And Roosevelt, the "big stick" diplomat who took the Panama Canal, was also the first American to win the Nobel Peace Prize.

"Strenuosity"

Theodore Roosevelt was born in New York City on October 27, 1858, to a wealthy and respectable family. The Roosevelts descended from the first Dutch settlers of New York, and his father was a prominent banker and philanthropist; his mother hailed from Georgia. As far as material advantages were concerned, the future President lacked for nothing in his early life; however, he was handicapped by frail health. Roosevelt suffered from asthma and weak eyesight, and his sickliness was such that he missed out on a conventional education with all the boyish rough and tumble associated with schooldays.

Theodore Roosevelt was educated by private tutors, and trips to Europe were undertaken in the hope of improving his health. In later life the 26th President was to dwell often on the contrast between the feeble, bookish youth and the robust outdoor type he was to become. Encouraged by his father, he resolutely beefed up his body through strenuous physical exercise: at boxing especially he became remarkably proficient and later he did well at Harvard in the sport (his eyesight, however, never improved – Roosevelt always wore glasses and in middle age he lost the use of one of his eyes entirely).

Through the conquest of his own frailties, Roosevelt developed a gospel of "strenuosity," and it is easy to see the great emphasis on muscular prowess as over-compensation for his youthful weakness. No doubt it was: but young America, so long in the thrall of cautious businessmen, was keen to flex its muscles, too. Roosevelt's zestful self-assertiveness would catch the nation's imagination, stirring many young men fitter than he was. "Roosevelt bit me and I went mad," newsman William Allen White was to say.

To the Badlands

Theodore Roosevelt graduated from Harvard in 1880, and in the same year married Bostonian Alice Hathaway Lee. He afterward prepared for a career in law, but abandoned his studies within a year to enter the New York State legislature. There he determined to learn the craft of politics from the bottom up; family and friends were shocked by his decision to enter so ungentlemanly a profession, but Roosevelt persisted and in the state legislature from 1882-4, he won a reputation as a vigorous Republican reformer.

The year 1884 was, however, a dark one for Roosevelt. His wife died in giving birth to a baby daughter, and within 24 hours his mother had died, too. Roosevelt also fought unsuccessfully at the Republican convention of 1884 against James Blaine's nomination as presidential candidate, and afterward refused to stand again for election to the New York state assembly. Instead he repaired to the Badlands of North Dakota to live a rancher's life in authentic Wild West country, declaring that he had given up politics for good.

In North Dakota, Roosevelt enjoyed the strenuous life to the maximum. He rounded up steers, served as deputy sheriff and, according to his *Autobiography*, soon earned the respect of cowhands who had called him "Four Eyes" because of his glasses. The open-air life was good for his asthma and it rebuilt his spirits, too. In 1886, Roosevelt returned to politics to stand for mayor of New York. He failed; but in December of that year, he married a childhood friend Edith Carew. When the couple set up home, it was not out on the wild frontier but at Sagamore Hill, Oyster Bay, Long Island.

"That damned cowboy"

Roosevelt's career in public life reopened in 1889, when President Harrison appointed him a civil service commissioner in Washington D.C. His reforming zeal again made him conspicuous, and as police Commissioner for New York (1895-7) he won nationwide fame through his methods of attacking corruption. These included prowling the New

Theodore Roosevelt, photographed in the 1880s in typically macho pose (he has removed the pince nez glasses which were a trademark). Roosevelt bought his Elkhorn Ranch in Dakota territory in 1883 while still serving as a New York legislator. Guns remained a lifelong interest; even as President he always carried a revolver with him, and he worried some law-abiders by even taking it into states where holding firearms was illegal.

York streets by night, in cloak and hat, to catch patrolmen consorting with criminals and prostitutes. Perhaps in the end his efforts were ineffectual – but they must have given many an erring officer a queasy moment.

Roosevelt returned to Washington in 1897, to serve President McKinley as Assistant Secretary of the Navy. It was a brave appointment for the mild-mannered President to make, for Roosevelt was a known imperialist. According to one Congressman, he "came down here looking for war. He did not care whom we fought so long as there was a scrap." When conflict with Spain arose over Cuba, Roosevelt

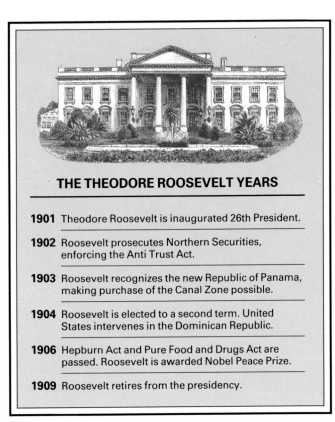

THE THEODORE ROOSEVELT YEARS

1901 Theodore Roosevelt is inaugurated 26th President.

1902 Roosevelt prosecutes Northern Securities, enforcing the Anti Trust Act.

1903 Roosevelt recognizes the new Republic of Panama, making purchase of the Canal Zone possible.

1904 Roosevelt is elected to a second term. United States intervenes in the Dominican Republic.

1906 Hepburn Act and Pure Food and Drugs Act are passed. Roosevelt is awarded Nobel Peace Prize.

1909 Roosevelt retires from the presidency.

The trust-buster

Mark Hanna was not alone among prominent Americans to be alarmed by the energetic young Roosevelt's accession. The United States in the 1900s was a country of over 75 million people whose growing national wealth was carved up by giant corporations headed by a few very powerful financiers: men like Harriman, Carnegie, Gould, Rockefeller and John Pierpont Morgan. And there was great consternation on Wall Street in February, 1902, when Roosevelt opened an attack on Big Business malpractices by deciding to prosecute a huge holding corporation known as the Northern Securities Company, controlled by J. P. Morgan and railroad king James Hill. In May, 1904, the Supreme Court confirmed that the company was founded on an illegal merger. Other suits were brought against other powerful combinations, and although critics have pointed out that Roosevelt's prosecutions were relatively few in number, the anti-trust cases did open a long era of struggle between government and big business which lasted until World War I.

Roosevelt also intervened in a coal strike in 1902, on behalf of the miners, confirming the progressive trend of his home policies. It was continued in his second term when the Hepburn Act of 1906, for example, regulated railroad rates; and a Pure Food and Drugs Act of the same year prohibited the manufacture, sale or transport of any adulterated foods, drugs, medicines or liquors.

Roosevelt also exerted himself as a conservationist and was prepared to circumvent lawyers to get his way. He believed that the nation's resources of timber and grazing land, water power, oil and minerals were a part of the American heritage; they were being stripped and despoiled at an alarming pace by a handful of private speculators. Among his protective measures, the area of national forests was increased from 43 to 194 million acres; the Inland Waterways Commission was created in 1907; and a Conservation Conference was held at the White House.

Roosevelt has often been described as a reforming conservative rather than a true radical. In an age of socialist theorizing, for example, the President never quite challenged the fundamentals of capitalism, and his trust-busting actions were directed against corporative wrong-doers rather than the corporative idea itself. Nevertheless, he did demonstrate that the President could act for the people against private wealth, and in that was truly progressive. The people, meanwhile, responded with a huge vote of confidence. Theodore Roosevelt was elected in 1904 to his second term by the biggest popular majority (some 2½ million votes) ever given to a presidential candidate, and the biggest electoral majority with 336 votes to 140.

did indeed press for armed intervention, and on the eve of hostilities it was he who ordered the fleet to the war stations which led to Dewey's famous victory at Manila Bay. In May, 1898, Roosevelt resigned from office in order to participate personally in the war in a volunteer cavalry regiment known as the Rough Riders, recruited from ranchhands, college boys and others. He fought with a reckless bravery, notably at the battle of San Juan, where despite grim casualties he led his men in a flamboyant uphill charge. "Are you afraid to stand up when I am on horseback?" he asked reluctant troopers on foot. The success of the action made Roosevelt a national hero, and on his return in 1898, he was elected Governor of New York State. His reforming program, however, alienated his political backer, Republican boss Tom Platt, who thought he could get rid of Roosevelt by maneuvering him into the vice-presidency (which can so often be a graveyard for political ambitions). Roosevelt, therefore, was duly nominated in 1900. But the plan backfired horribly on Platt when President McKinley was assassinated the next year. "Now look," fumed Senator Mark Hanna, boss of the Republican national machine, "that damned cowboy is President of the United States!"

APOSTLE OF PROSPERITY.

HE WHO SOWS WIND WILL REAP STORM —
BUT FROM GOOD SEED SPRINGS PROSPERITY!

STRIFE
T.R.

PROSPERITY

AGRICULTURE
FORESTRY.
MINING.

INDUSTRY
COMMERCE
NAVIGATION.

ARBITRATION
JUSTICE.
LAW.

LITERATURE
SCIENCE
ART.

TAKE SPADE AND HOE THYSELF; DIG ON —
GREAT SHALT THOU BE THROUGH PEASANT TOIL.
GOETHE'S FAUST II PART

The "big stick"

A major component of Roosevelt's popularity was his assertive stance in foreign policy. And this was embodied above all in his approach to the Panama question. Roosevelt had long been convinced that U.S. interests would be served by building a canal across the Isthmus of Panama (then a Colombian province). When Colombian legislators delayed granting the required permission to build, the President raged against "those contemptible little creatures in Bogota." In 1903, when a Panamanian rebellion broke out, Roosevelt supported it, and he was exceptionally quick to recognize the new state of Panama. In consequence, he was able to buy the Canal Zone for $10

Theodore Roosevelt is depicted on this Republican poster as the Apostle of Prosperity. Big business, however, suffered some setbacks through his attacks on the trusts.

million from the infant regime in 1904. Some years later he summarized the whole episode with the claim: "I took Panama and left Congress to debate, and while the debate goes on the canal does also."

Roosevelt was certainly decisive in his foreign policy. When the Republic of Santo Domingo failed to honor its foreign debts, he assumed supervision of the country's finances, justifying his action with the so-called Roosevelt

Corollary. This was an extension of the Monroe Doctrine which had basically told European powers to keep their hands off the Americas. The corollary was that if any unstable American country did fail to maintain civilized standards, the United States must be prepared to act as the policing power. "If we intend to say 'hands off' to the powers of Europe, sooner or later we must keep order ourselves," the President explained.

Clearly such an outlook might be used to justify imperialist actions anywhere in the Western Hemisphere. But in fact, Roosevelt was never quite so rash an adventurer as some critics feared. His restraint was, in a sense, as interesting as his ebullience. In particular, the one-time Rough Rider never tried to annex Cuba (as several foreign powers feared he might). And in 1905, he won real international respect for his initiatives in arranging the end of the Russo-Japanese war; it was for these mediations that Roosevelt was awarded the Nobel Peace Prize of 1906.

Roosevelt further exhibited his internationalism by becoming the first statesman to send a case for settlement to the International Court of Arbitration at the Hague. He also promoted the second Hague Peace Conference (1907), attended by 44 states, which declared against the arms race. "Speak softly and carry a big stick," was his oft-quoted maxim in foreign affairs. Obviously he was not a pacifist; but he was no wild man either, and his views were almost as well expressed in another quotation: "Don't hit at all if it is honorably possible to avoid hitting – but *never* hit soft!"

The energetic T.R. is depicted in this 1906 caricature as being given a Rough Ride through his championship of the Panama Canal purchase.

Retirement

The Roosevelts brought a new exuberance to the White House, having six uninhibited children who amused themselves by sliding down the mansion's staircase on tin trays, and kept a veritable zoo of pets ranging from flying squirrel and macaw to a pony named Algonquin, whom they once smuggled into an elevator. The unruliest child was Alice, the vivacious teenage daughter of Roosevelt's first marriage, who might be found on occasion with a snake in her purse. Roosevelt was philosophical: "I can be President of the United States or I can control Alice – I cannot possibly do both." When not working, exercising with tennis racket or medicine ball, or pillow-fighting with the children, Roosevelt entertained. Among his first guests was the great educator Booker T. Washington, invited to dine in 1901. That a Negro should sit at table with the President and his family outraged whites in the South, but in general the public loved Roosevelt's extrovert style, and he could easily have stood for a third term as President. He had, however, pledged in 1904 to honor the two-term tradition initiated by George Washington, and in 1908, having obtained the nomination of William H. Taft, he stood down.

It has often been said that Roosevelt's tragedy was to retire so young: he was still only 50 and in his prime. Though he went off hunting lions in Africa and toured Europe, too, his political ardor had in no way cooled. He was to fall out bitterly with Taft, believing that his protegé was pursuing too conservative a line as President. So deep was the rift by 1912, that Roosevelt opposed Taft for the Republican presidential nomination; and on failing he withdrew his followers from the Republican party to campaign for the White House on a third, Progressive Party ticket. The result only guaranteed a Democratic victory.

Theodore Roosevelt was always a strong friend of Britain and came to support the Allied cause in World War I, after earlier advocating neutralism. He was also a talented and prolific writer with some 40 books to his credit. He suffered from ill health in his last years – perhaps through overtaxing his constitution – and he died in his sleep on January 6, 1919, at his Sagamore Hill home.

Roosevelt is second from the right in this group observing the construction of lock gates at Gatun in the Panama Canal Zone. The President's ruthless pursuit of the zone for the United States has often been criticized as unethical. But Roosevelt certainly showed an extraordinary personal commitment to the enterprise. To inspect the work he broke a long-standing precedent that an American President should not leave the United States during his term of office.

WILLIAM H. TAFT

Weighing in at a hefty 350 pounds, William H. Taft certainly attained one distinction in office, as the heaviest President of all time. He was amiable and immense – the very archetype of a genial fat man – with a vein of real drollery in his character. Once, when offered a Chair of Law by a university, he replied that he feared a chair might not be adequate, but that a Sofa of Law might do.

If lovableness were the key quality for successful Presidents, Taft would have notched up rather more marks for distinction. Unfortunately, though, he lacked the more important qualities of will and vigor, and their absence was made all the more conspicuous in that he succeeded the energetic Teddy Roosevelt in the White House. Taft never wanted the presidency, and though he tried conscientiously to continue Roosevelt's progressive policies, he did so at his own pace – which involved mornings on the golf course and naps in the after-

Twenty-seventh President 1909-1913

noon. Nor was Taft prepared to circumvent Congress as his predecessor had done, for the judicial life had taught him to respect the often ponderous processes of law. His moderate approach so enraged Teddy Roosevelt that the ex-President launched an aggressive campaign against his protegé which tore the Republican Party in half.

"Make it the presidency!"
William Howard Taft was born in Cincinnati, Ohio, on September 15, 1857. His father was Attorney General in

Grant's administration and a minister to Austria and Russia under Chester A. Arthur. Taft graduated from Yale in 1878, and from the Cincinnati Law School two years later. Admitted to the Bar, he proved himself to be an exceptionally capable lawyer, and served as U.S. Solicitor General from 1890-92 and a federal circuit court judge from 1892-1900.

In 1900, Taft was appointed president of the Philippine Commission, and as the islands' civil governor from 1901-4 he encouraged Philippine development while doing all that was possible to conciliate the islanders themselves. His growing reputation brought him to the attention of President Roosevelt, and as U.S. Secretary of War from 1904-8 he counterbalanced "T.R."'s combative personality with a moderation that helped to serve the cause of peace. In 1906, Taft mediated in Cuban affairs, serving briefly as provisional governor on the island. Roosevelt acquired a real fondness for his genial adviser and, in 1908, obliquely offered him an extraordinary choice: "I am the seventh son of a seventh daughter and I have clairvoyant powers. I see a man weighing 350 pounds. There is something hanging over his head. I cannot make out what it is... At one time it looks like the presidency, then again it looks like the chief justiceship."

It is said that the modest Taft opted to be Chief Justice; but his ambitious wife, Helen, insisted "Make it the presidency!" So it was that the rotund judge and administrator was groomed for Chief Executive.

William Howard Taft campaigning in the elections of 1908. It turned out to be the fourth successive victory for the Republicans who carried the country by well over a million *votes. Taft failed to gain re-election four years later, however, due to a vehement conflict with his predecessor, Teddy Roosevelt, on Taft's antitrust and foreign policies.*

The great schism

With Roosevelt's backing, Taft easily won the Republican nomination, and in the presidential election of 1908, he triumphed over the Democratic contender William Jennings Bryan by a popular majority of 1,269,900 votes – 159 votes in the Electoral College. As President he followed a moderately progressive course, actually initiating more anti-trust acts than Roosevelt had done. His administration dissolved Standard Oil and introduced an 8-hour day for people on government contracts. In 1913, Taft endorsed the 16th constitutional amendment authorizing a federal income tax. His high protective tariff, however, and his conservation policies particularly angered Theodore Roosevelt. Taft believed in protecting the nation's natural resources but was not prepared to use the executive power as boldly as his predecessor had done. Where Roosevelt had snatched forest reserves without consulting Congress, Taft insisted on proper legislation. In a celebrated controversy between Secretary of the Interior, Richard A. Ballinger, and the conservationist Chief Forester, Gifford Pinchot, Taft supported his own official and eventually dismissed Pinchot. This as much as anything led to a decisive break with Roosevelt. Though Taft was renominated by the Republicans in 1912, Roosevelt ran against him in the presidential election of that year, taking with him most reforming spirits under the banner of the Progressive Party. Taft retained the Republican old guard, but he was overwhelmingly defeated by Democrat Woodrow Wilson and forced into third place behind Roosevelt. In the Electoral College, Wilson received 435 votes, Roosevelt 88, and Taft only 8. (In the popular vote, results were closer: Wilson 6,286,000, Roosevelt 4,126,000, and Taft 3,484,000.)

Taft left the White House with relief, retiring to the profession which was his true interest. He was Professor of constitutional law at Yale between 1913 and 1921, served on various commissions during World War I, and was a distinguished Chief Justice of the United States from 1921-30. William H. Taft was married from 1886 to Helen Herron, and the couple had three children. He died of a heart ailment in Washington, D.C., on March 8, 1930.

WOODROW WILSON

A college professor, antiseptic in appearance, Woodrow Wilson was among the most complex figures to serve in the White House. No one ever came more suddenly to the forefront of national politics – in little more than two years he rose from president of Princeton University to President of the United States – and his scholarly looks belied a tremendous personal dynamism. Wilson's "New Freedom" program initiated a mass of progressive legislation: a central U.S. banking system was set up for the first time since the Jackson era; new acts toughened up anti-trust measures, limited the use of child labor, established an 8-hour day for railroad workers, and provided workmen's compensation for federal employees. Wilson also backed the 19th amendment by which, in 1920, American women at last won the right to vote.

In foreign affairs, however, Wilson's record was shadowed by tragic ironies. Urging neutrality in World War I, he ended up taking the United States into Europe's Armageddon at a cost of 50,000 American lives. Afterward he set forth his famous 14-point program for world peace; its hopes were sadly disappointed by the Versailles Treaty of 1919, and the U.S. Senate even repudiated American membership of the League of Nations which he helped to create.

It was the final irony that Wilson, advocate of strong leadership in the White House, should end up incapacitated by a paralyzing stroke, with his second wife virtually

Twenty-eighth President 1913-1921

governing in his place. To this day, historians cannot quite agree on whether Woodrow Wilson was a presidential success or failure, but one thing is beyond doubt: he was a man of stature.

A Presbyterian upbringing
Thomas Woodrow Wilson was born in Staunton, Virginia, on December 28, 1856, to parents of Scottish-Irish descent. His father was a Presbyterian minister, and the young Woodrow was taught from childhood to read the Bible daily and know the values of moral thought and simple living. At first he seemed destined for the ministry, like his father, but at Princeton, which he entered in 1875, Woodrow Wilson developed strong political and literary interests. Debating was one of his particular passions: the English Liberal William Gladstone was among his heroes, and Wilson himself became an outstanding and brilliant orator.

He left Princeton in 1879, studied law at the University of Virginia, and opened a practice at Atlanta, Georgia, in 1882. But a legal career held no intrinsic interest for him. "The profession I chose," he was to say, "was politics; the profession I entered was the law. I entered the one because I thought it would lead to the other." In 1883, he abandoned his not very successful practice to do what he really wanted by entering John Hopkins University, Baltimore, to study history and political science. Wilson's thesis, published under the title of *Congressional Government* (1885), lucidly argued that the proper balance of powers envisaged by the Constitution had been usurped. Partly through a succession of weak Presidents, Congress had come to dominate the federal authority, and Wilson called for men of commanding character to restore policy-making and decisive leadership to the presidency.

Wilson's book was very well received. In the year of its publication he married Ellen Louise Axson and also began teaching at Bryn Mawr, so opening his long career as an educator. He taught at Bryn Mawr from 1885-8, at Wesleyan from 1888-90, and was Professor of jurisprudence and political economy at Princeton from 1890-1910, where he was also university president, from 1902-10.

Wilson was, by all accounts, a spell-binding lecturer and also earned a name as a reformer, especially through introducing the preceptorial system to Princeton (with this system, small classes and teachers offer something close to individual tuition). Some of Wilson's changes, though, led to

bitter academic feuding, and the struggles exposed a highly dogmatic streak in his character. Once, a colleague suggested mildly that there were two sides to every question. "Yes," snapped Wilson, "a right side and a wrong side." Such categorial thinking was to make him enemies in his future political career.

The presidential nomination

Through his professorial years, Wilson had never lost a yearning for political life, lamenting to a friend that it was impossible: "In this country men do not go from the academic world into politics." His reputation as a liberal and varied writings on political issues had, however, brought him some attention, and in September, 1910, he was offered the Democratic nomination for Governor of New Jersey. He was backed in the proposal by the state's Democratic boss, Senator James ("Sugar Jim") Smith, and

Revolutionaries take over a locomotive at Guernavaca, Morelos, during the Mexican Civil War of 1910-20. The inset portrait is of Emiliano Zapata, the revolutionary leader who headed a rising of landholders in his native state of Morelos. The upheavals in Mexico were of intimate concern to Wilson who believed it was America's destiny to promote her democratic ideals abroad.

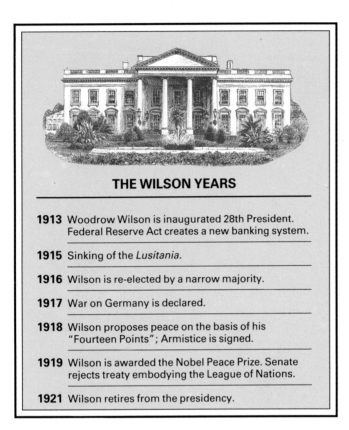

THE WILSON YEARS

1913 Woodrow Wilson is inaugurated 28th President. Federal Reserve Act creates a new banking system.

1915 Sinking of the *Lusitania*.

1916 Wilson is re-elected by a narrow majority.

1917 War on Germany is declared.

1918 Wilson proposes peace on the basis of his "Fourteen Points"; Armistice is signed.

1919 Wilson is awarded the Nobel Peace Prize. Senate rejects treaty embodying the League of Nations.

1921 Wilson retires from the presidency.

Nevertheless, backed by Democratic majorities in both Houses of Congress, Wilson was well placed to enact his faith in strong presidency, and to carry through the legislation for which he had campaigned.

He did not shirk the task. Almost immediately he made his commitment plain when in April, 1913, he delivered his first message to Congress – and addressed the two Houses in person. He was the first President to do so since John Adams, and Wilson often intervened in later sessions, too, to back legislation of keen interest to him.

An early achievement was the Underwood Tariff Act of October, 1913, which cut duties sharply, to the annoyance of some large industrialists. In December, the Federal Reserve Act created a new central banking system, so breaking the tyranny of private banks and creating a flexible currency: in inflationary times the new Federal Reserve Board could discourage borrowing; in slump it could boost the economy by making borrowing easier and pumping new money in.

In 1914, the Federal Trade Commission Act and the Clayton Anti-Trust Act continued the on-going assault on unfair and illegal business practices, while later legislation included the Keating-Owen Child Labor Act (1916) which banned goods manufactured by youngsters under 16 from interstate commerce.

These and other measures confirmed the vigorous reforming trend of what was called the "New Freedom" program. But it should be said that in one area, Wilson was markedly non-progressive: race relations. Born in the South, with typically Southern prejudices, Wilson believed that segregation served the best interests of blacks and whites alike, and his administration saw its increasing enforcement in government offices.

A moralist in the White House

The First Family's early months in the White House were extremely happy. Wilson's wife Ellen and his three talented daughters (who were known as the Three Graces) formed a close-knit group who involved themselves in social work in Washington. But they did not lack vivacity, and the President himself, for all his Presbyterian upbringing, had a fun-loving side to his nature too, which revealed itself best in a domestic setting. For the family he recited limericks

other machine men. Their long-term plan was to ditch the progressive William Jennings Bryan and replace him at the head of the Democratic party with a safer liberal, someone less worrying to business interests. And who could be safer than a college professor?

Unhappily for his sponsors, the inexperienced Wilson proved far from pliable. Backed by Smith, he was elected Governor of New Jersey and served from 1911-13, but he was no sooner in office than he openly broke with "Sugar Jim" and forced through a program of progressive legislation. The New York bosses turned against him, but the anti-machine Democrats lined up in his support. In the deadlocked convention of 1912, Bryan himself eventually supported Wilson – and so it was that the college professor won the presidential nomination.

"The "New Freedom"

Woodrow Wilson triumphed for the Democrats in the 1912 election only because the Republican vote had been split by the rift between Taft and Roosevelt. Wilson, in fact, won fewer popular votes than Bryan had in *losing* the 1908 contest! Had Taft and Roosevelt combined their forces, Wilson would have been defeated by a good million votes.

A World War I recruiting poster for the U.S. Navy, with The Sinking of the Lusitania, 7 May 1915, *as depicted by German artist Claud Bergen. Wilson called the sinking an "illegal and inhuman act," insisting on an apology and reparations from the German government.*

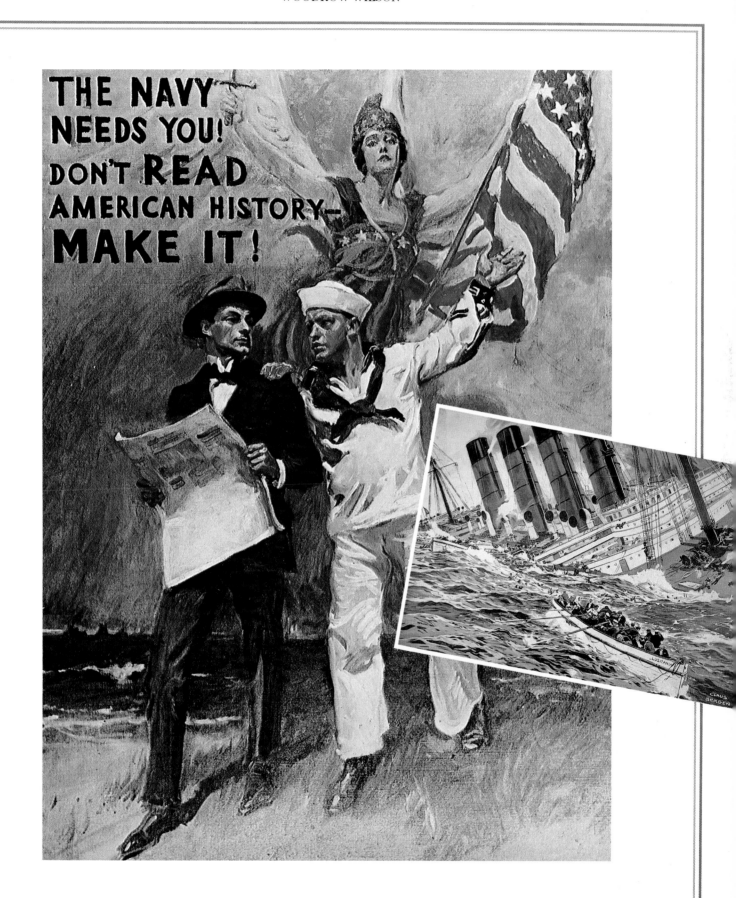

and did humorous impersonations (including one of Theodore Roosevelt). "He loved gay nonsense. He could play the fool enchantingly," said an intimate.

The laughter ceased abruptly in August, 1914, when Ellen Wilson died, a victim of nephritis. But in the year following his first wife's death, Woodrow Wilson met and wed a Virginia widow, Edith Bolling Galt, whose love helped to heal the wound.

Lively and affectionate as Wilson could be in private life, his public stance was always one of high moral seriousness, especially notable in foreign affairs where his attitudes were determined by his essentially liberal modes of thought. Wilson believed that militarism and imperialism were the vices of Europe's aged regimes and need play no part in the world politics of young America. "The force of America," he once said, "is the force of moral principle."

For some years beforehand, the United States had been trying to win influence in Asia and Latin America through a policy of economic penetration which Wilson's predecessor, Taft, had called "dollar diplomacy." Wilson made a conscious effort to terminate this clandestine imperialism. However, he was not opposed to intervention in order to promote the interests of republicanism and democracy. And his attitudes during Mexico's turbulent revolution of 1910-17 almost triggered a wholly unnecessary war.

Wilson refused to recognize the Mexican dictator, Huerta, supporting instead the constitutionalist Carranza. In 1914, when a Huertista general arrested some American sailors, Wilson took the drastic step of ordering the U.S. Navy to seize Vera Cruz; he was rescued from the affair only by offers of mediation from Argentina, Brazil and Chile. Later, Wilson unwisely sent American troops deep into Mexico in pursuit of the bandit "Pancho" Villa, who had been making unprovoked attacks on American civilians. Wilson's motives may have been perfectly honorable; but they roused understandable suspicion among Mexicans that the United States had designs on their country.

"Who keeps us out of war?"

The indescribable horrors of World War I tested Wilson's principled foreign policy to the utmost. When fighting began in Europe, in 1914, Wilson's first reaction was to issue a proclamation of neutrality. Few Americans believed in the early stages that it made any sense to participate in the carnage, though many had sympathies with one side or another. The majority (including Wilson himself) were naturally drawn to the Allies, but a sizable minority with German, Austrian or Irish connections leaned more toward the Central Powers.

As the war went on, however, it became ever harder to maintain a neutralist stance. British warships controlled the North Atlantic, forcing U.S. merchantmen to surrender just about any cargo destined for the Central Powers. Wilson was irritated by the situation, but appalled by the Kaiser's response. Early in 1915, the Germans declared the seas around Britain to be a war zone where all enemy and even neutral merchant shipping must be considered at risk. Wilson issued sharp warnings against any loss of American life or property, and tensions became acute from May 7, 1915, when a German submarine, without warning, torpedoed the British liner, *Lusitania*, off the Irish coast. Some 1,200 people perished when the ship went down, including 128 U.S. citizens.

Wilson did not yet force a showdown. He fought and narrowly won the 1916 election as the man "who keeps us out of war," and afterward made continued efforts to mediate an end to the fighting. But early in 1917, Germany resorted to wholly unrestricted submarine warfare; four American ships were sunk; and the infamous Zimmerman Telegram was published, revealing German proposals for a secret alliance with Mexico (which offered, as spoils of any war with the United States, the "lost territory in Texas, New Mexico and Arizona").

It was too much, and, in April, Wilson asked Congress for a declaration of war against Germany, proclaiming that "The world must be made safe for democracy."

THE WAR PRESIDENT

Having an innate dislike of militarism, Wilson had not properly readied the United States for war and had been criticized for America's lack of preparedness. Once committed to armed conflict, however, he proved a driving and decisive war leader – the most effective the United States had ever seen. It was not just that he mobilized the economy; he mobilized public opinion, too, in his "great crusade" for democracy. Patriotic feeling was, in fact, so intense that the liberal professor found himself swept toward virtual dictatorship in such measures as the stringent Espionage Act (1917), and the Sedition Act (1918) which made it a crime even to speak against the buying of war bonds, or to criticize the government in any way at all.

America's entry into the war tipped the scales decisively for the Allies, and the armistice of November 11, 1918, was concluded on the basis of Wilson's "Fourteen Points" for a fair peace. The President called for a "peace without victory," proposing instead of vengeance a series of principles that guaranteed, in particular, nations' rights to self determination, open diplomacy, and the freedom of the

One of Wilson's campaign autos in New York City, 1916, itemises key points in the Democratic platform. The election was fought essentially on U.S. policy toward the warring powers in Europe. "He Keeps Out of the War" was the Democratic slogan, and Wilson narrowly defeated his Republican opponent, Charles E. Hughes with 9.1 million to 8.5 million votes in the popular ballot; 277 to 254 in the electoral vote.

seas and of trade. To supervise the new order, a League of Nations should be set up offering collective security against aggression (Point 14).

The program won the support of liberals everywhere, but the Paris peace conference of 1919 fell far short of fulfilling them. Wilson, who attended the conference in person, was greeted by ordinary Europeans as a hero; the politicos were much sourer and more cynical. French Premier George Clemenceau, in particular, had understandable qualms about any over-generosity toward Germany. Wilson, he complained, thought himself to be Jesus Christ: "How can I talk to a fellow who thinks himself the first man in 2,000 years to know anything about peace on earth?"

In the event, the treaty demanded massive reparations from the defeated Germany. And though the League of Nations was founded, Wilson's expectation of U.S. membership was balked by a resurgence of isolationist feeling back home. Wilson returned with the treaty to a Republican Congress, and the Senate refused to accept the document without some important reservations. Wilson replied with doctrinaire insistence that "the Senate must take its medicine" and in the summer of 1919, set out on an arduous tour of the country to win popular support. His physical reserves were, however, at low ebb by now, and in September he collapsed, suffering a severe stroke which

left his left side partially paralyzed. For months he was almost entirely incapacitated, and his wife Edith tried to shield him from any affairs which might tire him further. All state papers passed through her hands; and she gave Wilson only the most important documents, which emerged from the sick room with shaky scrawls for signature. It was a disquieting time, known as "Mrs. Wilson's Regency," in which the President's second wife appeared to be governing the country.

Constitutionally the position was awkward, and there was some talk of impeaching the President because of his inability to carry out his obligations. Two Senators were, in fact, sent to satisfy their colleagues that Wilson was of sound mind; the President, loathing the visit of what he called "this smelling committee," convinced them that he still had his faculties. Despite a slight improvement in his condition, this sorry presidential epilogue dragged on until March, 1921, when Wilson at last vacated the White House.

Woodrow Wilson lived on quietly for another three years in a house on S Street, Washington, D.C. In December, 1920, he was awarded the Nobel Peace Prize, and on Armistice Day, 1923, he managed to make a brief speech from the balcony of his home. He was a very sick man and it proved to be his last public appearance. He died in his sleep on February 3, 1924.

WARREN HARDING

Warren G Harding

R anking the Presidents has been a favorite pastime of historians for many decades, and famous names tend to move up and down the lists as careers are reassessed with the passing of time. Ever since historians' opinions were first canvassed in 1948, however, there has been one fixed benchmark: in all ratings, Warren Harding finishes last.

What made him such a bad President? If his record as a smalltown editor and Senator was undistinguished, he was by no means the first nonentity to reach the White House. True, he had what President Wilson called a "bungalow mind;" but Harding was also a handsome and good-natured man well liked by the public in his day. He was genuinely mourned when he died in office, and the awfulness of his administration only became apparent after his death, with the public disclosure of scandalous malpractices by the poker-playing cronies who had maneuvered him into the presidency and crammed

Twenty-ninth President 1921-1923

their pockets when he was ensconced. Warren Harding was a bad President because he could never say no to his buddies. In his last days, he finally came to recognize the scale of their sordidness. "I have no trouble with my enemies," he confided to a newsman, "but my damned friends – they are the ones who keep me walking the floor nights."

The smoke-filled room
Warren Gamaliel Harding was born in Corsica (then Blooming Grove), Morrow County, Ohio, on November 2,

1865. His father was a country doctor, and the young Harding attended Ohio Central College before trying and abandoning the study of law. Afterward he worked in a newspaper office and in 1884, while still in his teens, he became owner and editor of *The Marion Star*. His poker winnings occasionally baled the paper out of difficulties in the early stages, but Harding gained more solid wealth and respectability through marriage to a rich divorcée, Florence Kling De Wolfe. Ohio machine politics elevated the handsome young editor through a succession of posts: he was state senator from 1900-4, lieutenant governor between 1904 and 1906, and in 1910, ran unsuccessfully for governor of the state. He was a U.S. Senator from 1914-21, and at this time entered a long and romantic liaison with a young admirer, Nan Britton, who bore him a daughter in 1919. It was to sully his name greatly after his death when the affair became known (it was disclosed that the couple made love in a White House closet for fear of Mrs. Harding's discovery). Outwardly, however, Warren Harding as Senator had a good "safe" look: a conservative Republican, he held no very controversial views, and in the deadlocked Chicago convention of 1920, was chosen as presidential candidate by a gathering of 15 party managers in what was to be immortalized as a "smoke-filled room." (The phrase was coined by spoilsman Harry M. Daugherty, who was leader of the so-called Ohio Gang of machine politicans backing Harding.)

Children with picket signs plead for the release of their fathers imprisoned for "anti-government" activities, in a demonstration of 1922. Under President Wilson in World War I exceptionally fierce Espionage and Sedition Acts had been passed, curtailing rights of free speech: some people were hauled before the courts merely for suggesting that the war was against Christian teaching. To President Harding's credit he eased the repressive atmosphere, notably by pardoning (1921) the socialist leader Eugene Debs who had been sentenced to ten years imprisonment in 1918 for violating the Espionage Act.

In the presidential contest which followed, Harding waged a front-porch campaign, staying at home and exercising his one great skill of managing the press – an old newshand himself, he even had a three-room house built especially for the reporters. Recognizing the national yearning for stability, Harding pledged a return to what he called "normalcy" (prose stylists shuddered; why not say "normality?"), and in the election he defeated Democratic candidate James M. Cox by an overwhelming 7 million popular votes (404 to 127 electoral votes).

"Normalcy"
Politically, Harding's administration was chiefly important for opening a new period of business ascendancy in government: Treasury Secretary was the multimillionaire banker and industrialist, Andrew Mellon, who proposed a series of highly reactionary measures. The administration also ended any expectation of the United States entering the League of Nations. Harding himself was notable in a minor way for delivering in June, 1923, the first presidential radio broadcast.

But scandal, above all, distinguished his presidency. The whole atmosphere in Washington loosened up when Harding was elected. His wife was a lavish entertainer, and the President held poker parties at the White House. Cigars were smoked; liquor flowed; and blatant corruption was practiced. Harry Daugherty, for example, having been made Attorney General, was involved in widespread graft twice leading to trial on criminal charges. Charles R. Forbes of the Veterans Bureau looted millions of dollars designated for hospital-building. Thomas W. Miller, alien property custodian, was imprisoned for accepting a bribe. And in the most disgraceful of all the scandals, the Elk Hills and Teapot Dome properties affair, Albert B. Fall, Secretary of the Interior, accepted bribes to lease U.S. naval oil reserves to private oil companies, ending up with a fine of $100,000 and a year's jail sentence for his part in the scam.

Not much of all this was generally known in the summer of 1923, when Harding returned from an Alaska trip. The President, though, had become a worried man – it was the time of his "damned friends" statement – and he appeared to some to be on the edge of physical collapse. Newspapers carried reports that he was suffering from food poisoning, but it was a stroke which took his life. Warren Harding died in San Francisco on August 2, 1923, and the public grieved . . . until the disclosures were made.

CALVIN COOLIDGE

It is an irony of modern history that the United States in the noisy boom time of the Jazz Age should have been presided over by a puritanical Vermonter legendary for reticence. "Silent Cal" was a popular nickname of America's 30th President, and the tales of his taciturnity have often been told. It is said, for example, that a lady once sat next to him at a formal dinner, gushing, "You must talk to me, Mr Coolidge. I made a bet today that I could get more than two words out of you."

"You lose," was Coolidge's only reply.

A small man, thin and anemic in appearance, Coolidge was as thrifty with public money as he was with words. He did not believe that the federal authority should either raise or spend cash: the well-being of the country was best guaranteed by letting businessmen get on with creating wealth untrammeled by government interference. "Perhaps one of the most important accomplishments of my administration has been minding my own business," he said at the close of his presidency.

Such a stance is easily caricatured as complacency – and the criticism was often to be made that he did not foresee the Wall Street Crash and the Depression which followed so soon after he vacated the White House. Nevertheless, Coolidge's attitudes suited the mood of his own less troubled times. He presided over an era of unprecedented prosperity, when businessmen thought it folly to tinker with the wealth-creating organisms of American capital.

Thirtieth President 1923-1929

Inactivity, wrote Walter Lippmann, was something much more than mere indolence for Coolidge; it was something "grim, determined, alert . . . a political philosophy and a party program."

The Boston police strike
John Calvin Coolidge was born in Plymouth, Vermont, on July 4, 1872. His father was a farmer and storekeeper prominent in local affairs, and the young Coolidge was brought up in an atmosphere of typically frugal and modest New England puritanism. He graduated from Amherst College in 1895, studied law and opened a practice two years later. Coolidge entered state politics as a Republican, and served as mayor of Northampton, Massachussetts, from 1910-11; he was a state senator from 1912-15, lieutenant governor from 1916-18, and governor from 1919-20.

Coolidge won national attention through his firm stance in the Boston police strike in September, 1919. The event was sparked when the city's policemen were refused the right to affiliate with the American Federation of Labor; the majority of Boston's policemen then left their posts and riotous disorders followed, with looting, street fights and threats of a general strike to cripple transportation and business. Coolidge delayed in intervening but when he did so he took action decisively, calling out the whole state guard and assuming personal charge of the police department. "There is no right to strike against the public safety by anybody, anywhere, at anytime," he insisted, and his gritty deter-

Mounted troops chase a car suspected of involvement in bootlegging; the back seat passenger is armed. In the Coolidge era Prohibition led to widespread law evasion, while police and political corruption helped to create a climate in which gangsters such as Chicago's Al Capone (inset) flourished.

mination won him many admirers at a time of widespread labor unrest in the United States. The strike was broken, public order was restored, and Coolidge was re-elected governor by a large majority. At the Republican convention of 1920, moreover, enthusiasm for him was such that he was given the vice-presidential nomination on the first ballot.

"Keep cool with Coolidge"
Elected on the Republican ticket with Warren Harding, Coolidge proved a wholly uncontroversial Vice President. When the worried and embittered President Harding succumbed to a fatal stroke on August 3, 1923, Coolidge was vacationing at his father's farm in Plymouth. Informed by reporters that the President was dead, Coolidge issued an official statement and then, with characteristic lack of show, had himself sworn in as President on the spot, by his father who was a Justice of the Peace: it was 2:43 a.m., and the ceremony was performed by the flickering light of a kerosene lamp.

Personally honest, untainted by any of the scandals which had disgraced Harding's presidency, Coolidge partly occupied himself during his first months with a White House clean-out. Prosecutions were brought against malefactors in high places, but in other respects the complexion of the government was not greatly changed. In particular, Andrew Mellon, financier and industrialist, remained in place as Secretary of the Treasury and a powerful force for conservatism. Coolidge's first presidential message, delivered in December, 1923, promised a commonsense approach to the economy, and so he was easily nominated by the Republican convention of 1924. "Keep cool with

Henry Ford, photographed in 1946 at the wheel of his first car which he had first operated 50 years earlier, in 1896. The pioneer of the U.S. auto industry formed his company in 1903, and before long his assembly line methods were transforming the face of American society. Ford's great innovation was to match prices with an average citizen's purchasing power. By the opening of the Coolidge presidency Ford was turning out 9,000 cars a day – about one every ten seconds – and he was seen to embody all the marvels of the American business system.

Coolidge" was to be his campaign slogan.

The Democrats, meanwhile, were hopelessly divided between progressives, pro-Klan Southerners and Eastern industrialists. Coolidge won the election overwhelmingly with 15.7 million popular votes (382 electoral votes). Democrat John W. Davis got 8.4 million popular votes (136 electoral votes) and Robert M. La Follette, leader of a new Progressive Party, got 4.8 million popular votes (13 electoral votes). The country was in a determinedly conservative frame of mind.

The business of America
In an oft-quoted passage from a speech of 1925, Calvin Coolidge declared that "the business of America is business." The nation's prosperity in the 1920s was remarkable: industrial output practically doubled in a single decade; real wages rose steadily, and unemployment was negligible. It was the age which saw the maturing of Henry Ford's mass production techniques adopted not only in the auto industry but in the manufacture of a host of other goods, including refrigerators, vacuum cleaners and radios. Successes triggered further expansion: the booming auto industry, for example, sparked a huge road-building program; the mass production of cheaper consumer goods

created a boom in outlets such as the Woolworth chain of five-and-ten-cent stores.

Laissez faire – let it happen – was the philosophy of the day. Coolidge's active contributions were chiefly in the areas of tax cuts and government economies. The President even resisted war veterans' demands for bonus payments. Ex-soldiers complained that they had served for next to nothing while war workers in industry had been highly paid. Congress was sympathetic to their demands for compensation and responded with a Soldiers' Bonus Act: it was passed in 1924, but only over the President's veto.

Farmers formed another group with grievances. They had suffered from a severe drop in farm prices resulting from overproduction, but true to his philosophy of inactivity, Coolidge refused to grant direct aid. In 1927, the McNary-Haugen Farm Relief Bill proposed government intervention to help farmers and was passed by Congress. Coolidge vetoed it; and he vetoed a similar bill passed by Congress the following year.

The Prohibition years
One effect of Coolidge's thrift was to reduce the national debt by $2 billion. In foreign affairs the President continued to oppose U.S. entry into the League of Nations,

Woolworth Building and City Hall, New York City. Built in 1913 by architect Gilbert Cass the 60-story skyscraper soared to 792 feet and was famed throughout the Coolidge era as the tallest building in the world. A true cathedral of commerce, the Gothic creation symbolized all the ambition and ingenuity of American capital.

United States and France. Frank B. Kellogg, Secretary of State, wanted to avoid any too entangling an alliance and so extended the proposal to a multilateral agreement which was eventually signed by 62 nations. It lacked any real bite, resting only on the goodwill of all concerned.

To most Americans, however, Coolidge's only major failing was probably his inability to control the excesses of bootlegging, gangsterism and speakeasy drinking which flourished under Prohibition. The ban on intoxicating liquors had become official and nationwide in January, 1920, when the 18th Amendment became operative. It was in the same year that Al "Scarface" Capone moved to Chicago where he built up his $60 million crime enterprise, and under Coolidge's administration wholesale lawlessness prevailed with deepening police and political corruption. Of course, the President himself could not be held accountable for all that happened. Yet the crime wave was part and parcel of the Coolidge era, like some mad, bad parody of the laissez-faire spirit.

"I do not choose to run . . ."
Calvin Coolidge married Grace Anne Goodhue in 1905; she bore him two sons (one of whom died of blood poisoning in the White House). She was an elegant First Lady, somewhat more sociable than her husband. And grimly reticent as he was, Coolidge himself possessed a buried quality of boyish humor which expressed itself in his sardonic one-liners and in a curious fondness for practical jokes. Sometimes in the White House he would press all the buzzers at once, then vanish to observe the confusion that resulted. Nor did he mind dressing up – whether as cowboy, Sioux Indian or Boy Scout – to please press photographers. And his clear, terse speech proved well suited to the new medium of radio broadcasting (much more so than some of the blowsier oratory of the time).

Coolidge was popular – hugely so in smalltown America – and as his second term drew to a close it was widely expected that the Republicans would renominate him for the presidency, despite the tradition against triple terms. It was not to be. In August of 1927, Coolidge informed reporters with typical precision: "I do not choose to run for President in 1928." From this decision he did not waver, despite continuing pressures brought to bear on him.

Vacating the White House on March 4, 1929, Calvin Coolidge retired from public life, and died on January 5, 1933, at Northampton. His genius for inactivity had always been such that when told Coolidge was dead Dorothy Parker is alleged to have asked, "How do they know?" It was a dry little one-liner of the sort Coolidge appreciated – and might almost have fashioned himself.

and though he urged participation in the World Court, a tribunal for settling international disputes, isolationists in the Senate demanded such reservations in the terms of entry that membership was impossible. Under Coolidge, the United States's main contribution to world politics was the Kellogg-Briand Pact, signed in Paris in 1928. This treaty, outlawing war, grew out of bilateral talks between the

HERBERT HOOVER

Herbert Hoover (signature)

Elected by a landslide on the promise of continuing Republican prosperity, Herbert Hoover had the misfortune to face almost immediately the dramatic stock market crash of 1929. The Great Depression followed, and Hoover had to endure his crisis-ridden presidency with advice coming at him from two opposing sides. One camp recommended inaction – let the economy sort itself out. The other camp urged action by greatly expanding federal enterprises. Hoover opted for a middle course, trying to restore public confidence while proposing limited government measures to halt the decline. He was humane and intelligent – but his policies did not work, and the man once puffed by the press as the "Great Engineer" was dubbed the "President Reject" when he was routed on seeking re-election. It was a humiliating outcome for what had up till then been an all-American success story.

Thirty-first President 1929-1933

international engineering firm.

In 1914, when war broke out in Europe, Hoover became involved in high-level relief work, supervising the distribution of food and supplies to the people of Belgium and northern France. When the United States entered the war, Hoover was recalled from Europe to become U.S. food administrator. He served in that capacity from 1917-19, and when the official relief programs for Europe were concluded he continued to supervise voluntary efforts to fight famine in the devastated continent.

As Secretary for Commerce from 1921-28, Herbert Hoover served both Harding and Coolidge, distinguishing himself as an intellectual leader of America's confident business community, and as a man with a remarkable aptitude for facts. "Facts to Hoover's brain are as water to a sponge," someone once said. "They are absorbed into every tiny interstice." With a humble Midwestern background to balance his millions, he came to be seen as

A self-made man

Herbert Clark Hoover was born on August 10, 1874, in West Branch, Iowa, to a Quaker family. His father was a village blacksmith, but both parents had died before the young Hoover was ten years old, and he was brought up an orphan in the family of his uncle. Hoover studied geology and engineering at Stanford University, graduated in 1895, and two years later was working as manager of some newly developed mines in western Australia. His career as a mining engineer later took him to China and other foreign parts; it also made Hoover a millionaire, as partner in an

an attractive presidential prospect, and was nominated by the Republican convention of 1928. In the election of that year, buoyed by the Coolidge years of prosperity, Hoover trounced the Democratic candidate, New Yorker Alfred E. Smith, with 444 electoral votes to 87 – 21.4 million to 15 million popular votes.

The Crash and Depression

In Hoover's election year a mania for speculation had gripped the country, sending stock prices soaring to levels

Hunger marchers photographed in Washington, D.C. The Depression which came in Hoover's presidency bewildered a nation which had been led to believe in the infallibility of the U.S. business system. In 1932 20,000 unemployed veterans marched on Washington to demand immediate payment of bonuses due to them. Some settled with their families on swamps bordering the Potomac, erecting ramshackle dwellings of tents, old packing cases and scrap metal. Such shanty towns there and elsewhere in the United States became known as "Hoovervilles" in implicit condemnation of the President's handling of the Depression.

which guaranteed catastrophe should the bubble burst. The crash came in October, 1929, when a sudden wave of selling sent prices on a hideous downward spiral: on "Black Tuesday" (October 29) the record figure of 16 million shares were sold. Businesses collapsed; savings were wiped out; working people lost their jobs. Hoover took immediate action to try and restore confidence, but though stocks rallied briefly, hopes of a true recovery were dashed by the coming of the worldwide Depression, which by 1932-3 saw U.S. unemployment reach about 13 million.

Hoover's instincts were always for individualism and self-help, but he could not (as ultraconservatives advised) merely let the slump bottom out. The scale of human suffering was too immense. Instead, constantly asserting that the bad corner would soon be turned, he tried to persuade bankers, businessmen, state governments and others to voluntarily stabilize credit, keep wages up and give to charitable enterprises. A Reconstruction Finance Corporation was founded in 1932 to lend to banks, railroads and insurance companies; Home Loan banks were set up to aid home owners meeting mortgages; the government also lent money to drought-stricken farmers.

These were all positive measures. What Hoover would not

do, however, was to use the national government for direct relief work. Despite the conspicuous hardships faced by millions, he refused federal aid to the unemployed. It was a question of principle: while Hoover sanctioned federal loans, he would not sanction federal handouts because, he believed, they would lead to an unconstitutional dependency of citizens upon the state. On this point he was wholly inflexible, and could appear callous, too. In 1932, many thousand unemployed World War I veterans marched on Washington, demanding early payment of bonuses promised to them. Hoover refused even to talk with their representatives, instead ordering the army to move the demonstrators out in what proved to be an ugly dispersal.

Renominated by the Republicans in 1932, Hoover was hopelessly associated with America's calamities and was massively defeated by Franklin D. Roosevelt. He retired ruefully from the White House, which he called a "compound hell." Afterward he partially restored his reputation through public works: notably, he served Harry Truman as coordinator of the European Food Program in 1947. Hoover was married from 1899 to Lou Henry who bore him two sons. He died at the grand old age of 90 in New York City, on October 20, 1964.

FRANKLIN D. ROOSEVELT

Franklin D Roosevelt

Pioneer of the New Deal, uniquely elected four times to the presidency, Franklin D. Roosevelt was first inaugurated on March 4, 1933. The weather that day seemed to match the condition of a nation shivering in the pit of the Depression: the sky was dark and a chill wind scoured the area before the Capitol where 100,000 people were assembled. The 51-year-old President-elect, paralyzed from the waist down by polio, had to be assisted to the stand where he stood supported by iron leg braces. But his spirits, as ever, were high and having read the oath he began his address with a now-famous message of hope. "This great nation will endure as it has endured, will revive and will prosper ... the only thing we have to fear is fear itself."

Roosevelt criticized the business leaders who had failed the country. "This nation asks for action, and action now," he went on, adding that he would unhesitatingly assume leadership of the great army of the people, asking Congress for executive powers comparable to those of a wartime President, "as if we were in fact invaded by a foreign foe."

Tens of millions of Americans, gathered around their radios, heard the inaugural through live hook-up and were stirred. To some it seemed that a great crusade was beginning; others were alarmed by the dictatorial powers which the President appeared to be seeking. Just about everyone, though, was aware that with this speech, America had reached some kind of turning point.

Thirty-second President 1933-1945

A pampered childhood

Franklin Delano Roosevelt was born in Hyde Park, New York, on January 30, 1882. His father was a wealthy landowner and vice president of the Delaware and Hudson Railroad. The young F. D. R. enjoyed a carefree upbringing in the leafy setting of Hyde Park: tennis, polo, yachting and riding to hounds were favorite pastimes in the millionaire neighborhood. Franklin was the only son of two doting parents and, with frequent trips to European resorts he experienced a childhood almost wholly sheltered from the jostlings of average American life.

A sense of civic responsibility was, however, part of his background, too. The Roosevelts set the patrician values of the country gentleman above those of the city slicker; Franklin's father had some pedigree in Democratic politics, and the thrusting Republican reformer, "Teddy" Roosevelt was a fifth cousin whom Franklin greatly admired.

Graduating from Harvard, Franklin Delano Roosevelt attended Columbia Law School from 1904-7, and it was during this period that he married Anna Eleanor Roosevelt, his orphaned sixth cousin, who was to contribute so much to his career and make her own reputation as a champion of the underprivileged. Teddy Roosevelt (her uncle and then President) was at the wedding on March 17, 1905; through frequent contact with him afterward, Franklin acquired a deepening interest in progressive politics. He campaigned vigorously to become a Democratic state

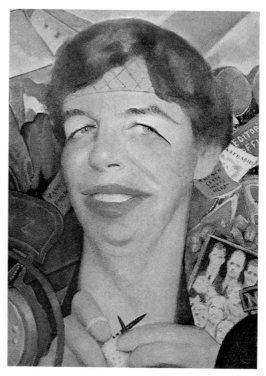

Above: *Eleanor Roosevelt depicted by W. Cotton in a cartoon of 1933. A spirited and controversial First Lady she became a national symbol for all supporters of freedom and social justice. "No woman has ever so comforted the distressed or so distressed the comfortable," an admirer once said of her.*

Left: *Franklin D. Roosevelt is a knight in armor attacking high finance in this 1934 cartoon from the German satirical magazine* Simplicississimus. *It has been said of FDR that he punctured one of America's great popular myths in dissociating the ideal of wealth from virtue.*

senator in 1910, and made a name for himself heading a reforming faction of Democrats who refused to accept as candidate for the U.S. Senate a man foisted on them by Tammany Hall. Franklin D. Roosevelt was an early supporter of Woodrow Wilson and for his loyalty he was given the post of Assistant Secretary of the Navy from 1913-20, when he was running-mate for the unsuccessful Democratic presidential candidate, Governor Cox.

Striken by polio
It was in August, 1921, that the 6 foot, athletic "preppy prince" of Democratic politics was stricken by polio, a viral disease which left him forever afterward without the use of his legs. Roosevelt retired for two years from public life, facing both physical and spiritual anguish before it became clear that the paralysis was permanent. Though he learned to walk a few painful steps with leg braces and two canes, motor nerves had been destroyed. It was a bitter blow, but in the end, as all who knew him affirmed, the battle with polio somehow deepened and strengthened his character. Never asking for sympathy, hiding his frustration just as he concealed (as much as possible) his disability, Roosevelt returned to legal work, extended business activities – and determined to get back into politics.

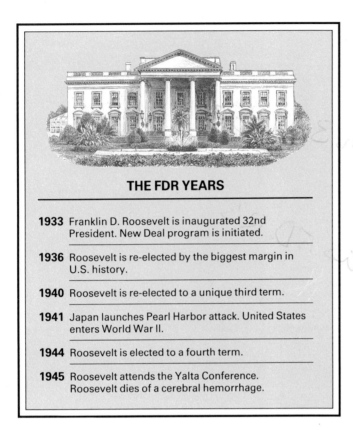

THE FDR YEARS

1933 Franklin D. Roosevelt is inaugurated 32nd President. New Deal program is initiated.

1936 Roosevelt is re-elected by the biggest margin in U.S. history.

1940 Roosevelt is re-elected to a unique third term.

1941 Japan launches Pearl Harbor attack. United States enters World War II.

1944 Roosevelt is elected to a fourth term.

1945 Roosevelt attends the Yalta Conference. Roosevelt dies of a cerebral hemorrhage.

In 1924, and again in 1928, he nominated the reformer Alfred E. Smith at the Democratic convention, and in 1929 succeeded Smith as Governor of New York. The stock market crash of that year ended an era of exuberant business confidence, and in the ensuing Depression, Roosevelt in New York distinguished himself from state officials elsewhere by the many imaginative economic reforms and welfare programs which he initiated to ease the situation. He was re-elected governor in 1930 by a huge plurality. As the 1932 presidential election approached, he began to look the most likely contender for the Democratic candidacy.

A New Deal

Roosevelt captured the Democratic nomination in 1932 on the third ballot, after rival candidates failed to combine against him. In his acceptance speech he declared: "I pledge you, I pledge myself, to a new deal for the American people," and he began a barnstorming campaign which took him 12,000 miles back and forth across the country to deliver some 200 speeches. President Hoover, carrying the banner for the Republicans, had been entirely discredited by the calamities of the Depression – and of Prohibition –

and Roosevelt won a thumping victory of 22.8 million popular votes to 15.8 million, 472 electoral votes to 59.

Between his election and his inauguration, the United States reached the Depression's nadir, a shellshocked holdover Congress presiding over the virtual disintegration of the banking system. Roosevelt in this period was developing his New Deal program, drawing in ideas from professors, economists, lawyers and many others besides political allies. His advisers, dubbed the Brains Trust, came up with many proposals at the core of which was a new faith in organized planning to replace the free market of classical economics. There was a determination, too, to bring relief to the most disadvantaged members of society – "the forgotten man at the bottom of the economic pyramid."

The Hundred Days

Action followed immediately after the inauguration: Roosevelt at once declared a national holiday and called Congress into special session. There followed a bombardment of bills, issued in quickfire succession through two electrifying months known as Roosevelt's Hundred Days. An emergency banking act was passed; new measures also regulated securities and insurance. A Civilian Conservation Corps was set up, taking on a quarter of a million unemployed young men for schemes of land-reclamation and dam-building. The Agricultural Adjustment Act gave the government sweeping new powers to help farmers. The Federal Emergency Relief Act introduced a federal dole for the unemployed. To cheer people further, Roosevelt began the dismantling of Prohibition by having the law changed to permit the making of beer and light wine again.

The alphabetical agencies

Other important measures in the first administration included the passing of the National Industrial Recovery Act which suspended anti-trust legislation in return for important concession to the unions. Under the Act's provisions, too, the National Recovery Administration (NRA) was established to enforce codes of conduct in industry.

The Tennessee Valley Authority (TVA) was also set up, comprising the first publicly owned electricity agency. This was an act of frank socialism. The purpose was to develop and conserve the resources of the Tennessee River valley, and the scheme took in parts of seven states covering well over 40,000 square miles in all. The TVA controlled the river system by means of over 20 major dams which generated cheap power for the people and provided thousands of unemployed men with jobs in construction.

With the NRA, the TVA and various other so-called

F. D. Roosevelt sits between Churchill and Stalin on the patio of the Livadia Palace at the Yalta Conference of February 1945. This was the last of the Big Three meetings and though the trio seem convivial enough they were deeply divided by the questions which victory in Europe posed. Despite his smile, the President was also under terrible stress through illness at the time. Addressing Congress on his return to the United States he was to remain seated, excusing himself on grounds of exhaustion. He also alluded to his paralysis – for the first time ever in a public speech.

"alphabetical agencies" (such as the AAA, RFC, PWA and WPA), Roosevelt appeared to some critics to be dangerously over-extending state control, giving the government in Washington too much power over people's lives and businesses. Although the Tennessee Valley Authority Act was sustained by the Supreme Court, some others were declared unconstitutional; the National Industrial Recovery Act and the Agricultural Adjustment Act were major casualties. And their nullification seemed to undermine Roosevelt's recovery program even as, in 1935, he launched his "Second New Deal" with measures to protect union rights and set up old age insurance.

THE STUNNING VICTORY

Despite vociferous critics, F.D.R. (as he was universally known) was extraordinarily popular with the public at large, and was re-elected in 1936 by the biggest margin in U.S. history: a plurality of 11 million votes, and an Electoral College vote of 523, to 8 for Republican Alfred M. Landon. Reasons for the stunning victory are not hard to find: Roosevelt had created 6 million jobs, restored faith in the economy and given countless dispossessed and disadvantaged people a sense of really belonging in America. The Democratic Party, ancient bastion of white Southerners, became under Roosevelt the natural home of ethnic groups and union supporters – the black vote, traditionally Republican, switched almost wholesale.

Roosevelt was, moreover, a brilliant communicator, immediately recognizable for his smile, cigarette holder and confident upward tilt of the head. He introduced radio "Fireside Chats" which made his reassuring voice familiar to millions, while Eleanor as First Lady adopted a high profile as moral crusader and had her own widely syndicated daily column "My Day." Eleanor was tireless: she might be seen one day entertaining sharecroppers in the White House, another doling out soup on a Depression breadline. The first Family included five children – four boys and one girl – and it was Eleanor's conscious intention to make the executive mansion as much a family home as it had been in the presidency of "Uncle Ted." Jews and blacks were welcome guests.

Roosevelt's second administration was marred, however, by wrangles with the Supreme Court which the President unwisely tried to reorganize along compliant lines. He failed – and his actions were a pretext for some conservative Democrats to break openly with the President. Continued economic difficulties were beginning to make it clear that the New Deal's success was only partial. And there was increasing talk that Roosevelt wanted a dictatorship when, in 1940, he made the controversial decision to seek a third term.

War clouds

One reason for Roosevelt's decision was the need to save the New Deal. "If you don't run," said a friendly Senator, "where will all the liberals go?" More compelling, though, was the situation in Europe where war had broken out in 1939. Roosevelt had always pursued a "Good Neighbor" foreign policy of cooperation with other democracies in the interests of peace. He was openly hostile to fascist Italy and Nazi Germany, and in May, 1940, persuaded a largely isolationist Congress to approve a massive increase in military expenditure against the possibility of a German attack. It was in this context that he broke the tradition against third terms and put himself forward for re-election. The American people responded by voting him back again. He defeated Wendell Willkie by a healthy margin (though reduced from the high point of 1936).

Roosevelt at the time of the election still appears to have believed that America might manage to keep out of the war without giving victory to the Axis powers. However, he now did more than ever to aid the democracies. In forceful speeches he enunciated the "four freedoms" at risk in the war: freedom of speech, of worship, from want and from fear. America, he said in a radio broadcast of December, 1940, "must be the great arsenal of democracy," and early the next year he pushed through the Lend-Lease Act by which over $50 billion was eventually expended on the loan or lease of military hardware for the Allies. In August, 1941, Roosevelt and Winston Churchill, meeting in Newfoundland, drew up the Atlantic Charter, a declaration of common objectives. And after the surprise Japanese attack on Pearl Harbor on December 7, 1941, ("a day that will live in infamy" in Roosevelt's words) the United States inevitably became a full participant.

The last campaign

As war leader, Roosevelt is particularly remembered for working closely with other Allied leaders at a series of conferences held, not only on the conduct of the war, but also to plan for the peace. The Teheran Conference of 1943 was the first at which the Big Three – Roosevelt, Churchill and Stalin – met in person, and the U.S. President established a surprisingly close relationship with the Soviet dictator. Roosevelt was to speak almost fondly of Stalin as "that old buzzard." At the Yalta Conference of February, 1945, victory in Europe was already assured, and the strains

Poster calling on Americans to "Avenge December 7" 1941, the day when Japanese bombers struck at Pearl Harbor. During the two-hour attack 2,392 servicemen were killed, 1,355 people were wounded and 960 were reported missing afterward.

in the alliance were beginning to tell. So, too, were the strains on Roosevelt himself: he had been re-elected to a fourth term in 1944, but the campaign had been dirty and left him with his slimmest margin of victory. At Yalta he was plainly suffering from fatigue and ill health. Churchill found him placid and frail: "I felt that he had a slender contact with life."

So it proved. Shortly before the San Francisco Conference which founded the United Nations Organization (a concept which the President had strongly supported) Roosevelt went for rest to Warm Springs, Georgia. There on April 12, 1945, he died from a massive cerebral hemorrhage. The 12 unprecedented White House years had taken their toll. But they left America reshaped, too, through the improved welfare and opportunity of millions of people – and the commanding new role of central government.

Pearl Harbor: columns of smoke frame the stricken USS West Virginia *and USS* Tennessee. *Two battleships were destroyed and six more were badly damaged while over 150 planes were wrecked in the assault on the Pacific Fleet's Hawaiian base.*

The United States declared war on Japan two days later. Roosevelt proclaiming that the event had taught the nation a terrible lesson: the war against the Axis powers was a world issue and Americans could no longer isolate themselves.

HARRY S. TRUMAN

"The buck stops here," read the now legendary sign on President Truman's desk, stating his unequivocal readiness to accept responsibility for his executive obligations. And few leaders have faced more awesome responsibilities than Truman when he began his first term. Stepping into the giant shoes of the stricken Franklin D. Roosevelt, the plain-speaking Missourian had to manage the conclusion of World War II, decide on the first use of the atomic bomb, oversee the creation of NATO and the Marshall Plan, and much more. F.D.R.'s sudden death had come as a shock, and Truman was fully aware of the scale of the difficulties facing him. On the morning after his inauguration he told reporters, "I feel as though the moon and all the stars and all the planets have fallen upon me. Please, boys, give me your prayers. I need them very much."

Yet the accidental President was always more than the average man his public image made him out to be. Behind the owlish spectacles lay a complex mind capable both of global thinking and quick decisions. For better or worse, it was Harry Truman who took the United States into a Cold War with communism, and his doctrine of Soviet "containment" was to remain the basis of U.S. foreign policy for over two decades.

A Missouri farm boy
Harry S. Truman was born in Lamar, Missouri, on May 8, 1884, and the "S" in his name was a curious anomaly. The

Thirty-third President 1945-1953

middle initial did not stand for anything: it was used because his maternal and paternal grand-fathers both had names beginning with S (Anderson Shipp Truman and Solomon Young), and to avoid offending either one by showing a preference only the initial was employed.

In 1890, Truman's father, a horsedealer, settled in Independence, Missouri, where he bought a small farm. Harry, like countless other country boys of his era, grew up adept at the chores of milking cows and splitting wood. His faulty vision was diagnosed early, and he had to wear glasses which prevented him from playing sports. Perhaps in compensation he read very widely and became a keen pianist (in his White House days, Truman seated at the piano offered many a photo opportunity for the pressmen).

Truman graduated from high school in 1901, and went on to try an assortment of jobs: working on *The Kansas City Star*, as a railroad timekeeper, as a bank clerk, on the family farm. In World War I he was commissioned a first lieutenant with an artillery unit, and he participated in the Vosges, Meuse-Argonne and St Mihiel actions. Promoted to captain, he earned the respect of his men for being a tough but fair-minded leader. On his return from Europe he married his childhood sweetheart, Bess Wallace: the wedding was held on June 28, 1919, at Independence, where she had lived all her life. The couple was to have one child, a daughter, Margaret, born in 1924.

U.S. servicemen stationed at Guam read reports of the first atomic bomb dropped on Japan. In the context of the long and harrowing struggle against the Axis powers their glee may be understandable – but it is disquieting too with the benefit of hindsight. The picture below shows the destruction at Hiroshima: on August 6, 1945, the Superfortress Enola Gay dropped a single device on this Japanese garrison town, destroying or damaging 96 percent of the buildings, killing about 75,000 people and injuring 100,000 more. Truman, who ordered the destruction, referred to using "the most terrible bomb in the history of the world," but seems not to have recognized nuclear warfare's threat to the very existence of the human race.

War in Korea: a U.S. Army mortar crew fires on communist hill positions, 1952. War had begun two years earlier when eight North Korean divisions crossed into the South and seized the capital, Seoul. Having no clear authority to intervene under international law, Truman nevertheless decided that the United States had the moral right to aid South Korea, and he authorized General Douglas MacArthur to lend support. The issue was then referred to the UN security council which set up an international command in which 14 other nations participated to counter North Korean aggression.

"Boss Tom"'s man

From 1919, Truman and a friend from army days ran a haberdashery business in Kansas city. The store failed, however, due to a general recession which wiped out many other small companies in 1921. While his partner went on to declare bankruptcy, Truman insisted on repaying every penny to his creditors, and it was while saddled with huge debts and looking for another job that he drifted into politics. Truman was introduced to bull-necked "Boss Tom" Pendergast, baron of all Democratic politics in western Missouri, and under his auspices was narrowly elected judge of Jackson County Court where he served from 1922-4. Truman had no legal qualifications but he attended law classes at night school to make itself worthy of his post, and was presiding judge from 1926-34.

A Baptist of scrupulous personal honesty, Truman was nevertheless tainted by association with the Boss Tom machine which he refused, out of loyalty, to disown. Truman was a U.S. Senator for ten years from 1935, and in the early period was widely regarded as no more than a stooge: "the Gentleman from Pendergast," as someone called him in the Senate. He responded by getting on conscientiously with his job. When the Pendergast outfit eventually collapsed amid a welter of indictments for voting fraud, Truman survived with his reputation intact. Indeed, it was greatly enhanced by his work as chairman of the

Committee to Investigate the National Defense Program, in which he campaigned vigorously against grafting war contractors. Truman never was a good public speaker – his voice was too flat – but he was an efficient legislator and a loyal supporter of Roosevelt's New Deal, so that in the 1944 contest for the vice-presidential candidacy he became the choice of the party managers, and was nominated on the second ballot.

A purely military decision

When Truman won the vice presidency, he and just about everyone else in Democratic politics was well aware that Roosevelt's job was really at stake. The President's declining health was a matter of general concern, and even before the convention opened Truman had expressed to his daughter Margaret a reluctance to become F.D.R.'s running mate: "1600 Pennsylvania is a nice address but I'd rather not move in through the back door – or any other door at 60." Nevertheless, the suddenness of Roosevelt's death, only five months into his new term, came as a shock. Inaugurated on April 12, 1945, Truman was fully aware of his own unpreparedness for executive action, never having been consulted by Roosevelt on issues of major importance. He felt exposed, and was to describe himself in the presidency as "the loneliest man in the world."

His first task was to oversee the victory plan which he

inherited on assuming office. The European conflict was already virtually concluded; on May 8, the incoming President was able to announce Germany's surrender. Japan, however, presented a continuing difficulty because her soldiers, retreating across the Pacific, were inflicting terrible casualties on the advancing Americans and could be expected to defend their homeland with even greater tenacity. An invasion of Japan would involve catastrophic loss of life, and it was in this context that Truman authorized the destruction of Hiroshima by atomic bomb.

It was an awesome decision which has been much disputed since. But to Truman the issue was straightforward. While acknowledging what a terrible weapon the bomb was, he believed that its use was justified on the grounds of the hundreds of thousands of lives saved by avoiding invasion. The longterm consequences for humanity of opening the nuclear era seem not to have preyed greatly on his mind. It was a "purely military decision to end the war," and long after his term of office had ended, Truman continued to defend the action.

The Fair Deal

Journalists in these early months were beginning to get the measure of the new President, discovering in him a feisty character whose pithy quotations were often delivered on his brisk pre-breakfast walk. Truman never much liked the attentions of press men, whom he called "news goons." Because of substantial renovations carried out between 1948 and 1952, he actually lived in the White House for only half of his presidency, and he did not enjoy the pomp associated with the office. His wife, Bess, cared for it even less, and did only the bare minimum required to acquit herself of the duties of First Lady. Both in the White House and at Blair House nearby, the couple lived frugally, so that everything conspired to reinforce the public perception of the President's ordinariness. "Harry Truman," said a contemporary, "proves the old adage that *any* man can become President of the United States."

In political life, though, Harry Truman showed himself to be much more than a merely average fellow. In domestic policy, for example, he surprised many observers by

New Yorkers greet General MacArthur with a traditional tickertape blizzard as he parades down Park Avenue, 1951. Though dismissed as commander of UN forces in Korea by President Truman he was given a hero's welcome on his return to the United States.

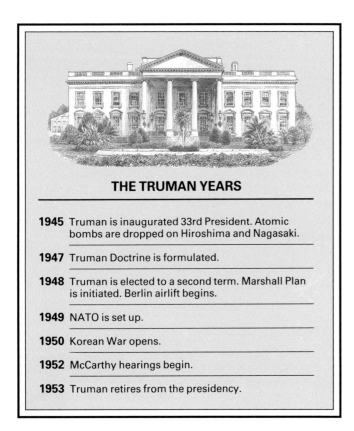

THE TRUMAN YEARS

1945 Truman is inaugurated 33rd President. Atomic bombs are dropped on Hiroshima and Nagasaki.

1947 Truman Doctrine is formulated.

1948 Truman is elected to a second term. Marshall Plan is initiated. Berlin airlift begins.

1949 NATO is set up.

1950 Korean War opens.

1952 McCarthy hearings begin.

1953 Truman retires from the presidency.

The Truman Doctrine

Foreign affairs was, however, the area on which Truman had greatest impact. Wholly inexperienced in world politics at a key moment in history, he began by continuing Roosevelt's policies. Truman went ahead with the San Francisco Conference of April, 1945, which founded the United Nations, and he initially respected the concept of three-power unity derived from F.D.R.'s wartime cooperation with Churchill and Stalin.

The international order began to change, though, as the West grew increasingly concerned about Soviet policy in Eastern Europe. The Potsdam Conference of July, 1945, was to be the last of the Big Three meetings: a general reassessment of policy was needed, and in 1947 the President initiated the so-called Truman Doctrine. An address to Congress in that year contained a policy statement committing the United States to "support free peoples who are resisting attempted subjugation by armed minorities or by outside pressure." Soviet attempts at expansion were, in other words, to be contained. In response to the statement, Congress passed a bill granting $400 million in aid to the Greek and Turkish governments threatened by communist takeover.

This was a historic act, ending the long American tradition of non-intervention outside the western hemisphere; the United States now saw itself as a world policeman for democracy. It was followed by the Marshall Plan of 1948, by which the U.S. in four years pumped $12.5 billion into the devastated economies of western Europe. Their recovery was rapid, and fears of communist takeovers in the region subsided at equal speed. The North Atlantic Treaty Organization (NATO), signed in Washington in 1949, further hardened attitudes toward the Soviet Union and affirmed the new U.S. role in Europe.

WAR IN KOREA

In foreign affairs, the inexperienced Truman showed a striking willingness to make his mind up quickly and firmly. Churchill, after the Potsdam meeting, spoke of the Missourian's "gay, precise, sparkling manner and obvious power of decision," and though the President was capable of vacillation, his essential confidence on big issues was remarkable. "If you can't stand the heat, get out of the kitchen," was a favorite maxim of his.

His policies had, however, made him enemies within the Democratic party: while the Southern conservatives were alienated by his stance on civil rights, liberals disliked his tough line on communism. Truman had to fight to win renomination in 1948, and there was a widespread belief

presenting a "Fair Deal" program of legislation more liberal even than Roosevelt's own New Deal had been. Fair Deal proposals were put forward and though the measures were frustrated by a conservative Congress, some important acts were passed. The minimum hourly wage was raised to 75 cents, and social security was extended.

Perhaps the President's greatest initiatives lay in the field of race relations. Truman was authentically concerned about the mistreatment of America's black citizens and in 1946, set up a President's Committee on Civil Rights which the next year made sweeping recommendations to abolish poll taxes, discrimination in industry, lynch law and much else. In 1948, Truman made the proposals part of his executive program despite consternation from Southern Democrats. All his remarks on the subject radiate a genuine sense of moral outrage at abuses. "My very stomach turned over when I learned that Negro soldiers, just back from overseas, were being dumped out of army trucks in Mississippi and beaten," he said, repudiating one group urging him to soften his line. And though many of his initiatives on civil rights were frustrated as his other Fair Deal measures were, Truman did manage through executive action to desegregate the armed forces.

Truman (left) presides as Secretary of State Edward Stettinius signs the United Nations charter in San Francisco, California, June 26, 1945. Proposals for a new kind of league of nations were first submitted by members of the wartime alliance against the Axis powers. Plans for the postwar United Nations organization were worked out at the 50 nation San Francisco conference. Each member state was to be represented in the General Assembly, while a Security Council with five permanent members (United States, United Kingdom, Soviet Union, France and China) would have prime responsibility for security.

that the Republican presidential candidate, Governor Thomas E. Dewey of New York, would win the election of that year. Truman, however, flatly refused to believe the opinion polls and fought a vigorous campaign which took him nearly 32,000 miles around the country. And despite a celebrated gaffe by *The Chicago Tribune* (whose election extra mistakenly proclaimed his defeat), Harry S. Truman returned to serve as elected President by a comfortable 24.1 million votes to 21.9, and 303 electoral votes to 189.

In his second term, the Truman Doctrine was severely tested. Between 1948 and 1949, the President was called upon to break a Soviet blockade of West Berlin by airlift. Meanwhile, Mao's communists established a People's Republic in China, and in June, 1950, North Korean troops made a surprise invasion of the South. If Korea fell to communism, Truman felt, the Soviet government would back similar acts of aggression elsewhere – perhaps triggering a third world war. So the President sent forces under General Douglas MacArthur to the defense of South Korea, also seeking and winning U.N. approval for intervention.

The split of MacArthur

Fighting in Korea was to drag on until the ceasefire of 1953, and had serious political repercussions at home. For one thing the war gave momentum to the witch-hunting anti-communist Senator McCarthy (whom Truman strongly opposed). And it also resulted in a clash of titans in the rift

between Truman and war hero MacArthur. The two men held wholly different views on the war's purpose. MacArthur wanted outright victory even at the expense of opening a war against China; Truman aimed more modestly to restore the territorial integrity of South Korea. And when the general defiantly declared his intention of pursuing North Koreans into China, the President relieved him of the command. "MacArthur left me no choice – I could no longer tolerate his insubordination," Truman was to say, but his decision caused a public outcry pumped up by the speeches which the soldier gave on his return.

In November, 1950, Truman survived an assassination attempt by two Puerto Rican nationalists. Also on the home front the President tried to prevent strikes in the steel industry by seizing the mills. The emergency measure was declared unconstitutional by the Supreme Court in 1952, however, in a judgment which survives as a key constitutional marker delineating the limits of presidential power.

In March of the same year, Truman made it known that he would not run for the presidency again. However, he did campaign energetically for the unsuccessful Democratic nominee, Adlai Stevenson, and continued to take an active interest in party politics afterwards. In July, 1957, the Harry S. Truman Library, a part of the national archives containing all the presidential papers, was dedicated in his home town of Independence. Truman died in Kansas City, Missouri, on December 26, 1972, at the age of 88.

DWIGHT D. EISENHOWER

Dwight D. Eisenhower (signature)

Reassurance was the great quality which Dwight Eisenhower gave to the American people. With all the prestige of a five-star general who had been the Supreme Allied Commander in World War II, he also brought to the presidency a smiling friendliness which made him seem to be everyone's uncle. And his manner was reinforced by his tastes; though by no means a fool, he mistrusted overt displays of intellectuality; he played bridge and golf; and he enjoyed quiet evenings watching television with his family in the White House.

From a liberal critic's standpoint, the shortcomings of his presidency were all too clear. Eisenhower enacted no sweeping reform legislation; his attempts to establish "modern Republicanism" in his party failed; and on the international stage his efforts to ease Cold War tensions eventually came to grief with the U-2 crisis and the severing of diplomatic relations with Cuba toward the end of his second term.

Yet a President of the United States may contribute more to national life than programs and policies. Imperceptibly, almost, the Chief Executive may lend a certain character to people's lives by entering the national psyche: either as a good fellow in the White House – or as a knave or charlatan. Eisenhower, emphatically, was a good fellow. "I Like Ike" was his election catchphrase, and many millions of Americans – even his political opponents – cheerfully subscribed to the sentiment.

Thirty-fourth President 1953-1961

The outbreak of World War II

Dwight David Eisenhower was born in Denison, Texas, on October 14, 1890. In the spring of the following year the family moved to Abilene, Kansas, where his father worked as a creamery mechanic. Both sides of the family were of German origin and shared religious conviction, so that the Bible was regularly read in the home. There was time for play too, and "Ike", as he was already being called, grew to be a keen sportsman who excelled in the school football and baseball teams. He did well scholastically, and in June, 1911, entered West Point.

As a cadet, Eisenhower maintained his sporting interests, proving to be an unusually talented halfback until a knee injury took him out of football. He graduated in 1915, and his first posting as second lieutenant was to Houston, Texas, where he met his future wife, Mamie Geneva Doud. The couple married in 1916, and were to have two boys, one of whom died of scarlet fever in his fourth year.

Eisenhower never saw active service in World War I, the Armistice canceling his orders for overseas duty, and through long years in the peacetime army he served in the rank of major. He was on the staff of General Douglas MacArthur in the American mission to the Philippines (1935-9), but returned to the United States when Hitler invaded Poland.

As chief of staff for General Walter Krueger's third army, he rose from colonel to brigadier general, and he so impressed General George C. Marshall through his grasp of

strategy that he went on to be given command of the Allied forces landing in North Africa (1942). This, the largest amphibious operation yet seen, was followed by victorious desert campaigns and in due course the invasion of Italy. Eisenhower was made a full general and in December, 1943, was given supreme command of the Allied Expeditionary Force in Western Europe.

General Eisenhower photographed on February 14, 1944, among the other men who planned and directed Operation Overlord, the Allied invasion of North-west Europe through Normandy. The operation carried out in June owed its success partly to effective coordination by Allied command under Eisenhower. Massive resources of air power also contributed to victory: 10,000 combatant and 1,000 transport aircraft were deployed.

Victory in Europe

It was Eisenhower who selected June 6, 1944, as the date for the D-Day invasion of occupied France – a stupendous operation in which the biggest invasion fleet of history blackened the English Channel with ships. Supported by thousands of aircraft and paratroops, the Allied armada poured a million troops onto the Normandy beaches, and in the year of hard fighting which followed Eisenhower showed himself to be a commander both of great firmness and of tact. The enemy was driven from France; the Allies

pushed inexorably into the Reich heartland; and on May 7, 1945, in a brick-built schoolhouse at Reims, Eisenhower received the German surrender.

Victory brought Eisenhower huge popularity, and he returned to Washington to serve as Chief of Staff (1945-8), also being promoted to the rank of five-star general. Already, both Republicans and Democrats were seeing him as a potential candidate for the presidency, but Eisenhower (who had not expressed any party allegiance) declined to stand in the election of 1948. Instead in that year he took up the post of president at Columbia University; in 1948, too, he published *Crusade in Europe*, his war memoirs, which became a bestseller.

In 1951, Eisenhower returned to military service as Supreme Commander of NATO forces in Europe, but pressure to get him to stand for the presidency had never abated; in 1952, he accepted Republican overtures and won the party's nomination on the first ballot. The fact that Eisenhower had no strong party loyalties (and might as easily have accepted the Democratic nomination) was no handicap in electoral terms. His simple humanity had an immense appeal only reinforced by his infectious grin. "Ike, with that puss you can't miss being President," Secretary of Defense Forrestal had once remarked. And indeed, he won a sweeping victory over the Democratic candidate, Adlai E. Stevenson, with 33.9 to 27.3 million votes in the popular ballot; 442 to 89 votes in the Electoral College.

In the White House

In office, Eisenhower presented a marked contrast to his immediate predecessors. Where Roosevelt and Truman had practiced a strong "hands on" approach to the presidency, Eisenhower deliberately returned to a more relaxed style of government. Far from wanting to expand the role of central government, he promised cuts in federal spending and called for more local control. Eisenhower refused to bully congressmen into backing government proposals: "You do not lead by hitting people over the head," he often said. And as far as details of policy were concerned he gave considerable leeway to his advisers. Believing in an orderly administration, he established a White House staff under Sherman Adams, his personal assistant, who acquired a unique power to influence whom he saw and what he read. In foreign policy Eisenhower took a stronger personal lead, but in this area, too, his chief adviser, John Foster Dulles, was given considerable authority.

Nevertheless, Eisenhower's leadership, if unemphatic, cannot be called weak. He had his own broad sense of direction on major issues, believing, in particular, in the need to negotiate from strength to ease tensions in world affairs. He firmly supported mutual security programs to fight communism in the Far East. And he also gave his name to the Eisenhower Doctrine, formulated in 1957, empowering the President to give economic and military aid to any Middle East government seeking assistance against communist aggression. In 1958, moreover, Eisenhower ordered U.S. Marines into Lebanon following an appeal for help from President Chamoun, who was facing an armed insurrection by Muslim opponents.

These tough stances, however, were matched by an authentic pursuit of peace. Eisenhower's pledge in 1952 was to visit war-torn Korea if elected; he made the trip, and on his return hastened the end of the fighting. In July, 1955, at a Geneva summit attended by Nikita Khrushchev, Eisenhower made every effort to promote détente through his "Open Skies" policy of mutual inspection of military installations. And the following year he effectively stopped the Anglo-French invasion of Egypt during the Suez crisis.

"Modern Republicanism"

In home policy Eisenhower was moderately progressive. Despite his own natural conservatism he came to believe in some social welfare activities which he promoted under the broad heading of "Modern Republicanism." These included the extension of social security benefits; the creation of a new Department of Health, Education and Welfare; support for federal aid in school construction; and a major roadbuilding program which would lead to the construction of more than 40,000 miles of new interstate highways. The Interstate Highways Act of 1956 had incalculable consequences in stimulating the auto industry, the continental bus services and the general mobility of all Americans – especially of black emigrants from the South.

Eisenhower has sometimes been accused of dragging his feet on civil rights issues. But it was under his administration that the desegregation of schools began as a result of a Supreme Court decision in 1954, although the President privately expressed doubts on whether the goal of equality could be achieved by legislation. And it was Eisenhower who in September, 1957, sent troops into Little Rock, Arkansas, to uphold the federal authority. One thousand paratroopers and 10,000 National Guardsmen helped keep order as the first handful of black children entered Central High School.

McCARTHY'S WITCH HUNT

A sinister backdrop to Eisenhower's early years was provided by the activities of Senator Joseph McCarthy, Wisconsin's anti-communist witch hunter who, as Chairman of the Permanent Subcommittee on Investigations of the Senate Committee on Government Operations, launched over 150 investigations in the period 1953-5. His venomous and sensational accusations against "card-carrying communists" in the State Department and elsewhere brought very widespread fear, and it can fairly be said that Eisenhower failed in his presidential duty by refusing to challenge the Senator's attacks. "I just will not – I *refuse* – to get into the gutter with that guy," the President explained privately. In the end, when McCarthy began to

*Anti-communist witch hunter Senator Joe McCarthy (inset)
was idolized by supporters such as these, pictured on their way
to a rally in Washington, D.C., 1954. By these people he was
hailed as the guardian of genuine Americanism and a
dedicated patriot. However, by his critics he was considered
irresponsible and his attitudes were gradually undermining the
nation's traditions of civil liberties.*

attack the U.S. Army, the witch hunt went too far. In
December, 1954, McCarthy was censured by the Senate in a
vote for 67 to 22, for unbecoming conduct.

There were other respects in which Eisenhower faced
difficulties. Though re-elected in 1956 by nearly 10 million
votes – the biggest popular majority up to that time – he
came into his second term facing a Democratic Congress.
"Modern Republicanism" was strongly opposed by the right
wing of his own party; and an economic recession afflicted
the country in 1957-8.

There were serious doubts, too, about the President's
health. In September, 1955, Eisenhower had suffered a
fairly severe heart attack; the following year he underwent

Eisenhower campaigns at Lubbock, Texas, in the 1952 election. Voters who chanted "I like Ike" continued to like him through his years in the White House. Though political commentators tended to view him as a passive president historians have revised opinions. Eisenhower has been likened to a tortoise: "all the while we never knew the cunning beneath the shell."

major abdominal surgery; and in 1957, he suffered a stroke. All in all, a sense that the nation was drifting began to prevail during Eisenhower's second term and when the Soviet Union put the first satellite, *Sputnik 1*, into space (1957), the event came as a considerable shock to American pride.

The President's personal popularity never really waned, however, and along with domestic problems there were events to celebrate, too. In 1959, Hawaii and Alaska were admitted as new states; the following year the great St. Lawrence Seaway was opened. As a First Family the Eisenhowers were both loved and admired. They appealed

to tradition through restoring the annual custom of the Easter egg rolling contest at the White House, first introduced by Rutherford Hayes's wife, Lucy, but discontinued for 12 years during and after the war. The President also initiated a new age by giving the first televised White House press conferences, and using helicopter transportation from the mansion's lawn.

The U-2 incident and Cuba
Toward the close of the Eisenhower era a series of events occurred which seriously altered the prospects for world peace. In May, 1960, a U-2 high-flying reconnaissance plane

was shot down over Soviet territory: the pilot, Gary Powers, survived and confessed to his espionage role. At that time a summit meeting had been scheduled to take place in Paris between Eisenhower and Soviet Premier Nikita Khrushchev, and the Russian leader used the episode as a reason to withdraw from the talks.

It has been argued that Khrushchev was, in reality, glad to get out of the conference. But the incident was, nonetheless, a genuine embarrassment for the United States. The State Department had initially denied that the flight had been made, and it was in somewhat shamefaced fashion that the President was forced to come clean, confessing not only that he had authorized high altitude spy flights over the Soviet Union – but that they were part of U.S. policy and would continue. Offered an opportunity to apologize for the incident, Eisenhower almost petulantly refused, providing the Soviets with moral victory and a legitimate and reasonable excuse to boycott the talks.

The U-2 incident came at a time when the United States was already facing difficult relations with Latin America. Continuing Truman's tradition, Eisenhower backed a number of right-wing military regimes there in the hope that they would offer guarantees against the spread of communism. However, local resentment against these often brutal dictatorships spilled over into demonstrations against the United States. In 1958, when Vice President Nixon arrived in Uruguay at the outset of an eight-nation goodwill tour he was mobbed by hostile students; in Peru and Venezuela similar scenes occurred, forcing the cancellation of the remainder of the trip. Many Americans learned something new and disquieting from these events: that their foreign policy and intervention made them actively disliked abroad.

The most dramatic developments, though, were in Cuba where, in 1959, Fidel Castro's revolutionary movement overthrew the repressive dictatorship of Fulgencio Batista. Eisenhower recognized Castro's regime, but relations with Cuba quickly worsened as foreign sugar holdings were expropriated and most of the island's major businesses were taken over by the government. Shunning American ties, Castro drew his country ever closer to the Soviet Union and China, and shortly before the end of Eisenhower's second term, the President broke off diplomatic relations with Cuba.

Farewell address
Before leaving the White House, on January 17, 1961, Eisenhower delivered a farewell address which struck an authoritative and cautionary note for the future. Eisenhower spoke of the need to maintain national security; but

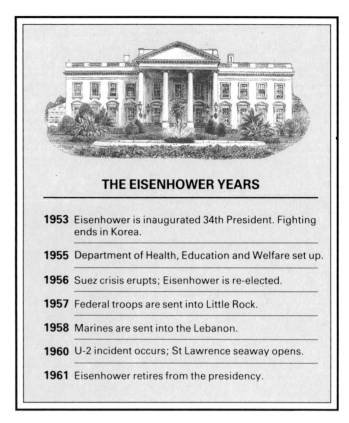

THE EISENHOWER YEARS

1953 Eisenhower is inaugurated 34th President. Fighting ends in Korea.

1955 Department of Health, Education and Welfare set up.

1956 Suez crisis erupts; Eisenhower is re-elected.

1957 Federal troops are sent into Little Rock.

1958 Marines are sent into the Lebanon.

1960 U-2 incident occurs; St Lawrence seaway opens.

1961 Eisenhower retires from the presidency.

he also warned against the growing power of the American "military-industrial complex:"

"The conjunction of an immense military establishment and a large arms industry is new in the American experience. The total influence – economic, political, even spiritual – is felt in every city, every State house, every office of the Federal government. Our toil, resources and livelihood are all involved; so is the very structure of our society."

"In the councils of government, we must guard against the acquisition of unwarranted influence, whether sought or unsought, by the military-industrial complex. The potential for the disastrous rise of misplaced power exists and will persist. We must never let the weight of this combination endanger our liberties or democratic processes. We should take nothing for granted . . ."

Afterward, Eisenhower retired to his farm in Gettysburg, Pennsylvania, and described some of his early experiences in *At Ease: stories I tell to friends* (1968), and his presidency in *Mandate for Change* (1963). Greatly respected as an elder statesman, he died in Washington aged 78, on March 28, 1969.

JOHN F. KENNEDY

On November 22, 1963, while being driven through the streets of Dallas, Texas, in an open car, President John F. Kennedy was shot dead, apparently by the lone gunman, Lee Harvey Oswald. Any assassination is a shocking event but in Kennedy's case the drama was especially numbing because to millions of people, not only in the United States but elsewhere in the Western world, he was a symbolic figure representing all the charm, vigor and optimism of youth. "We stand today on the edge of a New Frontier," Kennedy had proclaimed in accepting the Democratic nomination three years earlier. "Beyond that frontier are uncharted areas of science and space, unsolved problems of peace and war, unconquered pockets of ignorance and prejudice, unanswered questions of poverty and surplus." And who, if not this vital young statesman, was capable of leading the pioneering generation of young Americans?

History can be cruelly stark, and when the record is examined it may be seen that Kennedy the New Frontiersman, founder of the Peace Corps and promoter of the space program was also the President who approved the failed Bay of Pigs invasion of Cuba, extended U.S. involvement in Vietnam and, during the Cuban missile crisis of 1962, took life on Earth as close as it has ever been to the brink of nuclear extinction. Behind the glamorous image lay an essentially human figure – flawed and fallible as humans are. But he did not shrink from involving himself personally in the titanic issues of his day.

Thirty-fifth President 1961-1963

The naval lieutenant

John Fitzgerald Kennedy was born on May 29, 1917, in Brookline, Massachusetts. He was the second son of Joseph P. Kennedy, financier, who was to become Ambassador to Great Britain. The family took pride in its Irish origins and in its swift rise from lowly immigrant status to wealth and prominence. John F. Kennedy was educated at Princeton, Harvard and the London School of Economics, afterward studying at Stanford University's Graduate School of Business.

As a naval lieutenant during World War II, Kennedy commanded a torpedo boat (PT 109) in the Solomon Islands. Not long after midnight on August 2, 1943, the craft was hit by a Japanese destroyer and cut in half. With his back badly injured, Kennedy spent 15 hours in the water before leading the surviving crew members to an island and safety. For this action he was decorated, and he spent the remainder of the war years in hospitals and then as an instructor.

Serving as a Democratic congressman from Massachusetts (1947-53) John F. Kennedy won some reputation as a liberal in domestic policy while backing a firm anti-communist line in foreign affairs. Elected to the senate in 1952, he met and married the beautiful Jacqueline Lee Bouvier the following year. His back problems gave him continuing difficulties during this period and it was while convalescing after a series of spinal operations that he wrote *Profiles in Courage* (1956), which was a series of political biographies analyzing problems of leadership,

which won him a Pulitzer Prize in 1957.

In 1956, Kennedy narrowly missed the vice presidential nomination for the Democrats. He was re-elected to the Senate in 1958, and in 1960 openly sought the presidential nomination, building up so powerful an organization that after winning an impressive series of primary elections he gained the nomination on the first ballot.

The New Frontier
It was in his acceptance speech that Kennedy spoke of the New Frontier, a program involving a wide-ranging assault on American problems, designed to get the country moving again after the comfortable torpor of the Eisenhower years.

The Kennedy family photographed in 1938 when Joseph P. Kennedy (center) was U.S. Ambassador to Britain. The millionaire diplomat had four sons: John F. Kennedy, future President, stands behind him to the right with Robert, future Attorney General, at his shoulder. Six-year-old Edward is seated to the left.

The election itself was especially memorable for the TV debates which Kennedy held with the Republican contender, Richard Nixon. The first of their kind ever broadcast, they were watched by 70 million viewers and it has often been argued that Kennedy's more accomplished performance was the deciding factor in what turned out to be an

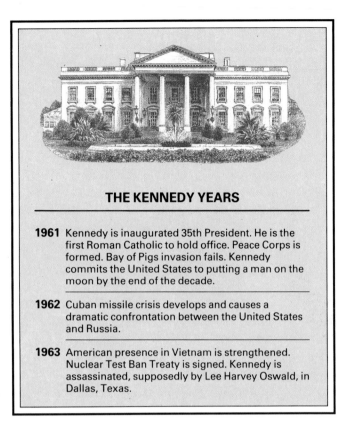

THE KENNEDY YEARS

1961 Kennedy is inaugurated 35th President. He is the first Roman Catholic to hold office. Peace Corps is formed. Bay of Pigs invasion fails. Kennedy commits the United States to putting a man on the moon by the end of the decade.

1962 Cuban missile crisis develops and causes a dramatic confrontation between the United States and Russia.

1963 American presence in Vietnam is strengthened. Nuclear Test Ban Treaty is signed. Kennedy is assassinated, supposedly by Lee Harvey Oswald, in Dallas, Texas.

The space program

In other respects, however, Kennedy was genuinely inspirational. Cold War rivalries had, almost by accident, stimulated an intense interest in space development and in April, 1961, the Soviet Union put the first man, Yuri Gagarin, into orbit. Kennedy replied in May by asking Congress to undertake a bold project, proposing that the United States should "commit itself to achieving the goal, before this decade is out, of landing a man on the moon and returning him safely to earth." It was an extraordinarily ambitious aim, and there were many critics who suggested that the money and technological expertise would be better lavished on improving conditions on Earth. Nevertheless, Kennedy pressed on, and the following year astronaut John Glenn became the first American to orbit in space. Also in 1962, the U.S. spacecraft Mariner II was launched to make the first interplanetary spaceshot: after traveling a distance of 180 million miles it flew past Venus, and was able to confirm its high temperature and the reverse direction of its rotation.

Kennedy's fascination with such projects did not derive from a mere desire to outdistance the Russians; in fact, he openly suggested that American and Soviet astronauts might go to the moon together. It stemmed rather from the vein of authentic idealism in his nature: the moon and the planets represented a challenge: "new hopes for knowledge and peace are there."

The Bay of Pigs and after

In foreign policy Kennedy made a deep impression despite the fact that his term opened with a disastrous enterprise. In April, 1961, a force of about 1,200 American-trained Cuban exiles invaded Cuba, at the Bahia de Cochinas (Bay of Pigs) on the island's southern coast, in an attempt to overthrow Castro's regime. The exiles failed ignominiously to promote the mass uprising they had anticipated. Though planned under Eisenhower, the scheme was carried out with Kennedy's full consent and even some limited U.S. air support. When America's involvement was disclosed Kennedy took full responsibility for a fiasco which had served only to confirm Castro's authority in Cuba while highlighting the mischievous and damaging role of the C.I.A. which had organized the invasion.

Despite this failure and his own firm anti-communism, Kennedy ardently desired to stop the arms race, declaring at the United Nations that the goal of complete disarmament was not a dream but a practical matter of life or death. "The risks inherent in disarmament pale in comparison to the risks inherent in an unlimited arms race ... Mankind must put an end to war or war will put an

exceptionally close contest: Kennedy won by 34.2 million to 34.1 million votes in the popular ballot; 303 to 219 in the Electoral College.

Age 43 at his inauguration, Kennedy was the youngest President since Teddy Roosevelt, and also the first Roman Catholic to preside in the White House. A remarkable aura of glamor – almost of adoration – surrounded his administration, causing people to speak of an American Camelot. The President himself displayed a great respect for intellectual and artistic achievement, while Jacqueline Kennedy as First Lady set standards of elegance and style which American women nationwide sought to emulate.

In his economic affairs Kennedy pursued expansionist policies founded on the principles of John Maynard Keynes. His domestic reforms included measures for civil rights, a revised tax structure, federal aid to education, a mental health program and medical care for old people. While firing the imagination of a new generation of young Americans the policies did not always impress a conservative Congress, however, and Kennedy has been criticized for his own mild-mannered and moderate championship of proposals which were often blocked in the end.

Left: *Inaugurated in January 1961, Kennedy delivered an address that seemed to some worryingly extravagant in its implied challenge to communism: "Let every nation know, whether it wishes us well or ill, that we shall pay any price, bear any burden, meet any hardship, support any friend, oppose any foe, in order to assure the survival and the success of liberty."*

Below: *Kennedy and Soviet Premier Nikita Khrushchev are pictured here on the steps of the United States embassy residence in Vienna, June 3, 1961, before going indoors for their first meeting. Despite the smiles the two leaders were deeply divided by Cold War issues, notably the question of Berlin. Khrushchev was in an intransigent mood and when the two men parted Kennedy forecast, "It will be a cold winter."*

end to mankind." In June, 1961, he held meetings with Soviet Premier Nikita Khrushchev in Vienna, but though the talks were cordial they did not prevent the construction of the Berlin Wall in August of that year or of Khrushchev threatening to sign a separate peace treaty with East Germany. The German city was to remain throughout his presidency a symbol of the tensions which divided East from West. "As a free man, I take pride in the words *Ich bin ein Berliner,*" he proclaimed in a speech to West Berliners in 1963.

The Cuban missile crisis

Cuba remained, however, the most disquieting focus of international rivalry. In the summer of 1962, the Soviet Union installed intermediate range missiles on the island, with hydrogen warheads capable of striking cities in both North and South America. It was an audacious move on Khrushchev's part, for the Soviet Union had never before placed missiles beyond its own frontiers and it reduced the warning time of a nuclear attack on the United States from 15 minutes to two. The bases were photographed by

Dallas, Texas, November 22, 1963: shots ring out and President Kennedy slumps forward, mortally wounded in the head and throat. A secret service agent bends toward the stricken president while Mrs. Kennedy huddles over her husband to support him. Governor Connally of Texas, who was also hit, takes cover in the front with his wife.

American U-2 reconnaissance aircraft, and when Kennedy asked for an explanation he was informed by Soviet foreign minister Andrei Gromyko that only anti-aircraft missiles were being installed. Confronted with the deceit, Kennedy imposed a naval blockade and insisted that Khrushchev dismantle the bases, removing the missiles. Any nuclear attack from Cuba would prompt a "full retaliatory response upon the Soviet Union."

It was a terrifying moment in history, and for a week the world waited in anguish. Kennedy's actions have been much criticized on the grounds that the United States had its own Jupiter missiles in Turkey, and would still maintain an overall nuclear supremacy even after the Cuban bases were installed. Nevertheless, the President regarded the episode as a deliberate provocation which might encourage the Russians to further and rasher acts. Appeasement, in the end, might set in train events which would lead inevitably to a third world war.

In those days of almost intolerable suspense, a U.S. invasion force assembled in Florida while the building of the bases on Cuba continued. Finally, Soviet ships thought to be bringing new missiles to the island turned back. "We're eyeball to eyeball," said Secretary of State Dean Rusk, "and I think the other fellow just blinked." Khrushchev had indeed backed down. The missiles were completely removed; the U.S. blockade was lifted; and with some sensitivity to Soviet pride Kennedy agreed to respect the territorial integrity of Cuba.

Prospects for peace

After the dramatic confrontation, tensions between the United States and the Soviet Union eased, and in the more relaxed atmosphere which followed the crisis the Nuclear Test Ban Treaty of 1963 was concluded, the three signatories – the United States, the Soviet Union and Great Britain – undertaking to "prohibit, to prevent and not to carry out" nuclear explosions except underground. It was the first arms control treaty concluded during the Cold War and, though France and China declined to sign it, represented a significant step toward détente. As a result of the Cuban crisis, too, a hot line was installed between Washington and Moscow – a direct telephonic link between the U.S. President and Soviet Premier for use in time of emergency.

Kennedy worked for peace in other ways, too. In March, 1961, he formed the Peace Corps, an agency of the State Department designed to harness the idealism and technological skills of Americans to the needs of emergent nations. The Corps consists of volunteers over 18 years old working especially as teachers and agriculturalists. Outspoken as he was in the causes of freedom and democracy, he well realized the limitations of U.S. power, calling, in a speech in 1961, on Americans to acknowledge the fact that the nation is neither "omnipotent nor omniscient – that we are only 6 percent of the world's population – that we cannot impose our will upon the other 94 percent of mankind – that we cannot right every wrong or reverse each adversity – and

Alleged assassin Lee Harvey Oswald crumples as Dallas nightclub operator Jack Rubinstein, known as Jack Ruby, shoots from a .38 snub-nosed revolver. The incident took place in the basement of the Dallas municipal building as Oswald was being transferred from the city jail to the county jail. Oswald died shortly afterwards, and Ruby was charged with the murder. He said that he killed Oswald to avenge Jackie Kennedy.

that therefore there cannot be an American solution to every world problem."

Those words carry a grim resonance when considered in relation to U.S. policies in southeast Asia. Kennedy believed that the United States was overcommitted in the area and refused to send American combat units there. He did, however, accept the broad lines of the domino theory that if one country fell to communism its neighbor would be in jeopardy. So it was that as the Vietcong continued to make gains against the Saigon government in South Vietnam, Kennedy increased the number of U.S. "advisers" to 16,732 by 1963, apparently hoping that the South Vietnamese could win their war for themselves with only marginal assistance. In this judgment he proved tragically wrong, and by expanding the American role he paved the way for a larger and more terrible intervention.

Death in Dallas

Speaking at the American University in Washington, D.C., on June 10, 1963, Kennedy expressed his hopes for world peace: "In the final analysis, our most basic common link is that we all inhabit this small planet. We all breathe the same air. We all cherish our children's future. And we are mortal."

Later that year the young President accepted what was considered a dangerous challenge of visiting Dallas where there was known to be some hostility to his administration. Kennedy, however, insisted on the removal of the protective

top from his limousine, and contrary to expectations there were no demonstrations – only friendly and cheering crowds. Riding with the President and Mrs. Kennedy were Governor and Mrs. John B. Connally, and as the motorcade turned into Elm Street the governor's wife could not restrain her Texan pride that the visit seemed to be going smoothly. "Mr. President," she said, "you can't say Dallas doesn't love you."

Seconds later shots rang out: Kennedy slumped, bleeding from the head, and though the driver raced the car directly to hospital, the President died without regaining consciousness.

The terrible event, captured on the blurred cine film of an onlooker, acquired the dimension of a national trauma, and the sense of shock and incredulity was only heightened when the supposed assassin, Lee Harvey Oswald, was himself murdered in the basement garage of Dallas Jail by a local nightclub owner named Jack Ruby. Oswald was found to have spent some time in the Soviet Union and to be known to the intelligence community. Suspicions that he may have acted as part of a conspiracy – and been silenced – have never been entirely dispelled despite the official verdict of the Warren Commission, set up to examine the affair, that he was a lone gunman. In all, the Kennedy assassination sent a wave of grief around the world, leaving a sense of great promise suddenly cut short, and prompting questions both large and small which even now remain to be answered.

LYNDON B. JOHNSON

[signature: Lyndon B. Johnson]

Thirty-sixth President 1963-1969

No President came to office in more traumatic circumstances than Lyndon Johnson, thirty-sixth President of the United States. He was sworn in on November 22, 1963, in Dallas; standing beside him was Jacqueline Kennedy, her dress still blood-stained where she had cradled her dying husband. The violence that ushered the tall Texan into the White House foreshadowed what was to become the most turbulent presidency of modern times. The horrors of Vietnam competed for attention with the worst riots in American history, racial conflict in the South, the assassination of important public figures, and burnings and rebellion on campuses across America. Johnson was unlucky enough to become President at the moment when several time bombs which had been ticking just below the surface of American society finally exploded. He would leave the presidency a bitter, worn out and disillusioned man, dying prematurely on his ranch, his own comment, "I do not believe I can unite this country," standing as an epitaph for his administration.

Yet it was Johnson who put the most comprehensive and effective program of civil rights and social welfare of any postwar President onto the statute book. This still stands as a major achievement to set against the chaos of the times. It was also one of history's ironies that the President who took up the demands of blacks and liberals was the first Southerner to hold the office since Andrew Johnson almost exactly a century before – and he, too, had become President after the assassination of a hugely popular predecessor, Abraham Lincoln.

A long apprenticeship

Lyndon Baines Johnson was born on August 27, 1908, on a farm near Stonewall, in the grasslands of central Texas. His parents were not rich and his family knew hardship during the Depression: Johnson himself was briefly unemployed. He entered the Southwest Texas State Teacher's College in 1927, graduating in 1930, and then teaching in Houston for two years. Yet he was fascinated by politics from an early age, and life as a teacher in Texas held no attractions for him. In 1932, he moved to Washington as secretary to a Texas congressman, and in 1935 became the Texas director of the National Youth Administration, a New Deal program to create part-time jobs for needy high school and college students. Within two years he had made his name, setting up what Washington regarded as a model state program, and he entered Congress in 1937 on the New Deal ticket as an FDR protégé.

Johnson then began building up the experience that would turn him into a veteran politician by the time he became President. He served five terms in Congress, interrupted briefly by a spell in the Navy after Pearl Harbor, and in 1948, was elected Democratic Senator for Texas. In 1953, he was made minority leader – at 44 the youngest ever – and, in 1954, won a national reputation when the Democrats gained control of the Senate and elected him

November 22, 1963; Vice President Lyndon B. Johnson is sworn in as President of the United States by Federal District Judge Sarah T. Hughes of Dallas aboard the presidential plane prior to returning to Washington, D.C. Johnson was flanked in the ceremony by his wife Claudia ("Lady Bird") and by the widowed Jacqueline Kennedy. The 55-year-old Texan was elected in his own right in a landslide the next year. "I am going to build the kind of nation that President Roosevelt hoped for, President Truman worked for and President Kennedy died for," he said.

majority leader. Johnson was not a partisan figure, and cooperated with Republican President Eisenhower on most issues. He was a master of negotiations in committee rooms and corridors, acquiring a deep understanding of how the American political systems works: "Johnson's instinct for power is as primordial as a salmon's going upstream to spawn," it was said.

He made his first attempt on the presidency in 1960, but was unable to match Kennedy's extraordinary charisma; he contented himself, instead, with the vice presidential nomination. He was never personally close to Kennedy but helped to carry the South and proved to be an extremely energetic Vice President, especially in supervising the infant space program.

A complex man
Despite his long experience, Johnson, when he succeeded to the presidency through the Dallas tragedy, was respected rather than loved. Coarse and earthy where Kennedy had been urbane and sophisticated, the new President was a man whose liberal instincts on domestic issues were sometimes hidden by a certain lack of tact. He had a prickly relationship with the media, and it has been said that he suffered from an inferiority complex about his glamorous

predecessor. Nevertheless, Johnson showed himself intensely loyal to Kennedy's policies both at home and abroad. In human terms, moreover, he was the most outgoing of men, liking nothing better than barbecues, hard drinking, and good company.

Completing the Kennedy term
While the country reeled from the shock of Kennedy's assassination, Johnson as a seasoned politician realized that he had to move quickly to establish himself in his own right as a legitimate successor to Kennedy. To do so he had to overcome the suspicions of black Americans, to whom he was a white Southerner, and the antipathies of liberals, to whom he was a backroom politician who had cooperated with Republican Presidents. He pledged to continue the New Frontier program, and was especially energetic in pushing through the Civil Rights Act of June, 1964, which had languished at the committee stage for years.

Then in August came the Tonkin Gulf Incident. The U.S.S. Maddox, operating in waters claimed by the North Vietnamese, was allegedly attacked by North Vietnamese patrol boats. Although doubts would later be raised about what had happened, a bellicose Congress passed the Tonkin Resolution almost unanimously, authorizing Johnson to

Martin Luther King Jr. is seen here third from the left on the balcony of a Memphis hotel – the same spot where he was shot the next day, April 4, 1968. The murderer was a white man, James Earl Ray, and blacks in cities all over the United States responded to the killing in a paroxysm of rioting which King himself, the apostle of non-violence, could not have condoned.

take action in Vietnam. So, by the time of the presidential election in November, 1964, the two themes which were to dominate Johnson's own term – Vietnam and civil rights – had already surfaced.

The 1964 election

Johnson's opponent in 1964 was Senator Barry Goldwater, a conservative at a time when the liberal tide was running high. Johnson's victory was the most crushing since 1937: he took over 61 percent of the popular vote. Instead of merely carrying on with the New Frontier, Johnson was now able to strike out on his own with a program he called the Great Society, "a place where the city of man serves not only the needs of the body and the demands of commerce but the desire for beauty and the hunger for community." The plan was to complement civil rights legislation with an anti-poverty drive, the War On Poverty, including the Medicare scheme to help the elderly, combined with tax cuts to stimulate the economy.

The sweeping victory included Democratic gains in the Senate and House of Representatives, where a working progressive majority was elected for the first time since 1937. This meant that Johnson could be sure of passing his most controversial measures in the teeth of opposition from Republicans and conservative Southern Democrats. This proved to be timely, for racial tensions had already plunged large parts of the country into open crisis.

Racial violence and civil rights

By 1964, blacks were taking the civil rights question into their own hands. The frustrations and resentments caused by discrimination and segregation could no longer be contained in the South, and in the big cities of the North and West racism, inner city decay, rising poverty and insensitive policing were increasing tensions which resulted in sustained rioting in Harlem in 1964 and the Watts district of Los Angeles in 1965. Harlem and Watts set the pattern for a series of riots that punctuated every summer of Johnson's second term, and left no important urban center untouched.

The riots – in Detroit, Newark, Harlem, Chicago, Cleveland, Watts and elsewhere – were the most sustained outbreak of civil disorder in American history. In Detroit in July, 1967, for example, at least 40 people were killed, 2,000 arrests were made, and 5,000 people were made homeless as dozens of city blocks were burnt out. It took 8,000 National Guardsmen reinforced by 5,000 paratroopers eight days to quell the riots. The root cause of the riots was poverty, compounded in the South by systematic racism. Inner city decay was an intractable problem where the only solutions were long term, but Johnson could move swiftly against the white supremacists in the South. He had the imagination to realize that the only way out of the crisis was to put the full weight of federal government and its machinery behind the blacks in their struggle, and to extend the protection of the Constitution to all citizens regardless of race.

The Supreme Court had declared all-white primaries illegal in 1944, and had come out against segregation in schools in 1957. Eisenhower had, with Johnson's help, passed limited civil rights bills in 1957 and 1960, but fierce opposition and entrenched obstruction in Southern state and county governments prevented their implementation. It was not until the early 1960s that the civil rights movement, under the charismatic leadership of Martin Luther King, forced the federal government to act. King, inspired by Gandhi's example, used peaceful protest to force the pace of desegregation: civil disobedience, consumer boycotts, and legal action. Typical was the campaign to desegregate Birmingham, Alabama. Thousands of blacks, reinforced by Freedom Riders (Northern liberals who drove coaches through the South defying segregation laws where they halted), marched through the streets, refused to board segregated buses, and entered whites-only restaurants; they were met with police dogs, clubbings, and even electric cattle prods. Despite the violence, the city could not function without blacks, and the city council finally gave in to the campaigners.

The Civil Rights Act of 1964 was the main plank in Johnson's legislative response. It forbade segregation in public places and hotels, and ordered the withdrawal of federal funds from any project that involved discrimination or segregation at any level. What made this and subsequent bills so effective was Johnson's realization that it was not enough merely to outlaw discrimination and segregation – the Supreme Court had been doing so since the 1940s – but that it was also necessary to set up practical ways of dismantling white supremacy at state and county level. This was done in various ways.

Perhaps the most important was the Voting Rights Act of 1965. It gave the Attorney General powers to send in federal registrars wherever discrimination in the compiling of

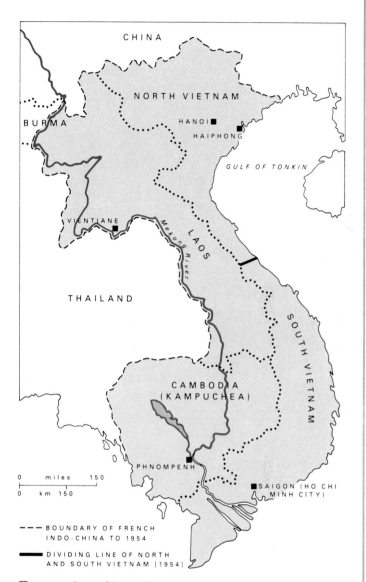

The countries making up French Indochina won their independence in 1954, but international agreement divided Vietnam along the 17th parallel (17°N). The communist North then began a long struggle against South Vietnam, aiming for reunification, while the United States became ever more embroiled in trying to prop up the South's regime.

voting registers was suspected: local officials throughout the South had to comply. As a result, campaigns to register black voters had added 250,000 new names to electoral rolls in the South by the end of 1965 alone. From then on, even diehard segregationists had to take account of the black vote. Governor George Wallace of Alabama, for example, ran for President in 1968 on a white supremacist ticket and won over four million votes. Yet within a decade he had

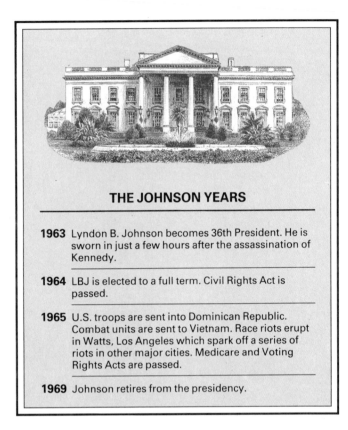

THE JOHNSON YEARS

1963 Lyndon B. Johnson becomes 36th President. He is sworn in just a few hours after the assassination of Kennedy.

1964 LBJ is elected to a full term. Civil Rights Act is passed.

1965 U.S. troops are sent into Dominican Republic. Combat units are sent to Vietnam. Race riots erupt in Watts, Los Angeles which spark off a series of riots in other major cities. Medicare and Voting Rights Acts are passed.

1969 Johnson retires from the presidency.

been forced to change his stance, needing and receiving black support to stay in office. Tragically, Martin Luther King did not live to see his dream partly realized. He was shot dead by an assassin's bullet on April 4, 1968, at a hotel in Memphis.

By the end of Johnson's presidency blacks had made great strides. Thurgood Marshall was sworn in as the first black Supreme Court Justice in 1967, the same year the first black mayors of large cities were elected, in Gary, Indiana, and Cleveland, Ohio. The racial violence and upheavals of the 1960s were the labor pains of a new, more equitable social order. Great problems remained to be solved, but Johnson's civil rights legislation was genuinely epoch-making.

War on poverty

It was easier to extend the protection of the Constitution to Southern blacks than to do something about the poverty of their counterparts in northern ghettoes. The economy boomed under Johnson, stimulated by tax cuts, but left pockets like Watts and Harlem untouched. Johnson did make war on poverty, as he had promised. During his presidency spending on health, education and welfare

tripled, rising from 15 percent of the G.N.P. to 25 percent; military spending as a proportion of the G.N.P. actually declined, despite the Vietnam War.

The Medicare program, greatly expanded under subsequent Presidents, began defraying the medical costs of the elderly in 1966. The drive against inner city decay was spearheaded by the Office of Economic Opportunity, which ran many community action programs with the innovative aim of getting the poor themselves to plan and run anti-poverty projects. Although not always successful, they did leave a valuable legacy of neighborhood-oriented health, legal aid and self-help projects.

Vietnam

On domestic issues Johnson made significant advances. Yet no modern President endured more hatred, a strength of feeling that echoes down the years in the chant "Hey, hey, LBJ, how many kids did you kill today?" In the end, Vietnam would destroy his presidency.

Johnson had no experience in foreign affairs before becoming President, and inherited a complex web of commitments in Southeast Asia from Kennedy, which he felt bound to continue. When Kennedy died, the point of no return in Vietnam had still not been reached: there were around 14,000 U.S. servicemen backing the Saigon regime in its struggle against Vietcong guerrillas fighting to unite the country under Ho Chi Minh's leadership, but they were "advisers" and did not mount independent operations.

This was to change very quickly. Johnson felt obliged to hang tough in foreign affairs, and forfeited much liberal support in 1965, when he sent the Marines into the Dominican Republic to stifle a popular uprising against a conservative regime. It was the escalation of hostilities in Vietnam, however, that turned disaffection into violent protest.

Johnson and the Pentagon believed that the quickest way to end the war was to bring the full weight of American firepower to bear. In February, 1965, the President ordered the bombing of North Vietnam; in March, Marines landed near Danang and American units went into combat – the Rubicon had been crossed. By the end of 1965, there were 185,000 troops in Vietnam, rising to 386,000 a year later, and over 500,000 by the end of Johnson's presidency. Young Americans fled the country in their thousands to avoid the draft. Vietnam, with all its attendant horrors, was the first television war, beamed into millions of homes. Shocked by what they saw, hundreds of thousands joined a mounting wave of protests, pickets and demonstrations. By the time Johnson left the White House, 222,351 servicemen had been killed or injured. The scars the Vietnam War left on

A G.I. photographed with a Vietnamese captive. Media images of the war's realities horrified the public and did irreparable damage to the Johnson administration. In 1968, with the military declaring that the communists were about to crack, North Vietnam and Vietcong forces launched the massive Tet offensive, seemingly foreshadowing further escalations of violence. The American public had enough and it became virtually impossible for LBJ to stand as a candidate for re-election in that year.

America have still not healed.

The United States lost the war perhaps because it was unwinnable from the start. The Vietcong could not easily be distinguished from civilians, and too often the American response was to bomb and shoot indiscriminately, as at My-lai in 1968 when over 200 Vietnamese died. Endless search and destroy missions were mounted against an invisible enemy in the countryside, while the cities were being infiltrated. By 1968, it was clear the U.S. military was becoming hideously entangled. Then on January 30 came the Tet offensive. In a coordinated attack on over 100 cities and towns, the Vietcong showed military flair and capabilities that belied Pentagon claims the war was being won. Hue, South Vietnam's second city, was taken, and even the defenses of the U.S. embassy in Saigon were breached. When the Vietcong melted away, they left Johnson's Southeast Asian policy in pieces among the rubble. The respected television journalist Walter Cronkite pronounced that "it now seems more certain than ever that the bloody experience of Vietnam is to end in a stalemate." Johnson, watching in the White House, said that if he had lost Cronkite he had lost America, and he was right. It was clear that Vietcong could not be bombed to the conference table, and in March, 1968, Johnson ordered a partial halt to the bombing. Peace talks began in Paris two months later; they would drag on for four more years of bloodletting.

The end of the presidency

In primaries early in 1968, Eugene McCarthy and Robert Kennedy, promising an end to the war, won enough votes to make it clear Johnson would split the Democratic party if he stood again, and in the same televised address that announced the bombing pause he ruled himself out of the race. Robert Kennedy was assassinated by a deranged gunman in June, and Hubert Humphrey ended up with the nomination. The Chicago convention, in 1968, was the most violent in American history. In what an official report called a "police riot," antiwar demonstrators were attacked, and Humphrey was nominated to the sound of pitched battles outside the hall and fist fights within it. Johnson's Vietnam policy was confirmed, but the Democrats would be crushed in the election that followed. It was a sad, squalid and violent end to a presidency that would without Vietnam have been remembered as a time of liberal advance.

Johnson retired to his ranch near Johnson City, Texas, and wrote *The Vantage Point* (1971), his version of the presidential years. He hoped to be remembered as "the man who saved Asia and Vietnam and did something for the Negroes of this country." He lived quietly with his wife, Claudia "Lady Bird" Johnson, whom he had married in 1934. The couple had two daughters. He died of a heart attack in San Antonio on January 22, 1973, the day before the Paris peace accords were signed.

RICHARD NIXON

R ichard Nixon, who became President in January, 1969, is remembered as the first chief executive to resign, driven from office by the Watergate scandal in 1974. Yet only two years before the day he bade a tearful farewell to the White House, he had seemed the most daring and successful of Presidents – the architect of a new policy of détente with Russia and China which promised to move the world beyond the dangerous tensions of the Cold War. He had made historic journeys to Moscow and Peking, returning with the first nuclear arms limitation treaty with the Soviet Union and the promise of normal relations with China. He withdrew American troops from Vietnam. Then, when acclaimed even by opponents, he overstepped the bounds of his office and was brought low by violations of the Constitution he had sworn to uphold.

Thirty-seventh President 1969-1974

Humble origins

Richard Milhous Nixon was born on January 9, 1913, in the small town of Yorba Linda, California. His Quaker parents were typical members of what Nixon would later call the "Silent Majority" – godfearing, hardworking and ordinary. The Nixons owned a small grocery store, and when Richard was a teenager they put him in charge of the vegetable section. It was the profits from the sale of potatoes and tomatoes that the youngster used to put himself through Whittier College, from which he graduated in 1934. He went on to Duke University Law School, qualifying as a lawyer in 1937.

For a few years he practiced law, gaining a reputation as a quick-witted and skillful young counsel. In 1942, he moved to Washington, D.C., where he worked for six months as a staff lawyer in the Office of Price Administration before enlisting in the Navy. Like his future opponent John Kennedy, he fought with distinction in the South Pacific, winning two battle stars and two commendations. In 1946, he entered Congress as Republican Representative for his home district in California.

A meteoric rise

Nixon's political career was marked by an extraordinary resilience, and from the start he showed a genius for self-publicity which even his opponents admitted. As a young Congressman he quickly made a name for himself in conservative circles, helping to draft an act that made union officials file affidavits swearing that they were not communists, and serving on the House Un-American Activities Committee with Senator Joseph McCarthy.

It was the Alger Hiss case which gave Nixon a national reputation as a hard line anti-communist – as well as the enduring hostility of many liberal Americans. Hiss, an official in the State Department, was accused of passing secrets to the Soviets, and Nixon caused a sensation not only through his exposure but through his willingness to exploit a widespread fear of communism. Hiss, who denied being a communist, was convicted of perjury. Nixon put the publicity he received to good effect in 1950, when he was

elected Senator for California, a remarkable feat for a first-term Congressman.

Vice President and defeat

Nixon was a tireless Senator, and his energetic campaign work, criss-crossing the country to speak on behalf of candidates or at party functions, soon made him a popular man within the Republican party. So in 1952, when Nixon was only 39, Eisenhower picked him as his running mate. Elected and then re-elected along with Ike in 1956, Nixon spent the next eight years as Vice President.

He became experienced in foreign affairs, representing Eisenhower abroad and visiting 55 countries. Three times he quietly filled in for Eisenhower during the President's illnesses, and he managed to negotiate a settlement in a bitter national steel strike in 1959. His experience, and Eisenhower's backing, made him the obvious Republican presidential candidate in 1960.

Although Nixon started the campaign as the favorite, he made a mistake toward the end of the campaign when he

Helmeted police look on as Vietnam veterans protest President Nixon's prolongation of the war, during convention week at Miami. Anti-war demonstrations peaked under Nixon on Moratorium Day, November 15, 1969, when some 250,000 people converged on Washington to march past the White House.

agreed to a series of televised debates with John Kennedy, whose charm contrasted with Nixon's slightly shifty television manner. The vote was the closest since 1888, with Nixon losing only by a whisker. He attempted a comeback, running for Governor of California in 1962, but lost again. Dubbed "Tricky Dicky" by journalists – and always sensitive to slights – he succumbed to bitterness. "Congratulations, gentlemen, you won't have Richard Nixon to kick around any more," was his bitter reaction to the press, apparently conceding that his career was at an end.

Victory in 1968

In 1963, Nixon joined a law firm in New York, but did not retire from politics as had been expected. He remained

Edwin "Buzz" Aldrin unpacks equipment on the moon's surface during the historic Apollo 11 mission of July 20, 1969. The first men on the moon, astronauts Aldrin and Neil Armstrong spent more than 21 hours on the lunar surface and collected 48.5 lbs of soil and rock samples. Armstrong also planted the U.S. flag and unveiled a plaque reading: "Here men from planet Earth first set foot upon the moon, July 1969 AD. We came in peace for all mankind." The pair then returned with Michael Collins in the command module to a safe splashdown in the Pacific. Minutes later, in quarantine aboard the carrier USS Hornet, *they were greeted by an exuberant President Nixon.*

popular with Republicans, began to speak and campaign again, then entered and won the Republican primaries in 1968, capping an astonishing comeback by walking away with the nomination. His presidential campaign was low on specifics: he talked vaguely of "secret plans" to end the war in Vietnam "on honorable terms," but public feuding by Democratic politicians was such that the people put the grocer's boy into the White House with 44 percent of the popular vote against 43 percent for the Democrat Hubert H. Humphrey.

Vietnam: escalation and disengagement

In his inaugural address Nixon pledged, "I shall consecrate my office, my energies and all the wisdom I can muster to the cause of peace among nations," and nowhere was there more need for peace than in Vietnam.

Over the next three years, Nixon followed a double-edged policy in Southeast Asia. On the one hand he tried to placate the antiwar movement by announcing the phased withdrawal of U.S. ground forces in early 1969; the first

troops left in July. But at the same time he compensated the Pentagon by escalating and extending the bombing campaign. His "secret plan" was exactly that: early in 1969, he was clandestinely sending B-52s against Cambodia and Laos, as the Pentagon had long and vainly urged Johnson to do. The bombings, which caused heavy civilian casualties in attempts to destroy Vietcong bases, were kept secret from Congress and the American people by a system of false bombing reports. They were meant to force concessions from the North Vietnamese in the Paris peace talks. But the strategy failed, and in April, 1970, Nixon lost patience and sent U.S. ground forces into Cambodia, only a week after announcing that a further 150,000 troops would be withdrawn from Vietnam. The sudden volte-face caused a storm of protest among antiwar activists. In one demonstration at Kent State University, in Ohio, jittery National Guardsmen opened fire, killing four students and wounding ten. Two black students were shot dead the same week in Mississippi, and the student movement was driven to a new pitch of fury. Shaken by the fierce condemnations, Nixon quickly withdrew the troops from Cambodia and reverted to airpower: more tons of bombs were dropped on Indochina between 1969 and 1972 than were dropped in all theaters of war during the whole of World War II.

The pressure grew on Nixon to break the impasse. Vietnam threatened to be a major issue for the Democrats in 1972, and public disaffection grew still more when *The New York Times* started to publish the Pentagon Papers in 1971, a leaked and shockingly frank Pentagon history of U.S. involvement in Southeast Asia.

Early in 1972 Nixon acted. In the Paris peace talks the link between U.S. and North Vietnamese withdrawal was dropped; the war was defused as a campaign issue when both sides declared "peace is at hand," and on January 23, 1973, with Nixon safely re-elected, the peace accords were finally signed. North Vietnam released 590 American prisoners, the last U.S. troops left Vietnam in March, and the bombing of Cambodia ended in August. The long nightmare was coming to an end. As the North Vietnamese gathered their strength for the final push against the Saigon regime, the United States was left to count the cost of involvement: 46,000 dead, nearly 200,000 wounded, and hundreds of thousands of Vietnamese, Cambodian and Laotian casualties.

Domestic issues

One reason why foreign affairs loomed so large in Nixon's first term was that he was the first President since Zachary Taylor to contend with both houses of Congress under the control of the opposing party. This limited his room for maneuver, and the flood of domestic legislation passed during Johnson's presidency soon dried up.

Domestic attention shifted to the judiciary. Nixon had long been convinced that the Supreme Court had moved too far to the left on race and civil liberties. In 1969, Chief Justice Warren, whose Court had handed down many landmark liberal decisions, retired. He was replaced by the respected conservative Chief Justice Burger, but the Senate rejected the names Nixon sent for confirmation to fill two other places on the Court, and in the end the Burger Court, like Supreme Courts before it, turned out to be stubbornly independent. In 1970, it gave 18-year-olds the vote; in 1972, it declared the death penalty unconstitutional; and in 1973, it struck down all state laws that prevented abortion in the first six months of pregnancy.

Nixon's presidency also marked the culmination of the American space program. On July 20, 1969, Neil Armstrong became the first man to step onto the moon's surface, and Skylab, America's first manned space station, was launched in 1973.

Détente

Détente with the Soviet Union and China was Nixon's most spectacular achievement. It is ironic that Nixon, who built his career on fighting communism, was the first President to set foot in Moscow and Peking, but it was his impeccable anti-communist credentials that made it possible. The "Silent Majority" knew Nixon was not "soft on communism," and trusted him where they might have turned on a more liberal President.

Détente was the brainchild of Secretary of State Henry Kissinger, an able, ambitious and occasionally ruthless man who believed the United States and the communist powers "circle each other like two blind men in a dark room. Over time they are capable of doing great damage to each other. Not to mention the damage to the room." Kissinger convinced Nixon that more stable relations with both the Soviet Union and China could be achieved if each side strove for strategic balance.

In February, 1972, Nixon flew to China. The one-time communist hunter joked with Mao Tse-Tung and crossed chopsticks instead of swords with Chou En-Lai. The visit lasted six days, the longest state visit by a President in history, during which Nixon toured the Forbidden City and walked on the Great Wall. The journey ended with a statement undertaking to expand ties between the two countries, and it was a landmark: the final American recognition of Mao's revolution, after over two decades of mutual hostility. U.S. support ensured China's swift admission to the United Nations, which put an end to the absurd situation where the country which contained a quarter of the world's population was not represented in the General Assembly.

The journey to Moscow in May, 1972, resulted in SALT I, the first Strategic Arms Limitation Treaty, signed to world acclaim in Moscow at the end of the visit. Even sworn political enemies congratulated Nixon and hailed détente as a great and remarkable achievement.

The 1972 election

Everything seemed to go right for Nixon in his re-election campaign. Détente had captured the popular imagination, peace seemed to be at hand in Vietnam, and the Democrats had split over the nomination of the liberal Senator George McGovern, who was distrusted by the conservative wing of the party. Nixon won a crushing victory, carrying every state save Massachusetts and the District of Columbia, with 61 percent of the vote.

Popular at home and admired abroad, Nixon was at the peak of his career. Yet it was during this triumphant campaign that the first signs appeared of "a cancer growing

THE NIXON YEARS

1969 Richard Nixon is inaugurated 37th President. Astronauts Armstrong and Aldrin walk on moon.

1970 Kent State shootings occur.

1971 Pentagon Papers are published.

1972 Nixon visits Peking and Moscow. Nixon is re-elected in a landslide.

1973 U.S. troops withdraw from Vietnam. Watergate affair becomes a national scandal.

1974 Nixon resigns under threat of impeachment.

on the presidency." On June 17, 1972, a burglary had taken place at the Democratic Party headquarters in the Watergate building in Washington. The break-in was bungled and the perpetrators were arrested, in an affair which led to scandal, outrage and the worst constitutional crisis since the Civil War.

WATERGATE

On March 19, 1973, the leader of the Watergate burglars, James McCord, wrote a letter to the judge presiding over his trial. The judge suspected there was more to the case than met the eye, and threatened to throw the book at the defendants unless they came clean. McCord, frightened, claimed important figures in the Republican Party had ordered the break-in and persuaded his co-defendants to stay silent about the connection with payments of hush money. Investigations began that soon uncovered trails leading to the White House.

From the beginning Nixon denied all knowledge of the burglary and cover-up. On June 22, 1972, he had issued a statement: "I can say categorically that no one on the White House staff, no one in this Administration presently employed, was involved in this very bizarre incident." He promised full investigations and punishment of the guilty, and appointed a Special Prosecutor, Archibald Cox. The Senate formed an investigation committee headed by the Senator from North Carolina, Sam Ervin, and the committee members were spurred on in their efforts to discover the truth by a series of reports in *The Washington Post*.

Top Presidential aides were soon implicated. Advisers Haldeman and Ehrlichman, Presidential counsel John Dean and Attorney General Kleindienst resigned under pressure in April, 1973, and Nixon's presidency began to sink under the weight of scandal. Impeachment was first whispered, then openly canvassed.

Paralysis at the top

Watergate was compounded by a series of other damaging scandals. The "secret" bombing of Cambodia was revealed, infuriating a Congress which believed it alone had the constitutional right to make war. In August, 1973, Vice President Spiro Agnew resigned in disgrace to face trial on charges of graft and tax evasion while serving as Governor of Maryland: he was fined $10,000 and given three years' probation. It was revealed Nixon himself only paid a total of $1,600 in income tax from 1969 to 1972, years when his annual income was over $500,000. Humiliatingly, he had to pledge publicly he would pay $500,000 in back taxes.

As the Administration began to lose the capacity to govern, world events seemed to run beyond its control. In October, 1973, the Middle East erupted in the Yom Kippur War, followed by an Arab oil embargo; inflation leapt into double figures and an energy crisis began as OPEC quadrupled oil prices. And all the time the United States, preoccupied with Watergate, turned in upon itself.

Decline . . .

In July, 1973, John Dean told conservative Senator Barry Goldwater that Nixon had been lying when he said he knew nothing of the cover-up. Before a horrified Ervin and a captivated television audience, Dean also detailed his accusations: that the President had improperly used the F.B.I. and C.I.A. to block investigations, that dirty tricks, bribery and corruption were endemic in the Administration, and that Nixon had installed a taping system in the White House which could prove everything. A battle royal then developed over the tapes.

Special Prosecutor Cox subpoenaed 64 tapes; Nixon, pleading "executive privilege," refused to give them up. When Cox pressed further, Nixon ordered Attorney General Richardson to sack him. Both Richardson and his deputy resigned rather than comply, until Cox was finally fired by

The Watergate affair approaches crisis point, July 1974, as the House Judiciary Committee decides to recommend the impeachment of President Nixon. The voting was 27 votes to 11, many Republicans joining with the Democrats on the committee in pressing for impeachment. On the strength of these figures it was clear that the full House would also vote against the President.

the third ranking official in the Justice Department. The outcry forced Nixon to appoint another Special Prosecutor and hand over some of the tapes – which were found to have been erased at vital points. What remained showed a Nixon very different from his public image: he was, in particular, notably foulmouthed – "expletive deleted" became a national catchphrase. In public, however, he continued to deny everything: "I am not a crook," he pledged on television.

. . . . and fall

The final act of the drama began in May, 1974, when the House Judiciary Committee began impeachment hearings. In July, the committee recommended three Articles of Impeachment, accusing Nixon of conspiracy to obstruct justice in the Watergate cover-up, abuse of power, and unconstitutional defiance of committee subpoenas. On the first two counts many Republican committee members voted with the Democrats, showing Nixon would lose his case in the House of Representatives. He pinned his hopes on mustering a third of the Senate behind him, but on July 24, the Supreme Court struck down his plea of "executive privilege" and ordered him to release the remaining tapes, which he finally did on August 5.

One contained a conversation with adviser Haldeman on June 23, 1972, the day after Nixon had issued his statement denying all knowledge of the burglary. Nixon ordered Haldeman to use the C.I.A. to get the F.B.I. to "drop the investigation, period." It was the long-awaited "smoking

gun," with the President's fingerprints clearly visible on it. The Republicans who had believed in his innocence deserted as it became clear they had been lied to. Goldwater told Nixon he would lose the Senate vote. It was the end.

Kissinger would describe how the distraught Nixon, worse the wear for drink, knelt with him in prayer and then broke down on the carpet, sobbing and banging his fist on the floor. Finally, on August 9, 1974, he wrote a short note to Kissinger: "Dear Mr. Secretary. I hereby resign the office of the President of the United States. Richard Nixon."

Lessons of Watergate

Damaging though the revelations of wrongdoing at the heart of government were, many saw the traumatic experience of Watergate as a salutary and valuable demonstration of a vital fact: the United States has a Constitution, and it can be made to work. It was not the press which destroyed Nixon, but the law as enforced by Congress and the Courts. As Senator Sam Ervin said, "One of the great advantages of having three separate branches of government is that it's difficult to corrupt all three at the same time."

Granted a Presidential pardon by Gerald Ford, Nixon retired to San Clemente, his California home, together with his wife Pat, whom he had married in 1940; the couple had two daughters. After the nightmare of Watergate, he attempted to rehabilitate his presidency, writing his memoirs and giving occasional interviews.

GERALD FORD

Gerald R. Ford

Gerald Ford was sworn in as thirty-eighth President on August 9, 1974, in the White House. He had been an obscure Congressman for most of his political life, and neither expected nor wanted any high office. Thrust into the Oval Office by Nixon's resignation, he had to restore battered public confidence in government without the authority of an elected mandate: almost the first words he uttered as President were, "I am acutely aware that you have not elected me as your President by your ballots."

It was a time of inflation and rising unemployment at home and fragile détente abroad. Many doubted Ford's capacity for government at the highest level: Ford himself had self-effacingly said, "I am a Ford, not a Lincoln" when he was sworn in as Vice President. Yet his straightforward manner compared favorably with the evasions of his immediate predecessor, and over time his virtues of modesty and amiable decency earned him popularity and a certain measure of respect. When he narrowly lost the election of 1976, he went into retirement leaving the presidency in better shape than he had found it. A caretaker administration it may have been, but it began the process of reconciliation between government and people so necessary after Watergate.

Early years
Gerald Rudolph Ford was born Leslie Lynch King, Jr. on July 14, 1913, in Omaha, Nebraska. When he was 2 years

Thirty-eighth President 1974-1977

old, his parents were divorced, and he moved with his mother to Grand Rapids, Michigan. There she met and married businessman Gerald R. Ford, who adopted her son and gave him his name. After high school in Grand Rapids, the young Ford went to the University of Michigan in 1932, graduating in 1935. He studied law, but his consuming passion was football. He was an outstanding player, voted Most Valuable Player in college football in 1934, and he could have had a lucrative career as a professional. Ford chose law instead, and after working as a ranger in Yellowstone National Park over the summer of 1936, he entered Yale University Law School. There he contented himself with coaching football rather than playing it professionally, and graduated in 1941, in the top third of his law class.

Pearl Harbor interrupted Ford's career almost before it began. He enlisted in the Navy, spent four years on active service from 1942, fighting in the Pacific and reaching the rank of lieutenant commander. In 1948, he entered Congress as Representative for his home district. He always retained the loyal affection of Grand Rapids voters: in 12 subsequent Congressional elections his vote never dipped below 60 percent.

Congressman and Vice President
Ford once accurately described himself as "a moderate in domestic affairs, a conservative in fiscal affairs, and a dyed-in-the-wool internationalist in foreign affairs." He was

Queues at gas stations became a familiar sight under Gerald Ford, though through no fault of the President. The crisis began in 1973 with the Yom Kippur war in the Middle East. Arab producers declared an oil boycott and then, learning the strength of united action, worked within OPEC to announce a gigantic price hike: from $3 a barrel before the war to $11.65 a barrel. In the United States gas prices doubled overnight and the inflationary effects, hitting all petroleum products and petroleum-powered machinery, afflicted the whole economy.

completely loyal to the Republican Presidents he served under, first Eisenhower and then Nixon. He was an inconspicuous but diligent worker behind the scenes, served on the Warren Commission investigating the murder of Kennedy, and became minority leader in the House in 1965. He seemed set for a career of distinguished but largely unnoticed public service, when Spiro Agnew resigned as Vice President in 1973. Nixon needed a successor untainted by the whiff of scandal, who could be relied on not to plot against him. Ford fitted the bill perfectly.

Ford managed with some dignity the difficult task of being Vice President when the President was tottering. Ever the loyal party man, he accepted Nixon's protestations of innocence and stoutly defended him in public. Although a team within the State Department did begin work to ensure a smooth transition in May, 1974, it was without Ford's knowledge or consent.

When he took over the presidency he nominated Nelson Rockefeller as Vice President under the 25th Amendment, which meant that for the first time in American history both President and Vice President were appointed rather than elected. Ford tried to clear the atmosphere by immediately declaring, "I expect to follow my instincts of openness and candor." He retained Kissinger as Secretary of State, and settled down to tackle the mass of problems that had been piling up as political attention was focused on Watergate.

Nixon pardoned

Even out of office Nixon sparked controversy. Within a month of taking office, Ford granted Nixon a Presidential pardon for all crimes he had "committed or . . . may have committed" while in office. It was not a popular action in many quarters. It was suspected – wrongly – that Ford and Nixon had struck a deal, with the ex-President making his resignation conditional on the promise of a pardon. It seemed inconsistent that Nixon's confederates should be jailed while Nixon accepted a pardon without admitting guilt. Ford defended himself saying his purpose was to draw a line marking the end of Watergate "in order to heal the wounds." Many came to accept his reasoning in time.

Recession and energy crisis

Ford's most immediate problem was the parlous state of the American economy. In 1974, oil price rises prodded inflation up to a postwar peak of 12 percent. In October, Ford convened a meeting of economists to discuss what should be done, and the orthodox solution of slowing the economy down was adopted. Unfortunately, the effect was to turn a slump into a full-blown recession: 1975 was the worst year for the American economy since the black days of the Depression. Production plummeted, factories closed, and unemployment leapt to 9 percent of the workforce, 8.25 million, another melancholy postwar record. Welfare spending, on Medicare and the food stamps program, had to be

Left: *Vietnamese women and children crouch in a U.S. helicopter evacuating refugees from a fighting zone towards the end of the Vietnam war. The last U.S. combat troops left in March 1973, though the United States continued to supply arms to the South. In the spring of 1975 the North Vietnamese armies intensified their push and the dispirited forces of South Vietnam completely collapsed. As the military situation worsened President Ford tried to persuade Congress to stem the tide with yet more arms supplies. Congress, however, refused, and in April Saigon fell.*

Right: *As the communists arrived, panic gripped the South and half the rural population fled to the cities. About 140,000 Vietnamese were evacuated before North and South were united under a single communist government (1976).*

increased to cope with the rise in poverty. By 1976, recession had pushed inflation back down to 5 percent, but the social costs were considerable.

Things were made worse by the energy crisis. Ever since OPEC had raised oil prices, the American people were made forcefully aware of how much they had come to depend on imported oil, 30 percent of which came from the volatile Middle East. In 1974 and 1975, there were periodic panics: drivers waited in line for hours, gas pumps ran dry, gas stations closed down. To Americans, used to cheap and abundant fuel, the shock was profound. Ford acted to reduce gas consumption, imposing new speed limits on federal highways, while Congress passed the Energy Policy and Conservation Act in 1975, aiming to boost domestic production and encourage other sources of energy. The era of cheap oil had gone forever, and new limits were imposed on economic growth as a result.

Abroad: détente and defeat

Foreign policy, which had remained under Henry Kissinger's direction, was not affected by the change of Presidents in 1974. Ford's experience of foreign affairs was minimal; nevertheless, he chose to involve himself energetically and, in late 1974, he braved the Siberian cold to meet the Soviet Union's General Secretary, Leonid Brezhnev, near Vladivostok. He returned with detailed agreements, negoti-

ated by Kissinger, putting limits on certain categories of nuclear weapons. Most observers felt he had coped well with his first steps on the world stage, and he returned with enhanced prestige.

Satisfaction was soon clouded by anguish, however, as in the spring of 1975, the final curtain was brought down on U.S. involvement in Indochina. The Vietcong and the Khmer Rouge in Cambodia launched their final offensives, driving all before them. Saigon and Phnom Penh fell within two weeks of each other in April. The U.S. fleet standing offshore evacuated 140,000 Vietnamese and 12,000 Americans, leaving behind many Vietnamese who had backed the U.S. and now faced an uncertain future. There were chaotic scenes as desperate crowds mobbed the airport and the U.S. embassy, and helicopters were thrown into the sea from the clogged flightdecks of aircraft carriers to allow others to land. It was an ignominious end to the first war America had lost.

Frustration increased in May when the Cambodian Khmer Rouge boarded the Mayaguez, an American ship, and held the 39 crew members. Ford sent in the Marines and all the crew were freed unharmed. The action met wide approval, although some cynics pointed out the number of crew released exactly matched the number of servicemen killed in the operation.

Détente with Russia continued with the signing of the

Helsinki agreement in the summer of 1975. It was not popular in many quarters: it recognized existing European frontiers, and critics accused Ford of ratifying Russian domination of Eastern Europe in return for vague and unenforceable Russian commitments to human rights.

In the Middle East, Kissinger's tireless "shuttle diplomacy" was rewarded with a peace agreement in late 1975 between Israel and Egypt, which provided for military disengagement in the Sinai Peninsula. It was the clearest foreign policy success of Ford's administration, preparing the ground for later advances.

Hostile Congress

In both foreign and domestic affairs, Ford was handicapped by a House of Representatives and Senate firmly under Democratic control and determined to reassert their authority over policy. Chastened legislators refused Ford's attempts to send military aid to the crumbling regime in Saigon, and blocked his efforts to back one of the sides in the Angolan civil war in 1976. At home, both the Senate and House regularly passed bills raising federal spending, undermining Ford's attempts to cut the federal budget. The result was that Ford used his powers of veto much more freely than previous Presidents, striking down 55 bills in all and getting 44 of the vetoes to stick – a tribute to his long negotiating experience in Congress.

Defeat in 1976

Ford always felt, understandably, that he could not have full authority as President until he had a mandate from the electorate. But before he could run for President he had to face a strong challenge from within his own party, where conservatives grouped behind Ronald Reagan. The two had a closely fought battle for the nomination: both won important primaries but Ford just managed to carry the convention. The fact that an incumbent President had had to fight so hard to get the nomination seemed to bode ill for the campaign against Democratic nominee Jimmy Carter.

Although Carter began with a big lead, Ford whittled most of it away during the campaign. He ended up losing by a margin of only 2 percent in the popular vote, 297 to 241 in the Electoral College, the narrowest victory since 1960. The first words the victorious Carter spoke as President were both gracious and appropriate; "For myself and for our nation, I want to thank my predecessor for all he has done to heal our land."

Retirement

Ford retired to Grand Rapids with his wife Elizabeth ("Betty" as she is popularly known) whom he had married in 1948. The couple had four children, three sons and a daughter. The ex-President devoted himself to his memoirs, and assumed the role of a respected elder statesman.

JIMMY CARTER

Jimmy Carter [signature]

When Jimmy Carter was sworn in as thirty-ninth President of the United States on January 20, 1977, he spoke of a "new dedication within our government and a new spirit among us all." His election was proof enough of that. Disillusioned with Washington insiders, voters had chosen a man whose entire political career had been spent within Georgia, the state of his birth, and whose campaign theme had been the pledge "I'll never lie to you." With Carter's arrival in the White House the presidency finally emerged from the long shadow of Watergate.

Watergate was not the only bitter memory Carter's election was meant to exorcise, for the new President had promised a long-sought amnesty for Vietnam draft evaders, enabling them to come home at last. He also spoke with a Southern drawl unheard in the White House since Zachary Taylor. He symbolized a resurgent, more racially harmonious South, and his arrival in the White House, carried by a tide of black votes, was evidence of how far the South had come in a very short time. Some even went so far as to see his presidency as the final healing of the North-South divide in American politics dating back to the Civil War and beyond.

When he began his term, Carter was almost universally seen as a thoughtful, decent and intelligent man. Yet in the end the fact that he was so much an outsider worked against him, as an unruly Congress blocked or watered down most of his domestic program. Abroad, diplomatic

Thirty-ninth President 1977-1981

successes with the Soviets, the Panama Canal and the Middle East were succeeded by the long agony of the Iranian hostage crisis, when the American people turned on the most powerful man in the world because he was unable to obtain the release of a few dozen diplomats. The tide of frustrated anger swept Carter from office: the President's intelligence and humanity had been overwhelmed by events, and the promise of his early days remained unfulfilled.

Georgia childhood
Few presidents had such deep and long-lasting connections with the place of their birth as James Earl Carter, born on October 1, 1924, in the small town of Plains, Georgia, where he would live and work all his life when not holding elected office. His parents were peanut farmers, neither very poor nor very rich, and from an early age the future President was helping out with chores in the fields and house, and selling bags of peanuts on the dusty town streets. He had the sort of rural Southern childhood that Mark Twain would have recognized: he had a gang of friends as a child, many of them black, and later remembered, "We hunted, fished, explored, worked and slept together. We ground sugar cane, plowed mules, pruned watermelons, dug and bedded sweet potatoes, mopped cotton, stacked peanuts, cut stovewood, pumped water..." This early experience of racial togetherness left him with a deep hostility toward segregation and discrimination that would stay with him for the rest of his life.

Jimmy Carter sits between Egypt's President Anwar Sadat and Israeli Prime Minister Menachem Begin as the three statesmen sign the historic Camp David agreement. The new understanding between Israel and Egypt resulted in part from two years of patient "shuttle diplomacy" by Henry Kissinger, but Carter played a crucial role in mediating the framework for a peace treaty, signed by both parties in March 1979. Negotiations had been conducted the year before at Camp David, the official country retreat of the President, in Maryland's Appalachian mountains. (Officially, Camp David "becomes" the White House whenever the President is in residence.)

He attended high school in Plains, with the ambition of one day going to the United States Naval Academy at Annapolis. To fulfill its entry requirements he spent a year in junior college at Georgia Southwestern, and a further year at the Georgia Institute of Technology. He went to Annapolis in 1944, graduating 59th in a class of 820 in 1946, and began seven years in the Navy during which he would rise from ensign to the rank of lieutenant commander.

He entered the then infant nuclear submarine program, becoming an engineering expert specializing in reactor technology. Then in 1953, his father died. After deep thought, the young officer decided to return to civilian life and the family farm, becoming the seventh generation of Carters to work the land around Plains.

From peanut farmer to governor

Under Carter's direction the family farm prospered. The peanut acreage was extended, and the family went into retailing peanuts as well as growing them. They also built up a sideline selling fertilizers. Jimmy became a prominent civic leader in Plains, but was often at odds with his fellow citizens. He and his family adamantly refused to join segregationist bodies like the White Citizen's Council, a courageous stand to take in those years. He was also deeply religious, fighting long and hard to open his Baptist congregation to worshippers of all races, finally succeeding in 1976.

Using his business connections and his status as a civic leader in Plains as a base, he was elected to the Georgia Senate in 1962. He made his first attempt to run for Governor of Georgia in 1966. At that time he was so unknown even within his own state that some Georgia newspapers dubbed him "Jimmy Who?" But by 1970, he had built up an effective organization, was elected, and moved to the governor's mansion in Atlanta. His victory was part of the changes that were sweeping through the South at that time. As blacks registered to vote and segregationists were in retreat, a new breed of young, liberal, white, Southern politicians was emerging. They were disliked by the older generation, and Carter's term of office was marked by acrimonious clashes with an older and generally more conservative state legislature. When he left office and announced he would run for President in December, 1974, very few people outside Plains took him seriously.

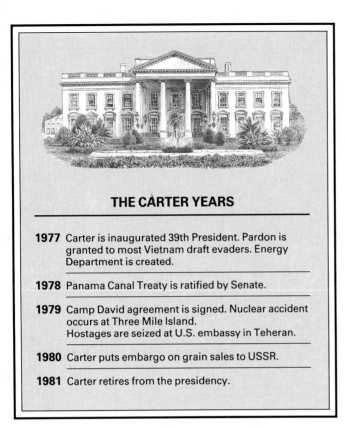

THE CARTER YEARS

1977 Carter is inaugurated 39th President. Pardon is granted to most Vietnam draft evaders. Energy Department is created.

1978 Panama Canal Treaty is ratified by Senate.

1979 Camp David agreement is signed. Nuclear accident occurs at Three Mile Island.
Hostages are seized at U.S. embassy in Teheran.

1980 Carter puts embargo on grain sales to USSR.

1981 Carter retires from the presidency.

Plains to Washington

Although it seemed that Jimmy Carter came from nowhere to take the Democratic nomination in 1976, in reality nearly two years of hard campaigning lay behind his sudden rise from obscurity. Often alone, he worked the towns and villages of Iowa and New Hampshire, and was rewarded with victories in the crucial early primaries, building up a momentum which took him to the nomination on the first ballot at the convention, with Senator Walter Mondale from Minnesota as his running mate.

The campaign against incumbent President Ford proved close, despite early predictions that Carter would win easily. He ended just 2 percent ahead, with 50.1 percent of the popular vote. Were it not for the fact that 92 percent of blacks voted for him, many newly registered in voting drives in 13 key states, and the solid support of the South, where loyalty to a fellow Southerner outweighed all other considerations, he would not have won.

Jeans in the White House

From the beginning the new President adopted a relaxed and informal style, creating a down-home atmosphere in the White House that many saw as a refreshing innovation. His first act after inauguration was to dispense with the usual limousine and walk down Pennsylvania Avenue with his family, waving to the cheering crowds. He immediately pardoned over 10,000 draft evaders, ending the last source of bitterness and division the Vietnam War had generated. His daughter Amy was enrolled at a public school, and the President appeared around the White House in jeans and sweaters, which he even wore for televised fireside chats, in the style of Franklin Roosevelt. But it would need more than an easygoing atmosphere in the White House to cope with the problems the Georgian inherited.

Economic woes and energy crisis

Once again, a sickly economy and the energy crisis were at the top of the domestic agenda. High world oil prices made inflation Carter's worst domestic problem during his administration: it rose from 4.8 percent when he took office to an unprecedented high of almost 20 percent when he left. It proved impervious to everything the government did. Carter kept federal spending down, interest rates up, and imposed voluntary ceilings on prices and wage increases. Here, as in other fields, he was hampered by a Senate and House full of Congressmen trying to increase federal spending to offset the effects of the slump in their districts. Party discipline grew laxer in the absence of experienced negotiators to act as mediators between an outsider President and insider politicians, and while President and Congress bickered, both inflation and unemployment crept remorselessly upward.

Nowhere was tension between President and Congress clearer than in energy policy. To Carter, the way ahead was clear. Domestic oil production had to be increased, energy conservation should be introduced, oil companies should be discouraged from withholding supplies, and all measures taken should be part of a coordinated national energy policy administered by a new Department of Energy. Yet Congress obstructed him at every turn. It did cooperate in the creation of the Energy Department in August, 1977. But when Carter moved to deregulate domestic oil prices, which he believed would lead to more conservation and oil exploration as prices rose, Congress blocked legislation until 1979. Despite Carter's efforts from 1977 onward, it took a wave of public outrage over large oil company profits in 1980 before Congress could be persuaded to pass legislation taxing windfall profits.

In 1979, an Iran in revolutionary turmoil cut off oil supplies to the United States. Once again there were panics reminiscent of the Ford years: drivers waited in lines, gas pumps ran dry, and in one case a man was shot dead in an argument over who had gotten to the pump first. There were some successes: domestic oil prices and production both rose, stimulated by deregulation, but so long as world oil prices remained high the energy crisis would not go away, and there was little an American President could do to alter the fact. A shadow was cast over one alternative, nuclear energy, by an accident at the Three Mile Island nuclear power station in Pennsylvania, in 1979, when over 100,000 people had to be evacuated from their homes.

Foreign policy and human rights

In keeping with his pledge to restore morality to government, Carter made a concern for human rights a central element of his foreign policy. He made this plain in his

Afghanistan, March 1980: the Soviet tank below was captured by rebels near the town of Khana close to the Pakistan border. Afghan guerrillas, sometimes as young as the boy soldier (right), resisted the invaders' military hardware, and in January 1980 President Carter announced punitive measures against the USSR, notably through an embargo on grain sales.

inaugural address, proclaiming, "Our moral sense dictates a clearcut preference for those societies which share with us an abiding respect for individual human rights, and our commitment to human rights must be absolute." It was, however, much easier to announce this policy than to put it into effect.

It often proved difficult to reconcile strategic interest with human rights. Carter was accused of double standards when he visited the Shah of Iran in December, 1977, for example, calling his country "an island of stability" and commenting on "the admiration and love which your people give to you." In fact, the Shah's arbitrary rule would last for little more than a year longer, as resentment that would flare into revolt in 1978 built up. The Iranians would not forget Carter's support for the Shah, and it was to have fateful consequences.

Nevertheless, human rights were at least placed on the agenda in a way they had not been during Kissinger's realpolitik. Many political prisoners all over the world had reason to be grateful for the American President's interest in their plight. When a popular revolt toppled the brutal Nicaraguan dictator Somoza in 1979, Carter resisted the temptation to prop him up, standing fast against conservative accusations he had "lost" Nicaragua. For a few years, American support for authoritarian Third World regimes was no longer automatic simply because they were anticommunist.

Success in Panama and the Middle East
The first half of the Carter administration was brightened by considerable achievements in foreign affairs, where great progress was made in two areas where previous Presidents had tried and failed to make headway.

The first was the final settlement of the Panama Canal question. Panamanian insistence that the Canal be returned to its jurisdiction pricked some American sensibilities – "we stole it fair and square" complained one aggrieved Senator – but could no longer be denied without seriously damaging U.S. relations with the whole of Latin America. After patient negotiations through 1977, in March and April, 1978, Carter succeeded where Johnson, Nixon and Ford had failed when he persuaded the Senate to ratify two treaties with Panama. The first returned the Canal to Panama by the year 2000, the second guaranteed the Canal's permanent neutrality. Impressive though this achievement was, it was overshadowed by perhaps the greatest achievement of the Carter presidency, the peace treaty between Israel and Egypt. In November, 1977, Egyptian President Anwar Sadat had made a historic visit to Israel, but since then the two old enemies had been

unable to agree a peace. In 1978, Carter invited Sadat and Israeli Prime Minister Begin to the Presidential retreat at Camp David. After days of complex negotiations, kept alive by Carter's patience and skill, tentative agreement was reached. It served as the basis for a peace treaty returning the Sinai Peninsula to Egypt signed in March, 1979. Although final peace in the Middle East was still elusive, critics and the American people were generous in their praise of Carter's efforts.

The end of détente
At first the Russians viewed the new President with unease. They reacted angrily to his outspoken support for Soviet dissidents and were displeased by his announcement of the establishment of full diplomatic relations with Peking in December, 1979. But the desire to obtain further agreements on nuclear arms overcame suspicions, and throughout 1978 and early 1979, negotiators worked on SALT 2, a second Strategic Arms Limitation Treaty. In a summit with General Secretary Leonid Brezhnev in June, 1979, in Vienna, Carter signed the treaty and the two leaders celebrated with a bearhug and kisses. Senate ratification was the next step.

Then in December, 1979, the Russians invaded Afghanistan, to save local communists who looked like losing a civil war. Carter bitterly recalled that "this action of the Soviets has made a more dramatic change in my own opinion of what the Soviets' ultimate goals are than anything they've done in the previous time I've been in office." In retaliation he withdrew SALT 2 from Senate consideration, effectively killing it, banned new grain sales to the Soviet Union, and persuaded the U.S. Olympic Committee to boycott the 1980 Moscow Olympic Games. Détente was effectively dead from the moment Russian tanks rumbled into Kabul, and a new era of hostility between the two superpowers began.

THE HOSTAGE CRISIS

In the space of a few weeks in late 1979, the Middle East, scene of Carter's diplomatic triumph only a few months before with the signing of the Egypt-Israel peace treaty, provoked the worst crisis of his administration and ultimately destroyed his hopes of re-election. In January, 1979, the Shah had fled Iran, driven out by revolt, and a theocratic anti-Western regime under the guidance of the Ayatollah Khomeini took his place. In October, the Shah begged to be admitted to the U.S. for medical treatment. The U.S. embassy in Iran warned that admitting him would provoke retaliation, but Carter decided on humanitarian grounds to do so. It was a fatal mistake.

Helicopter and aircraft wreckage in Iran betray the bungled plan to free the U.S. embassy hostages. Eight Americans were killed and five wounded in this attempt at a military rescue (which was to be achieved by means of a small commando force launched by helicopters from a battleship). The humiliation only intensified American feelings of frustration over the captives' continuing ordeal, and the whole calamitous episode completed President Carter's downfall.

On November 4, 1979, a large mob of revolutionary students, egged on by radical clerics, stormed the U.S. embassy in Tehran, overpowered the marine guards, and took 63 Americans hostage. Faced with this unprecedented violation of diplomatic convention, Carter froze Iranian assets in the U.S. and opened negotiations for the release of the hostages using the government of Algeria as an intermediary. The problem was that political instability in Iran was so great it was not clear who had the power to release the hostages. As days passed into weeks and weeks into months, an increasingly frustrated and angry public began to turn on a President apparently incapable of ending a national humiliation.

Carter unwisely gave in to the public desire for action, and ordered a military rescue attempt in April, 1980. It was a disaster: a helicopter collided with a transport plane at a desert assembly point in Iran, eight servicemen were killed, and the mission had to be aborted. Negotiations were set back for months, and Carter's popularity ratings plunged to depths unknown even to Nixon in the worst days of Watergate.

The hostages were finally released on January 21, 1980, the day Carter left office, in return for $8 billion of frozen Iranian assets. Carter, generously made special envoy by incoming President Reagan, flew to a U.S. base in West Germany to greet the hostages: he would later describe this along with Camp David, as the happiest moment of his presidency. Although he had been heavily criticized for his handling of the crisis, few were prepared to say what they would have done in his place.

Defeat in 1980

The campaign of 1980 was a lost cause for Carter from the start. He was facing a powerful opponent in Ronald Reagan, an extremely skilled campaigner whose relaxed television manner showed to good effect in a series of televised debates with a stiff and clearly nervous President. Inflation running at almost 20 percent at home and the open sore of the hostage crisis abroad had eroded confidence in President Carter far beyond repair. The final defeat was crushing: Reagan won 54 percent of the vote, and a Republican landslide gave the GOP control of the Senate and an increase of 33 seats in the House of Representatives. It was the first time in 48 years that an elected incumbent had failed to gain re-election.

Retirement

Jimmy Carter returned to the family peanut farm in Plains, together with his wife Rosalynn, whom he had married in 1946: the couple had three sons and a daughter. He wrote his memoirs, gave interviews, and settled comfortably back into the rural Southern background from which he came.

RONALD REAGAN

Ronald Reagan (signature)

R onald Reagan, sworn in as fortieth President in January, 1981, was at 69 the oldest man ever to be elected President. To many Americans he seemed to promise a return to an earlier and less complicated political era. He set the tone of his presidency in his inauguration speech, when he declared: "We are too great a nation to limit ourselves to small dreams ... we are not, as some would have us believe, doomed to an inevitable decline." Years of economic problems at home and reversals abroad had sapped American self-confidence, and voters found Reagan's optimistic vision of a brighter and better future irresistible. The one-time movie actor had landed his greatest role, the difference being, as he quipped, "in politics you not only have to get the part, you have to write the script as well."

His presidency would have its difficult moments. He would have to confront recession, rising international tensions, rising budget deficits and a stock market collapse; he would be damaged by the worst scandal since Watergate in his second term. But for most of the time Reagan remained a popular President, easily gaining re-election in 1984, with most people blaming his subordinates for failures and continuing to like the President. Although arguments over his administration may continue, it was if nothing else a public relations triumph. Not since Franklin Roosevelt had such a master image-maker occupied the Oval Office, and Reagan fully earned his nickname as "The Great Communicator."

Fortieth President 1981-

Small town background

Ronald Wilson Reagan was born on February 6, 1911, in Tampico, Illinois. While he was still a child the family moved to the small town of Dixon nearby, and it was there the future President grew up and attended high school. Both his parents were Democrats, and loyal supporters of the New Deal, and this most conservative of Presidents paradoxically began life as a liberal. At school Reagan became interested in acting and sports, as well as politics, and remembered, "I loved three things: drama, politics and sports, and I'm not sure they always came in that order." In his life the order was sports, drama and finally politics, as he developed successful careers in all his early interests.

Tall and athletic, Reagan graduated from Eureka College in 1932. It was a bad time to look for a job: the Depression was at its height, and so at first Reagan had to be content with a series of odd jobs, before his voice and self-assurance won him a post as a sports commentator with a radio station in Des Moines, specializing in baseball coverage. In 1937, he followed the Chicago Cubs baseball team to Los Angeles, and whilst there he was persuaded by his friends to take a screen test at the Warner Brothers studio in Hollywood. It was a good move; his dark good looks, mellow voice and presence landed him a contract, and he began the career which would make him a celebrity decades before he became a political figure.

Over the next 30 years Reagan starred in a series of

movies. Most of them were B-movies; he would be taunted in later life over *Bedtime for Bonzo*, in which he played an absent-minded professor and co-starred with a chimpanzee. Although in later years critics would poke fun at his films, he was in fact a very competent actor, and developed several skills that would stand him in good stead: no President would ever be as comfortable in front of the cameras.

It was during his Hollywood years that Reagan gained his first political experience. In 1937, he was elected to the board of the Screen Actor's Guild, the Hollywood trade union. After spending World War II making training films, with the rank of captain in the Air Force, he was elected president of the Guild in 1946, and served six terms. Around this time, his loyalty to the Democratic party began to falter. In 1952, he joined the Republican party, and in the same year married actress Nancy Davis. The couple would have a son and a daughter, to go with a son and a daughter from Reagan's previous marriage to the movie actress Jane Wyman.

During the 1950s Reagan combined work in movies and television with lectures and speeches in the conservative cause. In the early 1950s he antagonized many of his fellow movie stars when he enthusiastically cooperated with investigations of Hollywood undertaken by McCarthy's House Un-American Activities Committee. He was heavily involved in Goldwater's unsuccessful campaign for the presidency in 1964, endearing himself to right-wing Republicans with attacks on "big government" and high taxes. In 1966, he put his campaigning skills to work on his own behalf and was elected Governor of California by a margin of over 500,000 votes. He promised tax cuts and reduced spending: while his program was low on specifics it was masterfully presented.

He would be re-elected in 1970, but his two terms as Governor were mixed. He did succeed in cutting taxes and turned a $200 million state deficit in 1966 into a $50 million surplus by 1974. Critics charged this was at the expense of the poor, who bore the brunt of cuts in social spending. Students would remember him as the man who sent the National Guard to occupy the university campus at Berkeley to quell antiwar protests. In the state at large, however, he remained popular, and could have run for the Senate in 1974 when his second term ended. But Reagan had already set his sights on the presidency.

With the backing of conservatives he mounted a formidable challenge to Gerald Ford for the 1976 Republican nomination, and only just lost. In 1980, he crushed Texan George Bush in the race for the nomination, consoling him by bringing him onto the ticket as candidate for Vice

Ronald Reagan poses with co-star Diana Lynn in a publicity shot for the 1951 Bedtime for Bonzo, *certainly the most notorious of the President's early movies. Ronald Reagan made a total of 54 films in his early career as an actor, including many westerns, thrillers, comedies and war pictures. Not all were timekillers:* Warner Brothers' King's Row *(1942) was a major Hollywood production still respected for its powerful, if melodramatic, portrayal of smalltown America and in it Reagan gave a highly rated performance.*

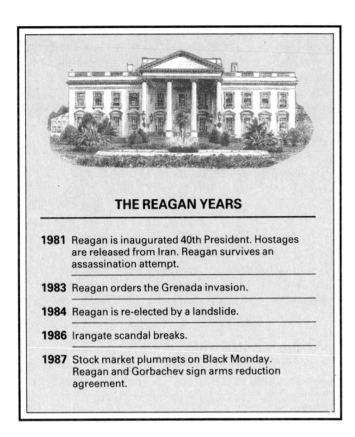

THE REAGAN YEARS

1981 Reagan is inaugurated 40th President. Hostages are released from Iran. Reagan survives an assassination attempt.

1983 Reagan orders the Grenada invasion.

1984 Reagan is re-elected by a landslide.

1986 Irangate scandal breaks.

1987 Stock market plummets on Black Monday. Reagan and Gorbachev sign arms reduction agreement.

was projected to save taxpayers a staggering $750 billion over his first term. Congress hesitated, and then on March 30, 1981, fate took a hand when John Hinckley, a mentally disturbed youth, shot and seriously wounded the President as he emerged from a Washington hotel.

Rushed to hospital, Reagan was able to walk into the emergency room and then collapsed. Doctors operated immediately, and although a bullet had pierced a lung and lodged less than an inch from the heart, Reagan made a rapid and complete recovery. The brave way the President coped with the incident, joking even when in pain, won him much praise, and a newly sympathetic Congress passed his budget in July.

Military build-up

The armed services were the one exception to the attack on federal spending. Reagan believed military weakness was one reason for American failures abroad during the 1970s, and was convinced the Soviets had gained an advantage in the arms race. So he gave the green light to projects long wanted by the Pentagon: the MX missile, the recommissioning of battleships, and SDI, the Strategic Defense Initiative, nicknamed "Star Wars," a futuristic plan to set up space defenses against incoming nuclear missiles. In Reagan's first term of office military spending increased by over a third: it was by far the largest peacetime military build-up in U.S. history.

The economy: recession and recovery

At first the American economy reacted badly to its new medicine. In 1981 and 1982, it slid into recession again: inflation fell from 13 percent to 5 percent, but unemployment leapt to over 10 percent of the workforce in 1982 for the first time since the Depression. It meant that gains in cutting federal spending were nullified, as welfare payments had to be stepped up, and the most Reagan was able to do was reduce the rate of growth of federal spending. Cutting it back proved impossible. Meanwhile, it was not until 1983 that the economy would emerge from recession, and not until 1984 would business really pick up.

Abroad: tensions and intervention

The invasion of Afghanistan confirmed Reagan in his belief that the Soviet Union was bent on world domination, and had to be discouraged by an assertive foreign policy that did not shrink from the use of military force. A new Cold War of rhetoric began: Reagan described Russia as "the Evil Empire." In Europe he prevailed upon his NATO allies to keep to the deployment of Cruise and Pershing nuclear missiles. In Central America he denounced the Sandinista

President. The campaign later that year against incumbent President Jimmy Carter was triumphant: Reagan worked his charm on television and let disillusion about inflation and the hostage crisis work to his advantage. Fifty-four percent of the vote swept him into office, and the conservative landslide gave the Republicans control of the Senate.

Change of direction

The new man in the White House had a new conservative prescription for the economy, part of a philosophy of government that aimed to reverse the trend of decades and "get government off the backs of the people." Reagan believed very strongly that "the taxing power of government must be used to provide revenue for legitimate government purposes. It must not be used to regulate the economy or bring about social change." Reagan proposed to cut taxes and reduce federal spending, to encourage private enterprise. The idea was that this would curb inflation and reduce unemployment as the economy got moving again.

In his first weeks he put this change of direction into effect when he presented Congress with a budget that cut taxes and reduced spending to the tune of $37 billion, and

The Irangate hearings cast a long shadow over President Reagan's second White House term. National Security Adviser John Poindexter was forced to resign, and great public attention focused on Colonel Oliver North who had organized the controversial arms deals and thought that combining them was a "neat idea." A much decorated Vietnam veteran, North was fired from the National Security Council by President Reagan who nevertheless called him a national hero. North himself testified: "I assumed that the President was aware of what I was doing and had, through my superiors, approved."

government in Nicaragua, and sent money, arms and advisers to El Salvador to counter leftist insurgents. Similar help was given on a larger scale to the "Contras," groups of disaffected Nicaraguan exiles raiding Nicaragua from its borders, in much the same way as Kennedy had supported Cuban exiles in their fight against Castro. Congress worried that the United States might be drawn directly into the conflict: an outcry in the Senate in April, 1984, forced Reagan to admit the C.I.A. had acted illegally in mining Nicaraguan ports and to call a halt to the operation. In the Middle East the Marines were sent into Beirut in August, 1982, to help supervise a ceasefire in the long-running Lebanese civil war.

The potential dangers of this increasing military involvement abroad were tragically demonstrated on October 23, 1983, when a suicide bomber drove a lorry packed with explosives into Marine headquarters at Beirut Airport, killing 241 U.S. servicemen. Only two days later came the most spectacular illustration of Reagan's more aggressive foreign policy with the invasion of the small Caribbean island of Grenada, ostensibly to protect 1,000 U.S. citizens caught in a coup. The action was swift; within a week the fighting was over. Forty-five Grenadians and 24 Cubans were killed, along with 18 U.S. servicemen. The action was

generally popular with the American public, who sent Reagan's popularity ratings soaring to new heights.

Relations with the Soviet Union, already tense, were made more difficult by a crisis of leadership in the Soviet Union during Reagan's first term. Death claimed successive leaders of an aging Politburo. In 1982, a period when Russia had four leaders in three years began. Brezhnev died, to be replaced by Yuri Andropov, who in turn died in 1984 and was replaced by Konstantin Chernenko. It was only in March, 1985, when Chernenko died and was replaced by the relatively youthful Mikhail Gorbachev, that the leadership vacuum was filled and serious discussions could begin.

The 1984 election: the Great Communicator triumphs
In 1984, the economy expanded rapidly, unemployment falling as production picked up, helped by the new "sunrise industries" as advances in computing and high technology were applied industrially. Despite increased poverty in some areas, and warnings that mounting budget deficits spelled economic trouble ahead, Reagan was more popular than ever. A mood of optimism and self-confidence was deftly orchestrated by the President through such events as the Los Angeles Olympic Games in 1984, replacing the doubts and complexities of the 1970s. So successful was

Reagan at deflecting awkward questions with disarming one-liners that some dubbed him "the Teflon President" – no criticism could be made to stick.

The 1984 election became a triumphal procession for Reagan. The Democrats nominated Walter Mondale, and named Geraldine Ferraro as the first woman candidate for Vice President, which made the election historic. Unfortunately for Mondale, Reagan handed him a defeat of historic proportions, too. He took 59 percent of the vote to Mondale's 41 percent, carried every state save Minnesota and the District of Columbia, and won by the widest margin ever in the Electoral College – 525 to 13.

Second term problems

Reagan's second term proved far bumpier than his first. Initially things seemed to go well. The economy prospered, the only dark spot on the horizon being a mounting federal budget deficit. This had been caused by the combination of tax cuts with increases in military and welfare spending, and meant that in 1985 the budget deficit had risen to over $200 billion. Relations with the Soviet Union improved: in November, 1985, Reagan met Gorbachev for the first time in a summit at Geneva. Little headway was made, but the fact that the two leaders were talking together rather than attacking each other was encouraging.

Then in 1986, the presidency started to run into serious trouble. In November, the Republican majority in the Senate was wiped out as the Democrats made big gains in the mid-term elections. Reagan had campaigned hard for his candidates, and this first rebuff from the voters was a blow. Then a meeting with Gorbachev in Iceland collapsed in confusion after an agreement on nuclear arms reductions seemed close. In 1987, Reagan suffered further embarrassment when the new Senate rejected his nominee for Supreme Court Justice on the grounds he was too conservative; then, much to the President's discomfiture, the replacement had to withdraw after admitting he had smoked marijuana.

IRANGATE

Most damaging of all were the revelations of the Iran-Contra scandal, which broke in late 1986. Several Americans had been kidnapped in Beirut by Islamic fundamentalist groups linked to Iran. Publicly, Reagan insisted that no deals would be done with terrorists. Then it was revealed that members of the administration had in fact been dealing with the Iranians, offering arms in return for the release of the hostages. Equally damaging was the discovery that the profits on the deals had been channeled

October 19, 1987, was Black Monday on the New York Stock Exchange. With only 20 minutes of trading left, prices plunged too fast for anyone to follow. By the time the 4 pm closing bell rang the Dow Jones industrial average had dropped 508 points – an amazing 22.6% – and roughly $500 billion in paper value had vanished. The calamity immediately became a global event hitting the stock markets of London, Paris, Frankfurt, Amsterdam, Zurich and Madrid, and Reagan's bewildered response on Wednesday (the crash was "some kind of a correction") suggested worrying lack of grip.

illegally to the Nicaraguan Contras, contravening a Congressional decision in 1985 to cut off aid.

In the outcry, subordinates denied the President knew about the diversion of funds to the Contras, but Reagan admitted, to public disapproval, that he had been dealing with the Iranians. In the storm, top aides were forced to resign, including White House Chief of Staff Donald Regan and National Security Adviser John Poindexter.

The President's relaxed, hands-off style of management, punctuated by frequent vacations at his California ranch, had been shown to have resulted in his not knowing what subordinates were doing, and allowing them to meddle in such important areas of foreign policy as the Middle East and Central America. For the first time, criticism began to pierce the Teflon armor.

In October, 1987, the President's troubles were compounded when, worried by the mounting federal deficit, Wall Street led stock markets around the world into the steepest nosedive since the Depression, raising fears that another recession might be on the way. Critics suggested that from being a lame duck President approaching the end of his second term, the incumbent was rapidly becoming a dead duck. Ironically, it was the old Soviet enemy which gave Reagan a chance to rehabilitate his reputation.

The Washington summit

The energetic new leadership of Mikhail Gorbachev provided just the impetus the arms reduction talks with the Soviets needed. Despite arguments over Star Wars, the fact that both sides badly needed an agreement led Reagan and Gorbachev to the signing of a historic treaty in Washington in December, 1987. For the first time actual reductions in nuclear arsenals were made, as both the Soviet Union and the United States agreed to remove and destroy all intermediate range nuclear missiles based in Europe. Although only 5 percent of the total nuclear arsenals of the two sides was affected, it raised hopes that larger reductions could be negotiated before the end of Reagan's second term. It was a solid achievement to set against the reverses the President had suffered.

Reagan and Gorbachev exchange views at the historic summit of December 1987. Though the prickly issue of "Star Wars" was temporarily set aside and there were some heated exchanges on human rights, the agreement undoubtedly marked a return to the spirit of détente politics. "This treaty represents a landmark in postwar history," said Reagan, and Gorbachev more tentatively agreed. "We can be proud of planting this sapling," he said, "but it is probably still too early to bestow laurels upon each other."

INDEX

A president's principal entry will be found on the pages denoted in bold type.